LAURA
ROBSON
THE BIOGRAPHY

LAURA ROBSON

THE BIOGRAPHY

TINA
CAMPANELLA

JOHN BLAKE

Published by John Blake Publishing Ltd,
3 Bramber Court, 2 Bramber Road,
London W14 9PB, England

www.johnblakepublishing.co.uk

www.facebook.com/Johnblakepub facebook
twitter.com/johnblakepub twitter

This edition published in 2014

ISBN: 978 1 78219 769 0

British Library Cataloguing-in-Publication Data:

A catalogue record for this book is available from the British Library.

Design by www.envydesign.co.uk

Printed and bound in Great Britain by CPI Group (UK) Ltd

1 3 5 7 9 10 8 6 4 2

Papers used by John Blake Publishing are natural, recyclable products made from
wood grown in sustainable forests. The manufacturing processes conform to the
environmental regulations of the country of origin.

Every attempt has been made to contact the relevant copyright-holders,
but some were unobtainable. We would be grateful if the
appropriate people could contact us.

Tina Campanella is an award-winning former tabloid and magazine journalist. You can tweet her at @littlebell1982.

CONTENTS

CHAPTER 1

BRITAIN NEEDS
A HERO

As the world counted down to Wimbledon in the summer of 2008, British sports fans found themselves struggling to muster up their usual exuberant enthusiasm.

It had been a dismal year for the country. The global financial collapse had begun, sparking well-founded fears of the biggest recession in recent history. Closer to home, record-high numbers of teenager-against-teenager murders in London had depressed the nation. The usual joy, inspiration and national pride that stemmed from our country's sporting achievements had been dampened by sweeping disappointments in the worlds of football, rugby, cricket and tennis, and it had been many years since the nation had idolised a Bobby Moore, Sebastian Coe or Virginia Wade.

It must have been difficult to imagine when Britain would next find something over which to come together in celebration – something to proudly recall in years to come.

There was talk everywhere from pubs to parliament that Britain badly needed some new sporting superstars, to inspire and enthuse the next generation of athletic heroes and to act as role models for teenagers all over the country.

As testament to this line of thinking, new initiatives to help focus disadvantaged youths through sports clubs were sprouting up all over the country, citing benefits that included healthier, safer and stronger communities, and exciting career prospects in the world of sport.

But, while other nations were determinedly battling it out in the European Championships, members of the England football team were instead spotted relaxing on sun loungers, enjoying an extended summer holiday. They'd failed to even qualify for the prestigious tournament, having been embarrassingly knocked out by Croatia in the qualifiers. It was the first time the England team hadn't competed since 1984.

England's rugby players had been disgraced both on and off the pitch during a disastrous tour of New Zealand – where lurid tales of all-night drinking, casual sex and even a rape allegation against four of the players had overshadowed the overseas test series. Despite the fact that in the end no charges were brought against any of the players, the team had returned to the UK with a shadow over their reputation that was hard to shake off.

At The Oval, England's cricketers had been well and truly shamed by their incomprehensible defeat at the hands of a New Zealand team whose player base would scarcely have supported an English county side. It was their tenth one-day international against the resourceful and plucky Kiwis that year, and their eighth loss – a totally unacceptable underachievement that was marked by persistently lack-lustre performances.

In tennis, British legend Tim Henman had repeatedly raised and dashed the hopes of a nation longing for a home-grown Wimbledon champion. A year previously, he had finally retired and vanished from the country's dreams of sporting glory, leaving all of Britain's heroic tennis hopes pinned on a solitary young Scot by the name of Andy Murray.

It was an intense amount of pressure to be heaped on one person and it didn't look like it would be relieved any time soon – because the wave of tennis juniors being coached to take their place beside young Andy weren't inspiring much confidence at all. Despite the money being thrown at the sport by the Lawn Tennis Association (LTA), the British youngsters being groomed for future sporting glory were being heavily criticised for demonstrating lacklustre performance in both focus and fight.

In an interview with the *Daily Mail* in January, after one young British hopeful was scratched from the Australian Open Boys' Event for persistent ill-discipline, one top British coach had admitted: 'It is often said that British juniors are lazy, ill-disciplined and lack fight on court – that's the reputation they've got unfortunately.' These were damning words, from a woman who knew what she was talking about – Judy Murray, tennis coach and mother of the then British No. 1s in both singles and doubles: Andy and Jamie Murray.

'We have to find a way to make them hungrier, set goals for them and then help them achieve them,' she added.

One of those goals, albeit long term, was the London 2012 Olympics, which, at that point, was four years away. It would be the ultimate opportunity to show off the country's wide variety of exciting talent, on the world's biggest sporting stage.

However, the overriding feeling among the general population was that Great Britain wasn't ready, and instead was just setting itself up for yet more disappointment and possibly even humiliation – this time on its own turf.

Morale was low in the sporting world.

The great British spirit was flagging.

But then, on a windswept bank in Roehampton, three days before the start of Wimbledon, a glimmer of hope shone out from among the young players battling it out on court. A relatively unknown 14-year-old was contesting the girls' final of the main junior Wimbledon warm-up event, against America's No. 2 ranked junior, Melanie Oudin.

She was a left-handed player, known in tennis circles as a 'lefty', with a surprisingly dominant serve. The new girl on the tennis block was giving the highly rated Oudin a tough time on the court – and in the process she was raising the eyebrows of the watching tennis world's cognoscenti.

The young player quickly took the first set against the top seed American, and for the rest of the game the small crowd gathered at the minor event watched her every stroke and volley with growing interest. Although she eventually lost to Oudin, those in the know walked away from the court convinced they had witnessed the tender beginnings of the next big British tennis starlet.

Mike Dickson, the *Daily Mail*'s tennis correspondent, leaned over to the young girl's mother and whispered: 'You do realise this is probably the last normal week of your family's life.'

His words proved to be prophetic.

Just days later, British tennis fans would be buzzing with excited talk about the hot new homegrown tennis hope.

Her name was Laura Robson and she would quickly become instrumental in helping reignite the country's passion for tennis.

CHAPTER 2

SPORTING PEDIGREE

It was January 1994, the height of Australia's blisteringly hot summertime, and the city of Melbourne had once more succumbed to its annual tennis fever. The Australian Open was well underway at Flinders Park and cries of both anguish and joy could be heard daily from the packed tennis courts.

And while tennis legends Pete Sampras and Steffi Graf were on their way to claiming their first major victories of the year, just a stone's throw away from the sweaty action, Laura Robson was busy making her entrance into the world.

Born in the city that traditionally begins the tennis year, and surrounded from her first breath by all the heady excitement of the international sport, some would say that it was in her DNA to someday become a racket queen.

But she had a long journey ahead of her.

She was the youngest of three children born to successful Antipodean couple Andrew and Kathy Robson, and it could easily have been Australia and not Britain who would claim her future glory as their own.

However, Laura's life in Australia was short-lived: when she was just 18 months old, the family moved to Singapore, where her father's job as an executive for Shell oil took him. It was there, in the refined surroundings of an expat country club, that she first picked up a tennis racket.

Laura was born into a family that highly values sporting skills and the hard work and dedication that it takes to turn talent into success: the whole Robson gene pool is over-flowing with sporting achievement.

Her great-grandfather Pat Fogarty is a legend at the Perth Australian Rules Football Club and even has a grandstand named after him there. Her mother was a professional basketball player in her native Perth, and her uncle, Larry Dwyer, was a star member of the Fremantle Dockers Premiership team. Add these achievements to those of her two cousins – who have represented Australia in hockey and kayaking – and it would have been amazing if Laura hadn't turned out to excel at some kind of athletic activity.

So, when the young family arrived in Singapore, it was only natural for Kathy and Andrew to immediately seek out some-where they could pursue the sporting hobbies of their choice. They found the Hollandse Club, a sprawling, private, tropical oasis located at the heart of the city that the Robson family would call their home for the next four years. The family were regular visitors to the club, which offered everything from squash, golf, hockey and swimming to football and tennis, and it soon became almost like a second home.

When Laura was four, the family began playing friendly tennis knockabouts among themselves with Laura drafted in as ballgirl. As a reward for her efforts, she was treated to ten minutes of play at the end of each match, and Kathy was immediately struck by her daughter's instant ability to hit the ball.

Enrolled in the club's under-7s coaching group, Laura's first training session was an astonishing experience for those around her.

'They were quite strict about the kids staying in their age ranges,' recalls Kathy. 'But after about five minutes the coach came back and said they would need to create a special group for her. By the age of five we could see signs of a special talent.'

While not a pushy tennis parent, Kathy encouraged Laura to enjoy the sport – but not to the detriment of her other interests, or for that matter to her childhood as a whole.

Early family photos reveal Laura to be a beautiful child with a wide and infectious smile and a penchant for dressing up. It's clear that her early years in the far-flung city of Singapore were happy ones.

A few months after her sixth birthday, however, the family made their final move and settled in Wimbledon, London – just a few steps away from the tennis capital of the world. Laura felt instantly at home in the cooler, greyer city, despite it being the polar opposite of the colourful place she had just come from.

The family bought a dog, Ella, and settled down permanently.

As a precocious six-year-old, Laura had a wide range of interests. She was an attentive child in class, an elegant dancer in her ballet lessons, musically gifted at the saxophone and obsessed with baking. But it was in tennis that she naturally shone, and she joined a junior tennis academy a year later.

It's safe to say it was sibling rivalry that started Laura on the road to serious tennis, as her first major competitor was her brother Nick. 'He's two years older than me and, as he was always that bit better, I would lose and sulk for the rest of the day,' Laura says. 'It's the reason I kept playing – I needed to beat him.'

Laura was 11 when she finally started winning.

'It was worth the wait,' she now admits. 'I was just more competitive and took training more seriously than he did.'

By the time Laura turned nine, members of the Robson household were all early risers. Kathy was up at 5am to take Nick to the pool for swimming training then back at 6am to take Laura to the tennis courts before both were whisked off to school.

Nick was swimming for Middlesex and approaching Olympic qualifying times and Laura had attracted the attention of various tennis coaches, including the Lawn Tennis Association's coach Carl Maes. Carl noted that, although Laura had trouble staying emotionally under control, he could see right away that she had a lot of potential.

But, with so many interests and commitments and so little time in the day, young Laura had a very adult decision to make.

Along with her talent at tennis, she had begun to excel in her ballet lessons, and had been offered a scholarship to the Royal Ballet School. She also loved to spend hours in the kitchen with rolling pins and icing, and at night she fell asleep with cookery books under her pillow, dreaming of being a baker. In the years to come, she would sometimes take over a small part of the kitchens at the hotels she stayed at on tour. There she would relax by baking trays of splendid cupcakes and cookies for her friends and family.

Laura's dilemma was that, in order to be a professional tennis player, she would have to put aside everything else – including her schoolwork – and focus exclusively on the sport. It was a tough decision, but one she wouldn't regret. She started taking her school lessons at home and began to work hard at the sporting career she was determined was her destiny.

Most British children being groomed for tennis glory are packed off to live at prestigious training academies in foreign climes.

Laura's fellow tennis ace and friend Heather Watson left her home on the island of Guernsey when she was 12 to live and train at the Nick Bollettieri Tennis Academy in Florida, while Andy Murray left Scotland for Spain in his early teens, to train on the clay courts of the Sanchez-Casal Academy.

Overseas training meant being uprooted from friends and families and, although seen as a small sacrifice to pay for sporting glory, it was a lot to handle for a young child like Laura, who was so close to her parents.

'When it got more serious, we did look at some academies, but it came down to us not wanting to split the family up,' says Kathy. 'I would probably have had to have gone and lived wherever with her and for us the family unit was just too important. She had a brother, a sister and a dog and all that stuff is more important when you are growing up. We took the view that if she was going to be good enough then she was going to be good enough.'

The Robsons were a family who prided themselves on their normal, middle-class home life and didn't want that to change. None of their children, no matter how gifted, would take precedence over any of the others, and all three would have their feet rooted firmly on the ground.

Laura's tennis career would be separate from her family life, which would remain normal, and Kathy would be supportive but not pushy. It was largely as a result of her mother's excellently practical attitude that Laura would grow into the remarkably grounded and balanced young lady she is today.

She would go after glory with everything she had, but she would also always know that she had a life to live 'off the courts' too. Her loving and supportive family would be there to both applaud and console her, and at the end of each day, whether she'd done well or things had gone badly, she would return home to the same house and do the same household chores that she always had.

Other young tennis players haven't been so lucky. Countless pushy tennis parents, over the years, have been the cause of numerous deeply ingrained emotional issues that have blighted their children's careers – and their lives. And, although some would say that it is this kind of backing that produces world-class players, surely many might argue that it is too high a price to pay for professional recognition.

'It's a huge issue on the junior circuit,' says former Wimbledon champion Pat Cash. 'Parents being very aggressive, very abusive, cheating.'

Richard Krajicek, from Holland, another former champion, suffered mercilessly as a result of his father's unreasonable behaviour.

'If I didn't practise well my dad would make me run home behind the car,' he says. 'Once he was upset with me and he spanked me pretty good. I'd just come back from the States and he didn't know about jetlag. He thought I'd tanked the match, that I didn't try.'

Krajicek struggled emotionally and physically because of the relationship, adding: 'A few days later he said to me: "I've heard about this jetlag, I shouldn't have done it – but all the other times you deserved it."'

This gives a heartbreaking insight into the pressure that only parents can put on their children.

Between the ages of 20 and 30, Krajicek didn't speak to his father, after finally learning to stand up for himself.

The Dutchman won Wimbledon aged 24.

Krajicek's own son is now playing junior tennis, and as a father he has a totally different attitude to his boy's career.

While Krajicek junior was playing under-12s tennis, his father noticed his son getting upset by a series of cheating opponents, despite the fact that some of them were his friends. Richard understands all too well the reason why the other children were resorting to underhand tactics.

He says: 'I told him that, although his opponent was a friend, he'd rather have problems with you than lose the match and have problems at home.'

Showing where his priorities lie, he adds: 'Maybe the way I approach it now my son is going to have a good relationship with me but he's going to be a terrible tennis player.'

Kathy Robson's determination to put the welfare of her

daughter and that of the whole family before Laura's tennis career is all the more commendable because pushy parents are actually more usually associated with women's tennis than with male players.

It's a trend that was begun by the father of Suzanne Lenglen, the flamboyant French player who is widely recognised as the first female tennis celebrity. Coached rigorously by her father, he controlled every aspect of her training and devised monotonous techniques, such as laying a handkerchief down at different positions on the court, and repeatedly forcing her to hit it with her racket.

At all Lenglen's games her father sat within earshot of her and loudly reproved his daughter for the slightest of errors.

It paid off: Lenglen won 8 Grand Slam singles titles and 31 Championships between 1919 and 1926. In those seven years she lost only one match.

But his actions set a sadly dangerous precedent.

In more recent times, four-time Grand Slam winner Mary Pierce is known as much for her father Jim's abusive behaviour towards her and her opponents as for her tennis prowess. Mary now admits that Jim was physically abusive towards her while coaching her as a youngster, once even shouting: 'Mary, kill the bitch!' while watching his daughter play in a junior match.

When she turned 18, Mary finally found the courage to break away from her father, aided by the Women's Tennis Council, the governing body of the women's circuit.

Jim was subsequently banned from the 1993 WTA (Women's Tennis Association) Tour, and Mary eventually had to get a restraining order against her father to prevent him from attending any more of her matches.

'It's like a weight off me,' she said at the time. 'When I miss a shot it's not the end of the world anymore.'

At the height of her game, Serbian tennis ace Jelena Dokic also struggled to cope with the behaviour of her father, who was also her coach, who displayed constant outbreaks of aggression.

Instances of this included stomping on a journalist's mobile phone at Wimbledon, claiming that the draw was rigged at the Australian Open, calling members of the Edgbaston Priory Club 'Nazis', and threatening the Australian Ambassador to Serbia with a rocket launcher.

Dokic eventually parted ways with her father, Damir. In 2011, she informed the press that he wouldn't be at the Australian Open, admitting: 'He can't watch my matches because he gets too stressed'.

This was somewhat of an understatement.

American coach Nick Bollettieri has long experienced the detrimental effect that parents can have on their offspring, when they act as coaches. 'Having mum and dad so closely involved is not the most productive route to success,' he has diplomatically said. 'Too close a relationship in terms of sport, more often than not, proves a negative.'

There are exceptions, like Serena and Venus Williams's mother and father, Oracene and Richard, and Andy and Jamie Murray's mother, Judy. But, on the whole, pushy parents are more often than not a hindrance to their children's success.

'There have been plenty of examples where parents have really pushed an individual and that isn't so healthy,' says Tim Henman. 'In an ideal world, the passion and the drive should come from the player.'

It's clear that Kathy Robson made the decision to leave Laura's career to the experts, opting instead for providing stoic support and firm gentle persuasion.

It would prove to be a winning combination.

CHAPTER 3

A STAR IN TRAINING

Despite the decision to remain firmly on British soil for her training, Kathy still wanted the best coaching for her daughter. Teaming up with British coach Alan Jones was a natural first step towards glory.

Jones had an impressive track record. In the 1980s, he had guided Jo Durie to win the Wimbledon girls' title and she had gone on to become one of the top five tennis players in the world.

No Brit had won the girls' title since.

Alan Jones could see Laura's obvious talent, but in his opinion it was another of her qualities that stood out.

'My wife and I have had plenty of young players of school age pass through our house over the years and they've had one thing in common – it's impossible to get them to do their homework,' he told the *Daily Mail* in 2010. 'Not Laura. She would get straight down to it without any trouble. Even at that age you could see she was bright, had strong discipline and a work ethic.'

This coach had a very specific approach to Laura's training and he is now credited with laying the foundations for the young player's future success. But he also insists that Kathy's shrewd parenting was central to her younger years on the tennis courts.

'Time and time again I come across parents who are much too focused on instant results and short-term outcomes for their children,' he explains. 'The strategy was always to try and give Laura an adult sort of game and make her go for her shots even if it meant losing matches that she should have won.

'She would sometimes lose to girls who would loop the ball and play safety first, getting it in all the time and winning by making a few mistakes. But in the long term it is better to have a bigger game. Luckily, Laura's parents bought into that.'

Tennis star Jo Durie, who is still close to her former coach, also helped guide Robson through various ups and downs during her early years of professional training. Jo well recalls her first encounter with the promising player, and the immediate impression she made on the former World No. 5 when they first got on a practice court together.

According to Durie, something about Laura stood out from the other girls they were working with. 'Straight away you could tell she hit the ball really well,' Jo Durie commented. 'A lot of the time it went into the back fence, but there was an unusual sense of timing.'

Durie and Jones coached her to compete in a series of under-12 championship matches, where they taught her some important lessons. 'I remember her losing in a first round,' says Durie. 'We asked her and Kathy afterwards if she wanted to win under-12 titles just by making fewer mistakes than her opponent, or end up being good at 18 by learning to hit the ball properly and hard and lose a few more matches than might be expected.'

At the time, Robson was training at the Hazelwood Lawn Tennis Club, which had a brand-new elite tennis academy on its premises in North London. The brainchild of coach Alan Jones and backer Stephen Marks (the head of French Connection UK), the academy had opened in 2003 and was a new concept in British tennis training – modelled on the holistic hothouse approach that had proven such a success for Nick Bollettieri in Florida.

The Bollettieri Academy, where training was intense and totally focused on perfection, had produced Andre Agassi, Monica Seles and Maria Sharapova, so it certainly had a proven track record. But traditionally cautious British parents didn't generally favour the hothouse method of sports training that Jones envisioned with his academy.

Directing this radically hard-line approach at future British tennis stars may have raised a few eyebrows, but the LTA was firmly behind the scheme. 'The bottom line is we want to create champions who will then inspire others,' said Marks, while Laura was a Hazelwood pupil.

She was one of just sixteen students at the school, where fees were £25,000 a year and training – which included Pilates, sports science lessons, school lessons, movement classes and an extremely high class of tennis coaching – was extremely intense. In the morning, Laura had two-and-a-half hours of footwork and training. After lunch, she had two hours of school lessons, before it was time to play tennis. At the end of every day, she had an hour of stretching.

'Ultimately you come here to aim for the top 100 in the world,' said Hazelwood coach James Lenton in 2005. 'We're using that as our benchmark. No one comes here to be treated like royalty.'

The team had a no-nonsense approach to training, which was perfectly in line with what Kathy Robson was looking for. She wanted Laura to stay with her family, but focus hard on her chosen career in tennis.

Since arriving in London, Kathy had been shocked at the British attitude to female sports, which differed markedly from that in her native Australia. 'Women's sport in Britain is a disgrace,' she bluntly told a reporter who visited the club in 2005 to write about its facilities.

Laura was 11 and in training, and Kathy was watching from the sidelines with Ella, the Robsons' puppy.

'It scares me,' Kathy went on, 'the idea of girls and young women over here seems to be to hang around in shopping malls in big earrings. In Australian schools, to be good at sports is the ultimate. Over here, if you're good at sport, you're butch.'

Kathy didn't pull any punches, and her words resonated with the reporter, who wrote in the *Daily Telegraph*: 'All hail that woman. She is frighteningly right.'

There was no mollycoddling at Hazelwood, which was breaking down sports training barriers in the country and starting a veritable revolution in tennis coaching. It was just what British tennis needed.

Although the bulk of Laura's training was done in Britain, she did attend short training camps overseas, including some at La Manga in Spain. Former British No. 1 Elena Baltacha was also at the camps and knew Laura already from Hazelwood, where they both trained. She took Robson under her wing on the trips and often babysat her and another girl after training.

Baltacha remembers Laura being disciplined about doing her homework, and, while she occasionally had to intervene to stop some enthusiastic bed-trampolining, she had a soft spot for her young charge.

'Laura was probably about 10 and I was around 20,' she recalls, before referring next to the girls in her charge: 'They were quite good mostly, but I did have to tell them off for chatting after lights out. I had to pretend to call the head coach to scare them into going to sleep.'

Living so close to Wimbledon's famous courts, it was only natural that Robson would watch the big matches that were regularly taking place just a short walk from her home. She learned a lot from closely examining the form of experienced players like Martina Hingis, whom she greatly admired. She dreamed about one day playing on Centre Court.

When Laura was 10, she was given her first opportunity to play on the hallowed courts at the All England Lawn Tennis Club, and she was understandably very excited. The LTA had specially selected a group of young, promising female tennis players, for an exhibition on Court Three that was set to take place on the middle Saturday of Wimbledon. To prepare them, the elite group spent two days at a training camp, so that the show game would be faultless.

Laura's family managed to procure some tickets, and on the morning of the exhibition she woke up raring to go. But, sadly, when she looked outside she could see the familiar summer rain that so often hindered Wimbledon matches. She got dressed in her tennis whites and trainers, and made her way to the club.

When the exhibition was due to begin, the rain still hadn't let up, and it continued to pour down throughout the afternoon, and Laura's first ever moment on a Wimbledon court was unceremoniously cancelled. So, instead of playing tennis, she tucked into strawberries and cream and soaked up the atmosphere. For her, it hadn't been a wasted trip by any means.

By now, Laura was being noticed by more than just former tennis stars and top coaches: in that same year, she signed with sports management agency Octagon, who would carefully manage her career off the courts. With global experience in athlete management, Octagon would negotiate sponsorship contracts and marketing opportunities for Laura and, when the time was right, build her personal brand, which would be key to securing her financial security in the years to come.

Her agent at Octagon was Abi Tordoff, who grew close to the youngster during their time working together and would go on to protect her from the sustained media attention she would receive in just a few short years' time.

The first sponsorship deal Laura signed was with famous sporting brand Adidas, followed shortly by the deep-pocketed Wilson company, most famous for its rackets. This resulted in her getting a steady supply of chic tennis wear and rackets, and access to the Adidas Player Development Programme, which provided top-notch coaching and training to those lucky enough to be involved with it.

Such exposure was invaluable, and word about Laura's

burgeoning talent soon reached the ears of one of the greatest tennis trainers in the world: Martina Hingis's mum, Melanie Molitor. The 11-year-old was subsequently invited to Switzerland to train with Melanie and Martina.

Flying over to accept the invitation, Robson couldn't believe her luck. 'It was like a dream come true,' she said in a later interview. 'I used to watch Martina a lot. I liked the way she played because it was so smart and I tried to bring some of that into my game.'

It was an inspirational experience. When Laura returned to Britain, she began to hit the junior tennis circuit with every ounce of focus and skill she could muster.

CHAPTER 4

JUNIOR GLORY

After extensive training and nurturing at the hands of some of the greatest tennis players in the world, it was time for Laura to start making a name for herself against her peers.

In 2006, she played in a constant stream of matches and tournaments – national and international – winning and losing and, more importantly, gaining valuable experience along the way. In December, she was lucky enough to enjoy a few weeks of training with the left-handed former American pro Nick Saviano, before heading to Florida to compete in two major junior events.

First up was the Eddie Herr International Championships at the IMG Academy: a competition that had previously served as a springboard to the professional tennis tour for players such as Roger Federer, Maria Sharapova, Andy Roddick and Anna Kournikova.

This tournament attracts the top junior players from around the world and as such it was an important event for Laura. In the first round, she comfortably beat China's Yuxuan Zhang, before breezing past Canada's Michelle Dandik to the quarterfinals. There she faced the USA's Jacqueline Crawford, where she lost the first set 3-6, but bounced back to win the next two 6-0 and 6-2.

Laura was excited and nervous, but determined to stay focused.

In the semifinals, she faced another American, Julia Jones, and once again lost the first set. But she took the next two sets and found herself facing Jessica Ren in the final. No. 1 seed Ren was a right-handed player from Sheffield who had started playing the game aged seven and was rising through the tennis ranks at the same fast pace as Laura was.

Along with Jessica Ren's sister, Jennifer, Guernsey girl Heather Watson and sisters Amy and Beth Askew, Jessica was being touted as a possible future British star, and as such would provide stiff competition for the thus far unseeded Laura.

In fact, Jessica and Laura had faced each other a number of times on court already, and Jessica had won at their previous few meetings. Both young hopefuls had played tremendously and their games were usually a close match.

But Laura eventually won 7-6; 7-5 and was pronounced the under-12s winner.

'I played amazing in the tiebreak,' a flushed Robson told reporters after the match. 'I just went for anything and I just didn't miss. I felt comfortable in the second set knowing that I had just won the first set in a tiebreak. I just had nothing to lose really.'

Talking about her opponent, she said: 'Last time I played her I was up and she came back. She never stops fighting. It kind of makes you angry at her, but you do realise sometimes that you have to do something else.'

Crediting her trainer Saviano with helping Laura to finally conquer her rival, she explained the work that the pair had been doing together: 'He was trying to fix my serve and forehand, because they were always flat. He has improved them, because he's got me to spin and stuff.'

It was clear that Robson had played close attention to post-match interviews and had remained professional in her summary of the game. But she was still a youngster and the telltale signs of her age that crept out during the interview were endearing: Robson told the interviewer that she might go out for dinner that night to celebrate her win, but she definitely wouldn't be missing training the next day.

'I just love the game too much to do that,' she said wistfully. 'I could never go without tennis for more than a week without missing it.'

A few days before Christmas, Laura found herself competing in the Orange Bowl Junior Tennis tournament, which was seen as the major end-of-year test for up-and-coming players and, as such, was fiercely competitive. Laura powered through the first stages. So did Jessica Ren, who was also competing in the tournament.

By the time Laura and Jessica faced each other in the semifinal, Ren had played seven matches without dropping a set and Laura must have felt nervous. Despite beating her a few weeks before, Ren was still a formidable foe.

Laura started out strong and it was clear that the two players were closely matched.

Robson took the first set 6-4 – the first Ren had lost in the tournament so far. Ren took the second 6-1. The final set was long and tiring and it looked like Laura might just take the game, but Ren came back in the last four from 5-4 down to beat her 7-5.

It was a disappointing loss, especially when Ren then sailed past Germany's Christina Shakovets to take the title. Jessica was the first British female to ever win the singles title at the Orange Bowl, and the media began to rave about her.

But Laura's time was coming.

In 2007, Laura began training at the brand-new National Tennis Centre (NTC) in Roehampton, close to her Wimbledon home.

Opened by Queen Elizabeth II on 29 March of the same year, the high-performance centre was a Mecca for tennis training. With sixteen outdoor courts, covering all the Grand Slam surfaces, six indoor courts, a gymnasium, and sports science and medical facilities, it also housed the administration of the LTA, which had previously been based at the Queen's Club in Kensington. Inspired by the elite national tennis centres in the consistently successful tennis nations of Belgium, France, Spain, Italy, the USA and Switzerland, it was hoped that the new premises would bring about a revolution in British tennis culture.

The huge centre had been commissioned in response to a 1999 review by the LTA into its sustained failure to produce world-class players. In fact, the only British players to make the world top 50 in that decade had been Tim Henman, who did so independently of the LTA system, and Greg Rusedski, who actually learned to play in his native Canada.

Most tennis clubs, including Queen's, were better known

as social clubs for the wealthy rather than centres of sporting excellence. The NTC's aim was to promote competition over social tennis, and finally begin to produce top-quality British players.

Aside from her activity at the NTC, Laura also spent time learning at The Bisham Abbey Academy, a teaching centre with a national coaching staff of 70, which had a sterling track record for high-performance training.

Laura had so far worked with several coaches, but in the early part of 2007 she chose to train mainly under Martijn Bok. This bespectacled former professional Dutch tennis player was by now an ambitious coach, who prided himself on getting the best out of his players.

Along with head of the LTA, Carl Maes, and head of women's tennis at the NTC, Nigel Sears, Bok began to prepare Laura for her first tournament on the Junior ITF (International Tennis Federation) Tour. It was the beginning of an intensely demanding year and marked her entry into the serious world of competitive tennis.

Laura's first match on the Junior ITF Tour took place in May, when she entered the qualifying tournament for the Tennis Sweden Junior Cup. She won two matches to qualify, swiftly followed by two more wins to reach the quarterfinals before she was knocked out.

A month later, she qualified for the Prokom Cup in Poland, and powered her way to the final before losing in three sets to Magda Linette: a right-handed Polish player who was two years her senior. Laura was so angry she threw her runners-up trophy on the floor and smashed it to bits.

It was an ominous sign: Laura definitely needed to work on her composure. Although she was a very talented youngster, Bok could see that her emotions could easily get in the way of her future success.

'When I first got to work with her I couldn't believe what I was seeing,' Bok would recall to the *Guardian* a year later. 'She would go insane, really nuts on court.'

Her trainers began to work on her focus and her temper, as well as her tennis technique.

In July, she travelled to Holland, where she won the coveted Windmill Cup. As autumn descended, she flew to Denmark for the HRT (Horhsolm Rungsted Tennisklub) Autumn Cup where she made it as far as the quarterfinals, before immediately heading to Finland for the Nokia Junior Cup.

Showing impressive form, Laura was on a roll. She won three matches in straight sets to qualify, even beating Russian starlet Ksenia Kirillova to reach the final. There she faced Russia's Polina Rodionova and won.

As 2007 drew to a close, Robson returned to the IMG Academy in Florida to go after another Eddie Herr title – this time in the under-14s category. In the quarterfinals she found herself facing her best pal, Eugenie Bouchard. Robson had met Canadian tennis player Eugenie when they were both nine and the two had quickly become firm friends.

Being of a similar standard and experiencing the same tennis-focused childhood, they both perfectly understood the pressure, excitement and sorrow of pursuing a pre-teen professional career. They had helped to keep each other focused in a competitive world that demanded maturity at a young age. As their friendship and careers had progressed in tandem, they also had fun together on what were often lonely tours, far away from home.

Facing each other professionally on court was another

matter entirely. Both girls were competitive and wanted to win, but they didn't want to lose their friendship because of their rivalry. It was a perfect opportunity to practise the finer points of separating the personal from the professional, and, when Laura triumphed to go through to the semis, there was no drama: Bouchard congratulated her enthusiastically.

Laura beat Jacqueline Crawford, as she had done the previous year, and then cast aside Monica Puig 6-0; 4-6; 6-0 to win the Eddie Herr for the second year running. All in all, she'd had a satisfying and successful first run on the junior circuit. A month later, Laura celebrated her 14th birthday.

With four junior titles and some impressive achievements behind her, she was making headway in her career. But she was still unseeded and relatively unknown.

All that was about to change.

CHAPTER 5

SUCCESS ON THE CIRCUIT

While most British teenagers were catching up with school friends in the playground and recounting what Santa had brought them for Christmas, Laura was on her way to do battle in Eastern Europe.

Since the 1970s, when the women's professional tennis tour began, one of the main ways in which it has changed is in the nations who have dominated the rankings. Early on, it was the Americans who governed the leader board, which was no surprise, seeing as the WTA (Women's Tennis Association) itself was founded by an American – former world No. 1 Billie Jean King.

Rosie Casals, Nancy Richey, Tracy Austin, Chris Evert and Jennifer Capriati – these iconic Americans were at the top of their game and other countries struggled to topple the USA's reign of tennis glory.

But, in more recent years, a tidal wave of Eastern

European talent has swept through the female tennis circuit, and with their height and power they have proved to be formidable new foes for other tennis-playing nations...

In 1952, former Soviet dictator Joseph Stalin put his government's propaganda department in charge of Russian sports. It was decided that the younger generation had to be fit enough to protect the motherland, and a nationwide system of physical education was implemented to that end. But to a large degree it was also a propaganda tool, designed to show the superiority of the Soviet Union's communist approach to society through their dominance of competitive sports.

Its main benefit was that all children were given an equal opportunity to play such sports and to be trained to a high standard. But there were frightening drawbacks: mandates were set among coaches to produce high-quality athletes – and if they failed to do so they might face serious consequences.

In the 1970s and 80s, their strict, factory-style training methods produced a steady stream of sporting stars, as the Soviet Union ruthlessly tried to prove they could compete with the disapproving West.

While America and the West believed in freedom and choice as the path to success, the Eastern bloc's enforced and focused training methods certainly produced results. Superior players like Martina Navratilova were a product of their almost brutal training regime, which stole childhoods, and made whole generations of children miserable and fearful.

However, Anna Kournikova believes that it was actually the fall of the Soviet Union in 1991 that signalled the beginning of the real Eastern European tennis takeover.

'We always had amazing tennis schools and clubs in Russia, it's just that the opportunities never were really there when it was still the Soviet Union for them to travel,' she says.

Money was also at the heart of the issue.

While the rest of the world's players were pulling in thousands of pounds in prize money, those in the Soviet Union never saw the financial fruits of their labours – because all winnings went straight to the government.

In January 1988, Russian tennis player Andrei Chesnokov stunned the tennis world by saying that he was on a $35-a-day allowance from the then Soviet Tennis Federation.

At the time, he was on his way up from 50th in the world, having just had successful weeks at Wellington and Sydney, where he had finished runner-up both times and should have received $30,000 in prize money.

'When I was at Orlando, the prize money was $75,000 and I got $630,' he later told a reporter. 'Can you believe that?'

Chesnokov, along with female player Natalia Zvereva, were the first to bravely question the system, and finally decided to stand their ground – and keep their prize money.

It was a dangerous form of defiance, which caused waves in Moscow. 'When she returned... the Soviet Sports Committee met with her and told her that she would have to hand over the cheque if she wanted to go and play any more tournaments,' says Chesnokov.

After the fall of the Iron Curtain, suddenly there were opportunities for great wealth. Spurred on by the potential for fame and riches, young females in Eastern Europe were immediately committed and dedicated to their respective sports, displaying the rigorous work ethic that was handed down to them from the Soviet system.

'I was the first post-Soviet-era player to leave Russia, and practise in better circumstances, in a better environment,' says Kournikova, who trained with Nick Bollettieri in Florida. 'Once kids and parents saw what I did, they realised that there was that opportunity.'

By 2004, the 'ova' era, as it was nicknamed, had produced three Grand Slam winners in one year: Anastasia Myskina won the French Open, Maria Sharapova conquered Wimbledon and Svetlana Kuznetsova took the title at the US Open.

Their focus was both unswerving and unnerving – and for Laura, facing Eastern Europe's most up-and-coming players on their home turf would certainly prove to be a challenge. But it was one she rose to admirably.

She reached the quarterfinals of the Slovak Junior Indoor Tournament in Bratislava, beating Poland's Paula Kania and Russia's Anna Arina Marenko, before losing to the Czech Republic's Tereza Bekerova.

Next, Laura made it to the quarterfinals of the DHL Cup, played in the Czech Republic – beating Czech Klara Koprivova, Slovakian Zuzana Luknarova and Czech Monika Tumova, before losing to Zarina Diyas from Kazakhstan. These were impressive wins, made even more so by the cool and calm way in which she dealt with her eventual defeats.

Laura was a passionate girl – keeping her emotions in check didn't come easy to her at all. But she was beginning to learn to control them.

In February, back on British soil, Laura had a decision to make. Wimbledon 2008 was approaching and she would be aiming to enter the girls' singles tournament – as a Brit. But, despite speaking with a Home Counties accent and having spent her most formative years in England, Laura was still technically Australian.

Although she has never commented directly on the subject, it is thought that she was determined to gain a British passport before tennis's most high-profile and best-loved tournament, so that she could represent the country in which she had lived for most of her life. However, a 2008 article that appeared in the *Daily Telegraph* hinted at a slightly more cynical reason.

'Some tennis experts believe the move will allow her to become a tennis sensation in a country which has failed to produce a genuine Grand Slam contender for years,' wrote journalist Rob Davies.

The article also quoted a tennis insider as voicing this opinion: 'Some are saying that because of the poor state of British women's tennis, the people who are looking after Laura's career believe she will do better as a big fish in a small pool.' The person added: 'Her earnings potential as a future British No. 1 is huge and she could very well go on to earn more than £10 million from tennis and sportswear endorsements.'

Whatever the reason, her father, Andrew, officially applied for British citizenship and was successful. Laura followed suit and legally became a British citizen.

In June, with Wimbledon just days away, Laura entered the Roehampton Junior tournament, generally accepted to be the Wimbledon junior warm-up event. Onlookers watched in amazement as she breezed past Martina Borecka, USA's Mallory Burdette, Australia's Johanna Konta, fellow Brit Naomi

Broady and Holland's Lesley Kerkhove, to secure a place in the final against top-class junior Melanie Oudin.

It was during this match that onlookers stood up and took notice of the unseeded and unknown Robson – even though she eventually lost against the American girl. Every serve and stroke was mesmerising, imbued with a competitive desire that made the atmosphere tense and the stakes feel infinitely high.

It was after this match that journalist Mike Dickson uttered his prophetic words: '*You do realise this is probably the last normal week of your family's life...*'

Wimbledon was coming and Laura was gunning for glory.

CHAPTER 6

WE LOVE YOU, LAURA

Laura was 14 years and 166 days old when she played her first match at Wimbledon. She was already an impressive 5ft 7in, her serve had already reached speeds of 107 mph, and she had lost only 9 of the 27 matches she had played that season.

But no one honestly expected her to progress very far in the tournament – not her coaches, not her family, not the crowd.

This is because it was Wimbledon – the most coveted tournament of the season – and she would be playing against girls much older and more established on the junior circuit. Girls who were as hungry for Wimbledon glory as she was, young women who had already tried and failed to win, indeed even individuals who had beaten her before.

It would be good experience for a young tennis hopeful: a chance to experience the pressure of a big match or two and ready her for future success.

So no one could have expected what would happen next.

In her first match, taking place on Court 19, the sun shone down on Laura as she faced her opponent, the USA's Alexa Guarachi. The British player made short shrift of the blonde, who was three years her senior, and took her down 6-0; 6-4.

Next she had to play American top seed Melanie Oudin – the girl Laura had pushed herself so hard to try to beat just days before at Roehampton. At 17, Melanie was three years older than Laura. A defensive counterpuncher, her speed and footwork had been integral to her early success and had certainly got her noticed during this, her first professional season. She was even being touted as the new successor to the Williams sisters. Anyone in the know would have bet on Oudin defeating Laura again. But Miss Robson had other plans.

Laura rose early, and had a morning practice to prepare herself for the competition. Waiting for her match to begin, she felt good about her form.

Four hundred spectators crammed themselves around Court 7 to watch the battle begin. Among them were NTA (National Tennis Academy) coach Carl Maes, Fed Cup captain Nigel Sears and, interestingly, Billie Jean King.

Laura looked determined as she walked out on court, her fists clenching in anticipation. She started with purposeful groundstrokes, throwing Oudin off-guard and pinning her to the baseline. Fully in control, her solid hits dragged the American into parts of the court she wasn't entirely comfortable in.

It was blisteringly hot. One tennis fan fainted in the intense heat, but Laura didn't break a sweat. Murmurs of appreciation came from the crowd as she showed sparks of the competitive fire that lurked within her. She kept her focus, and uttered only a few small grunts of encouragement to herself as she clearly outclassed her opponent.

After just half an hour, Robson had taken the first set, 6-1.

Those who had just been sunning themselves courtside suddenly gave the match their full attention, and were shocked when Laura took the second set, 6-3, to triumph over a floundering Oudin. It was an impressively mature performance, and the British fans were beside themselves.

'It was really good,' said Robson in her first proper post-match interview. 'There were so many people supporting me, lots of British fans, so it was a really good atmosphere.'

But, while she celebrated her win, she knew she had to keep focused on her game. Beating Oudin was just one small step towards Wimbledon glory. British hopes were faltering after Andy Murray had crashed out of the tournament, so all British eyes were on Robson the following evening, when she was scheduled to meet Holland's Lesley Kerkhove in the third round.

As the match approached, Virginia Wade settled into her seat to watch the proceedings – keen to see the new girl in action.

Kerkhove put up a good fight, but Laura put up an even better one, assaulting her opponent with a barrage of super powerful hits that the Dutch girl struggled to return. Virginia Wade began to wonder if she was watching a future British champion in the making. And, when Robson won 7-6; 7-5, she was glad she'd been there to see it.

The next day, Laura's face appeared in the national newspapers. There was general curiosity and interest in the phenomenon that was Laura Robson. Who was this ice-cool young girl, who was causing such a wave of excitement to pass through the British crowds?

Everyone wanted to know.

Whereas just days before she had walked from locker room to court and back again without turning a single head, she progressed into her quarterfinals match against ninth seed Bojana Jovanoski under the glare of photographers' lenses and television cameras and the gaze of fascinated spectators.

Laura was understandably nervous as she made her way on court. It was a lot for her to handle. Nothing and no one could have prepared the fresh-faced teenager for the burden of expectation that was suddenly being foisted upon her. She was still showing signs of nerves as the match began, and she dropped three games in the first set.

But then something changed.

As Laura focused solely on the task in hand, she found that the crowd, cameras and pressure faded away. And after that point the Serbian didn't have a chance.

The British player quickly retrieved the deficit with a series of crisp groundstrokes that were too accurate for her opponent, and took the set 7-5. Even when she surrendered her serve at the beginning of the second set, spectators were becoming slowly more convinced about how the match would end.

Robson had settled to her task on Court 18 and as she clinched victory on the 16-year-old Serbian's serve – with Jovanoski dumping a forehand into the net – Laura became the face of Wimbledon, 2008.

The deafening cheers could be heard echoing around the All England Tennis Club, and as she made her way back to the locker room a swirl of young boys enveloped her, begging for her autograph.

Laura was in the semifinals – a British girl on her way to Wimbledon glory, lifting the spirits of a nation that had recently felt so let down by their sports stars. *'Tell Laura We Love Her'*, screamed the newspaper headlines, and reporters clamoured to get quotes from her parents and her circle of coaches.

'I hope we can see her playing on Centre Court one day,' Kathy told them. 'That's her dream, what she wants. We're just along for the journey.'

Carl Maes was cautiously optimistic when asked about Laura's future, saying: 'I was full time with Kim [Clijsters] when she was 14 and I travelled extensively with Justine Henin when she was 14. Laura plays that level of tennis. But she needs to keep on making the jumps she has in the last six months.'

Laura needed to stay grounded. It must have been exciting for her to have become an overnight media sensation, but she still had a job to do.

Her semifinal clash was with Romana Tabakova, and took place on a jam-packed Court 3. Thousands forsook the delights of Henman Hill to watch tennis's new British darling take on the Slovakian.

The stakes were high for both girls, but during the first set Laura steadily chipped away at her opponent, determination etched on her young face. She was surprisingly calm and composed, and the crowd could hardly believe she was just 14.

When Tabakova double-faulted in each of her service games, Robson was invited to take advantage and it was clear that the set was inevitably hers.

'Come on, Laura, mess her up!' shouted her brother Nick.

After Robson took the first set, Tabakova was under pressure. And in a display of bad form, she took a long toilet break in an effort to break Laura's stride.

It worked – but only temporarily.

At 4-3 down on her advantage, Tabakova tried another tactic – a sly, underhand serve. Not technically illegal, it was nonetheless a shocking display of sportsmanship, and earned the Slovakian a chorus of boos from unimpressed spectators.

Stranded on the baseline, Laura put her hands on her hips and gave the umpire a quizzical look. The point was given to Tabakova, but the watching crowd were now fully behind Robson, who had so far played fair and true. When Tabakova later asked for confirmation that a forehand was long, the umpire didn't have time to respond before a voice from the crowd boomed out: 'Well out, love...'

Laura finished the match off with a 7-5 second set win.

The court erupted into cheers and Laura had to struggle through a tide of autograph hunters to make her way to the packed press conference.

Robson was in the final of the girls' singles at Wimbledon – the first Brit to make it there since Annabel Croft in 1984, and the only Brit left in the 2008 tournament.

Everyone wanted to hear what she had to say.

For the first time in her life, bodyguards formed a protective circle about the youngster to shepherd her through the crowds, while her delighted grin was being captured by dozens of photographers.

'It's really, really good,' she told the press scrum, after being asked how she felt. 'An overwhelming experience. Indescribable. I didn't think I would get to the final at the start of the week.

'I had some good results in the past three or four months so it was kind of expected – just not this soon.'

When she was asked about Tabakova's underhand tactics, Laura gave the reporters their first experience of the dry, sharp wit she would eventually become known for off court: 'It was the first time I've ever seen that in my life,' she remarked innocently. 'It worked so fair play to her. But I don't think the crowd liked it very much.'

The journalists grinned silently to themselves.

Laura had been forced to learn her media duties quickly, and she was tackling the press as impressively as she had her opponents. But she was still a teenage girl – the youngest player at Wimbledon that year – and it was this that captured the nation's hearts...

'I'll just do my usual routine before the final,' she said humbly about the weekend ahead. 'I'll have dinner at home and then not do much in the evening.' But, as a twinkle appeared in her eye, she added: 'But I'm really looking forward to tomorrow because I get to pick out a dress and stuff for the Champions' Ball.

'I'm looking for something a bit simple – Jelena Jankovic wore a bright-pink one last year. I don't think I'll be going down that route. So, something simple I guess. I like blue.'

The press lapped up her every word, laughing at her barbed comments before concealing a round of '*aws*' when she shyly admitted she was nurturing a crush on a fellow tennis player.

'Who will you invite as your guest to the ball?' asked a reporter, to which Laura responded that she had no idea.

'Have you got your eye on anyone?' they pressed, keen for column inches.

'No...' she said. 'Apart from Safin.'

She was referring to Marat Safin, a Russian with smouldering good looks, who at that very moment was losing to Roger Federer on Centre Court.

Bringing the talk back to sport, Laura next gave the press pack a brief glimpse into her life as a tennis star in training. Britain was hungry for any scrap of detail about their new teen prodigy – even her eating habits.

She described how her strict diet meant that she had to cut out a few favourite dishes. 'I have to watch what I eat a lot with the nutrition,' she said. 'I like pizza but I don't really get to have it that often.'

Over the next few days, tennis fever swept through the country.

Annabel Croft had commentated on the match between Laura and Tabakova, and told the press: 'I think Laura is fantastic. There was a packed court and she was completely unfazed by it.'

Bookmakers Ladbrokes immediately offered odds of 20–1 against her winning the Wimbledon women's title by 2020, and spokesman David Williams said: 'People are really backing Laura and the odds have plummeted. It's the lowest price we've ever offered for someone so young.'

Carl Maes, now bristling with pride, said: 'She plays at the same level [as Clijsters did] and, on grass, perhaps even a bit better.'

Laura was riding the crest of a wave of publicity that was carrying her like royalty to her final match – which would be against 16-year-old Noppawan Lertcheewakarn from Thailand. But, waking up to find the press outside her bedroom window on the day of the final, she found herself struggling to quell her rising nerves.

She'd had a restless night's sleep.

The normally ice-cool, newly crowned princess of tennis would have a lot to overcome before the Champions' Ball that evening – which she had bravely asked Safin to accompany her to. His response had perked her up as she readied herself for the match. *'To Laura, I'm sorry I couldn't come to the ball but good luck.'*

And so, with her heartthrob behind her, her family in the crowd and the hopes of the nation resting heavy on her shoulders, she stepped out onto Court One. She was greeted by the sight of 11,000 eager spectators and instantly felt sick as she scanned the hopeful look on so many of their faces.

As the match began, the crowd was unusually subdued and the atmosphere seethed with anticipation. Every spectator simultaneously quashed their rising excitement and refrained from roaring out the hopes of success they were collectively harbouring. Perhaps it was an awareness of her tender age, or maybe it was the memory of so many past British hopes crumbling to dust. But, aside from the odd quiet chant and a sporadic 'Come on, Laura!', nobody dared risk putting the teenager off her stride.

Having steeled herself for the challenge, Robson made an assured start to the match – her power overwhelming the diminutive Lertcheewakarn as she secured an easy break.

The third seed struggled to contain Laura's aggressive style and Laura quickly raced to a 3-0 lead. But she began to stutter when her opponent picked herself up and stormed back to 3-3.

It took all Laura's strength to find fresh momentum, largely with the help of her punishing serve and forehand – and she took the set without conceding another game. But she was clearly rattled and Lertcheewakarn only needed one opportunity to capitalise on her failing confidence: when Robson squandered a break at 3-2, the tenacious Thai found her fight and Laura simply fell apart.

She had come so close to achieving something so great, but now she could feel victory slipping away and she was angry and scared. The country was counting on her to win – in fact, the country believed she *would* win – and now a little voice was telling her she was letting everyone down.

Her new ice-cool composure melted, and to the crowd it was suddenly very clear just how much hard work it usually took to keep that calm exterior intact. Laura was still a child emotionally and now, unfortunately, she reacted like one. She threw her racket to the ground, screamed and admonished herself with a stream of negative words and angry gestures.

With her focus more on her own failure than the game, there was nothing she could do to prevent Lertcheewakarn from drawing level with her 6-3 success.

It had all come down to the third and final set, and Laura had to regain her composure before it began. She dug deep and, with England's sporting fate in the balance, she somehow found her inner strength.

She quickly went 2-0 ahead in the decider and all of a sudden her momentum was back. This time it was unstoppable.

'Robson's Rockets' – as her explosive serve and forehand were dubbed after the game – took Lertcheewakarn apart, shot by shot.

After an hour-and-a-half of heart-stopping drama, the last shot was played and the crowd began to roar. Laura looked over to her mother and whispered: 'I can't believe it.'

It was a sentiment that was being echoed throughout the country. Laura Robson had won a Wimbledon title – for Britain!

Laura's father, Andrew, put his fingers in his mouth and whistled wildly, but he was drowned out by the deafening screams of joy. Her brother, Nick – who had shared his bedroom with Laura so that her coach could take her room for the tournament – winked at the camera.

Finally, Britain had something to celebrate.

And it was all down to a 14-year-old schoolgirl who had only held a British passport for four months.

Laura watched proudly as the Union Flag was draped over the trophy table. Ann Jones, Wimbledon winner in 1969, walked proudly out on court with a smile on her face and the girls' singles trophy in her hands.

As she presented it to Laura, who raised it high above her head, the crowd roared anew. It was a victory for everyone.

Kathy Robson was still stunned when the reporters gathered around her to hear what she had to say: 'It's a lonely place, being out on a tennis court, but she has shown the right spirit,' she said emphatically. 'Laura is just a 14-year-old girl, that's the way we see her and we want to keep it simple. I'm so proud of her, as I am proud of all my children. Laura has done this by working hard and playing tournaments since she was seven.'

When asked how the family planned to celebrate, Kathy smiled, continuing: 'I think my husband will take me out for a meal. I don't know if Laura will want to be seen with us – she's 14, she doesn't want to be seen with her family – but if she does we could take her to Pizza Hut, or somewhere like that. She does like pizza.'

Displaying the kind of down-to-earth parenting that had

made Laura into the grounded young woman the nation had fallen in love with, Kathy was adamant that Laura's win wouldn't go to her head.

'She's just a member of the family. The jobs she does round the house still go on,' Kathy said firmly. 'She still has to make her bed in the morning and put the dishes away.'

Laura was refreshingly honest when she spoke to the BBC: 'It was so good today, as all the crowd were behind me and it was an overwhelming experience. I didn't feel relaxed and thought I was going to be sick when I walked out on court because there were so many people watching.

'In the second set, I went a bit mad but I got it together and that is how I won I think.'

Her excitement was visible for all to see, and she blushed when she was asked whether she would be going to the Champions' Ball with her heartthrob Marat. After revealing the contents of his good luck letter, she quipped: 'I think he's a bit too old for me anyway…'

Over on Centre Court, Venus Williams had just won her fifth Wimbledon title, after defeating her sister Serena.

It was likely that Laura would be given a wildcard into the main Wimbledon draw in 2009, where there was a chance she would come face-to-face with Venus Williams, the American powerhouse.

So how did Laura feel about the prospect of that terrifying moment?

'I'll take her down!' she said boldly, buoyant with her tender success.

CHAPTER 7

POST-WIMBLEDON

That night, Laura changed out of her tennis whites into a classy short black satin dress. She slipped a pair of hot-pink high heels onto her usually trainer-clad feet. She had chosen the dress that morning from a selection of 150 laid out by Wimbledon dresser Elizabeth Piner, in the changing rooms at Centre Court.

As Wimbledon's newly crowned princess, she had been the first to pick out her outfit and she wanted to look chic and grown up for her first big ball. Photographers clamoured for her attention as she arrived at the Inter-Continental Hotel on Park Lane. With her chestnut locks falling in ringlets to her shoulders and her long legs suntanned from a life spent outdoors, she looked stunning – a girl on the very cusp of womanhood.

She grinned broadly for the cameras, before going inside to be congratulated by every tennis idol she had ever dreamed of meeting. It was a fairytale night, and one that didn't end until 2am for the tired teenager. But in the newspapers the next day, everyone who was anyone had something to say about Robson – and not all of it was simply gushing praise.

While tennis fans were busy renaming Henman Hill 'Robson's Ridge' in honour of her triumph, a host of more seasoned tennis pros were discussing her future more carefully.

Venus Williams was rooting for Robson, and offered her some wise advice: 'I think it is amazing what she has done. I hope that she continues to develop,' she said. 'It's so important to develop your game during the stage in her career that she is at now. Winning is awesome but really developing your game is the vital point. I hope that she and everyone around her focus on that.'

Tim Henman was particularly impressed with Laura's handling of the media, and pointed out just how important that aspect of the game is.

'You hear her speak off the court and she's very self-assured and knows what she's on about,' he said. 'She looks like she's got some real potential.'

And Britain's last Wimbledon women's champion Virginia Wade, who lifted the title in 1977, said: 'I'm really proud of her for what she did on Saturday, and I do think she's got what it takes.'

But Annabel Croft – who had last won the Wimbledon girls' title in 1984 – was more cautious in her praise. She reminisced about her own career beginnings, and offered some tips for her young successor in the *Daily Mail*.

'Laura's game is already so smooth, complete and

accomplished,' she wrote. 'While I have little doubt that Laura is at the beginning of an extremely promising career, I also know she will have to deal with things few 14-year-olds have to face, and handle pressures most adults rarely experience.

'Tennis beats you up emotionally and places enormous demands on you... One of the hardest things you have to come to terms with as a player is the realisation that your weaknesses are on display for everyone to see every time you are on court.

'It honestly felt like the end of the world every time I lost a match. I felt like I was riding a rollercoaster and I had no perspective.

'What I didn't realise then, but I do now, is that tennis is not the whole world. And I hope Laura knows this too.'

Laura was now in training not just for tennis super-stardom, but also for a life that would be spent largely in the public eye. She had been given some media training by a few well-chosen Sky Sports reporters, but interview questions could be unpredictable and embarrassing. Everyone agreed she had a strong head on her shoulders and a supportive family behind her, which would certainly help with the years she would now undoubtedly spend in the limelight.

But there were concerns that Laura would never have a normal teenage life. Instead of being surrounded by gossiping schoolgirls, all with different hopes and dreams, Laura would be bonding with fiercely ambitious girls who all wanted the same thing – tennis glory.

She would spend most of her time with coaches, fitness trainers, physiotherapists, nutritionists, sponsors, lawyers and the flighty media, all of whom would be older than her.

Dating would be nearly impossible and the international tour could be a lonely and soulless place.

And with so much pressure on her young shoulders it would be easy to quickly burn out, instead of moving onwards and upwards.

'Is Laura ready for that?' mused Croft. 'From what I've seen she certainly has what it takes. I wish her the best of luck.'

They were wise words, from a woman with the wisdom and experience to know what she was talking about. Laura, her family and her coaches were thinking exactly the same thing.

Laura's coterie agreed that she shouldn't be over-exposed after the veritable avalanche of publicity that had greeted her victory, and as a result she would be sitting out the under-18 US Open competition that would take place at Flushing Meadows in September.

In essence, she wouldn't be going after another junior Grand Slam title so soon after her Wimbledon win – a sensible precaution that fitted in with the new age restrictions brought in by the WTA Tour, designed to prevent the well-known 'burn-out' of teenage prodigies that had prematurely ended so many promising careers. History is littered with their tragic tales.

In 1979, Tracy Austin became the youngest ever US Open champion, beating Chris Evert at the age of just 16. A year later, she became world No. 1, before defeating Martina Navratilova in an infamous tiebreak at the US Open in 1981. But back injuries, the result of years of intense training while she was still growing, forced the pig-tailed blonde to retire at just 21.

In 1985, a severe shoulder injury ended the startlingly successful early career of American Andrea Jaeger, before she had even turned 20. As a teen she had terrorised the tour, winning ten singles titles and earning more than $1.4 million in prize money and millions more in endorsements. She is now a nun.

Jennifer Capriati was the youngest player ever to break into the world's top ten, doing so at the age of 14. She won Gold at the 1992 Olympics, but struggled to cope with the resulting pressure to perform and took time out from the game the following year. Her struggles during that time were well documented by the press, and included arrests for shoplifting and possession of drugs.

Laura's family and support network were keen to tread carefully in the next stage of her career – the tricky transition from juniors to seniors – in order to avoid a similarly devastating downfall.

'The nicest thing for Laura would be that we can leave her alone for the next six months, so she doesn't start walking with her head in the clouds,' said Carl Maes.

To that end, she flew to Amsterdam the day after her win for three weeks of low-key, unofficial adult tournament play – more for practice than anything else.

On the way there, her celebrity presence was announced on the plane and Laura squirmed with embarrassment. 'I was sitting right at the back and literally the whole plane turned and stared,' she later recounted. 'That wasn't very fun.'

Laura didn't want to be famous. She just wanted to be the best tennis player in the world.

After Holland, Laura took a break and went on a well-deserved family holiday, before returning to training in Britain, and to face a stream of inevitable questions from the media on when she would be playing next. The country was hungry to watch her progression, but Maes was guarded in his response to the onslaught.

'It hasn't been decided exactly where she'll play,' he said. 'It's sensible not to grab every opportunity that comes your way and take your time.'

Robson tried to get back into normal life after her stratospheric rise to the top. She was carefully shielded from the media and spent her time working on her form, playing with her dog and indulging in her passion for scary films. For the next few months, the media admired her from a distance, allowing her to embark on the quest for her first professional ranking points relatively unwatched.

She made her professional debut on the ITF women's circuit with little fanfare, playing entirely unannounced at an obscure bottom-rung tournament in Limoges, France in September. She won two matches to qualify for the main draw and followed these victories with a first-round win against Alice Balducci from Italy – a player ranked 875th in the world.

With her first ranking points safely under her belt, she went on to play No. 2 seed Marina Melnikova, before having to retire at 2-4 down in the first set due to a shoulder injury.

While Laura was quietly beginning her senior career, the LTA were very publicly reaping the rewards of her Wimbledon win. Just weeks after the tournament's end, they unveiled a £25 million sponsorship deal with Edinburgh-based insurance group Aegon, which was a huge indication of the renewed faith Laura had inspired in British tennis.

Robson was next given a wildcard into the main draw of a £40,000 ITF women's tournament at Shrewsbury's Welti Club – her first professional debut in Britain. It was a similarly low-key affair, but proved to be extremely valuable for Laura's confidence and status.

Dressed in a pink-and-white top and grey skirt, and with her hair in a messy plait, her first round was watched by just 75 tennis enthusiasts. It was a far cry from the heady heights of Wimbledon. There were no ballkids, a skeleton line judging crew and no spectator seats in the hangar-like centre.

Instead, viewers had to crane their necks on the balcony to catch a glimpse of the British heroine in action.

But it was a perfect opportunity for Laura to hone her skills against more experienced and seasoned players – a well-thought-out dip of the toe into the shallows of the women's tour before she turned 15 in January, and could go after her next big title at the Australian Open.

It was a tough match, against fellow Briton Sarah Borwell, who at 29 was nearly twice her age and ranked eighth in the country. But the tenacious spectators weren't disappointed with her performance. Her handling of Borwell's serve – previously timed at 120 mph – was outstanding, as was her refusal to give up when things got tough on court.

There were plenty of groans and self-scolding from the youngster, but she kept her focus and emerged triumphant, with a 7-6; 2-6; 6-3 victory over the older player.

Despite her defeat, Borwell was full of praise for Laura. 'I know we tend to get excited about new players but I was impressed,' she said after the match. 'I lost to Ana Ivanovic in the second round of Wimbledon two years ago and Laura reminds me of her.

'I thought I would be able to hit her off the court a bit but she moves well and sees the ball very early.

'She hits very aggressively and that shocked me a bit at the start. After watching her matches at Wimbledon, I thought she might struggle against more powerful players but she has this awareness of where the ball is going. She also returns extremely well.'

But Laura did have an Achilles heel – one she struggled to hide from her opponents – and Sarah could see it.

'Her attitude is the sign of someone who is going to get up there pretty fast,' she said. 'It depends how she handles the pressure but she expects a lot of herself, like all top players.'

Borwell's insight was spot on – and plainly evident in Robson's own analysis of her performance: 'It was a tough match and I didn't play as well as I would have hoped,' she said. 'But I'm looking forward to the rest of the week.'

Robson was ambitious and hated to make a mistake, however small. The pressure she was placing on herself was enormous and it was just as well that her coaches were keeping her as far removed from the public eye as possible.

The added pressure of huge publicity, at such an early stage of her transition to the senior circuit, could be disastrous.

Robson's next opponent would be the girl she succeeded as Wimbledon girls' champion: 17-year-old Urszula Radwanska. The highly rated Pole was on her way to breaking the top 100 after a steady and accomplished ascent on the senior tour.

One half of Poland's answer to the Williams sisters – at the time her older sister Agnieszka was ranked 10th in the world and was herself a previous winner of the Wimbledon girls' trophy – Urszula was a bright young thing on the circuit, progressing steadily and tipped for great success.

So, when 14-year-old Laura – essentially a younger, newer version of herself – began to steam ahead during their second-round match, Radwanska went to pieces. She began violently hitting her racket on the ground with such force it was a wonder it survived. But her display of anger didn't help her game and Laura won 6-3; 6-3.

While Radwanska fumed to herself in consolation, Robson was diplomatic. 'I was pleased with my performance,' she said carefully. 'Radwanska is a tough player so I knew I had to play a good match in order to win.'

Speaking in his role as head of the women's game for the LTA, Carl Maes was more candid: 'That can't have been easy for Radwanska,' he conceded. 'Here she was losing to a 14-year-old. She got very upset. Radwanska probably wasn't expecting to lose to someone younger than her.'

Laura had been playing exceptionally well, keeping her cool under extreme pressure and was through to the quarter-finals.

Her next opponent was just a little bit more terrifying.

Having served two years in the Israeli army, Tzipi Obziler was a tough, 35-year-old player not to be trifled with. She was old enough to be Laura's mother, was ranked 120 in the world and had just represented her country at the 2008 Summer Olympics in Beijing in both singles and doubles.

For this match, going under the radar was simply not an option. Word had spread that England's sweetheart was flying through her first senior event on home soil and the media now wanted in on the triumph. When Robson began her quarterfinal face-off with Obziler, it was in front of a crowd of 200 and filmed by a handful of TV cameras.

Robson's nerves must have been made of steel, because in little over an hour she had vanquished the veteran 6-3; 6-3. She was feisty, quick and almost faultless, pouncing swiftly to gain breaks and remaining composed throughout.

'This match was the best of the three she has won this week so far,' said LTA Head Coach Nigel Sears, who was clearly impressed. 'She completely outplayed someone with a decent ranking, it was top quality. Laura showed remarkable composure and made scarily few errors – it was a very smart match she played.'

It was a good result for Laura, but an even greater one for the LTA. Despite the fact that Laura's career had been developed independently of the British Tennis Association, Laura's coach, Martijn Bok, was centrally funded, and Laura had the run of the LTA facilities to improve her game.

And it was a very different way of approaching training for the LTA, who had previously taken total charge of the most promising young players and sidelined their maverick parents completely. But Laura's parents, (just like Judy Murray with Andy and Jamie) had gone their own way from the very beginning and produced great results – before eventually receiving financial help from the LTA to continue doing so.

For the LTA, Laura's success was public proof that the governing body's more open-minded approach to professional training was working – and they were pleased.

'In 18 months I expect she will be playing on the main tour,' Sears was quoted as saying.

'She is far from the finished article but is developing fast, and it will be exciting to see when she is the finished article.

'I'm not really surprised about anything she does any more. It's down to the hard work she has already put in and her level of strength and fitness tells you that fitness trainer Steve Kotze is doing good work with her day in, day out.'

Robson was playing at the standard of someone around the top 100, despite the fact that she hadn't even played enough tournaments yet to officially rank at all. If anyone had been wondering, it was now obvious that Wimbledon hadn't been a fluke. And there was further proof in the fact that Britain's Elena Baltacha and Katie O'Brien – both established top 150 players and ranked two and three in the country behind No. 1 Anne Keothavong – were already out of the tournament in which she had thus far survived.

It was a phenomenal achievement.

But, in the semifinals, Robson finally ran out of steam. After losing in three sets to second seed Maret Ani from Estonia, Laura was philosophical. 'I can cope with playing at this level, but they have more experience,' she admitted.

'I can definitely play with them,' she repeated. 'It's just a question of getting the experience.'

Time was on her side.

CHAPTER 8

SEEDED

In October 2008, Laura made her main draw debut in the WTA Fortis Luxembourg Open on a wildcard – the youngest British player in history to do so.

She was still just 14, barely a teenager, and she had only just earned her first world career ranking of 550. It was a great starting point to ascend from, but it was just that – a starting point.

Robson was certainly rocketing on in her career, and had made a good impression on the women's ITF circuit, but the WTA tour was a whole new ballgame. This was where the best players in the world competed for huge prize monies and vital points to boost their rankings. It was a serious place, and not one that was often frequented by youngsters like Robson.

Her first-round opponent, world No. 42 Iveta Benesova, had never even heard of the Wimbledon girls' champ before she saw her name on the draw sheet. But she was certainly taken aback by the power and precision that the youngster attacked her with during the first set. Within 20 minutes, and after dropping just one game, Robson was a set up, and it was clear the Czech player didn't quite know how to deal with the teenager.

It was a dream start to Laura's debut on the WTA tour, and it didn't seem at all like Benesova was playing a girl a decade younger and more than 500 places below her in the rankings. In the gallery above the indoor court, a little scrum of seasoned players had appeared to watch the newbie, who, as far as they were concerned, had come out of nowhere to play her first match.

If she had been on the junior circuit, it's safe to say that Robson would have continued to steamroll her way to glory, after successfully putting the frighteners on her poor opponent. But, as Laura was about to find out, things were very different on the main circuit.

After her initial shock, the left-handed Benesova soon got the measure of her sporting foe and turned the game around with ease. It was like she'd been shocked by the initial strength of a wasp sting, and now she exacted her devastating punishment on its perpetrator.

Robson couldn't maintain her dominance and began to slide in the second set. Hitting her head with her racket in frustration, she knew what was happening: she was being naturally outclassed and there was simply nothing she could do. As the match drew to a close, Laura let out an anguished cry that was half scream, half sob. But the 25-year-old Czech won the battle of left-handers 1-6; 6-2; 6-3.

'I started very well,' the young British player said in self-consolation after the match, before admitting: 'The second set maybe didn't go as well and she started playing very well.'

Laura had flexed her adult muscles, but she still needed a lot more experience before she moved into the adult leagues full-time. It was certainly no reflection on her tennis ability, or her future potential.

It was time to head back to the ITF and even the world of junior tennis for a while, and she did so as the newly pronounced No. 5 seed. 'Everyone on the tour has been really friendly and I've enjoyed it,' she said respectfully. She stayed on in the Grand Duchy for a while to learn from the players, thoroughly humbled by her experience.

Then she took that experience home to the ITF circuit, with a renewed determination to climb to the top.

Her first tournament upon her return took place at Sunderland's Puma Centre, where the winner would receive £772.

It's safe to say that Laura didn't enter the competition for the promise of a huge payday. But it was here, on a dreary November day, that she claimed her maiden senior title – she hoped it was to be the first of many. It may have been the lowest level of tournament on the ITF senior circuit, but Robson was overjoyed to power through the Futures Event and beat fellow Brit Samantha Vickers, a 17-year-old ranked 1,052 on the world list, in the final.

Robson was 14 years and 9 months old, and her grin as she sealed the win was infectious.

A few days later, she made the headlines again: she had been shortlisted for the BBC's Young Sports Personality of the

Year, alongside diver Tom Daley and paralympic swimmer Eleanor Simmonds.

The panel who chose to shortlist Laura included former winners Harry Aikines-Aryeetey and Kate Haywood, various representatives of the Youth Sport Trust, and BBC Sport presenters John Inverdale and Jake Humphrey.

Jake explained their decision to include Laura, saying:

Laura is just what British tennis is crying out for – a winner. It's important to remember the pressure she had to deal with on the way to winning Wimbledon.

She had previously competed in much lower-profile events in front of a few hundred spectators, yet at SW19 she looked like she was born to play on Number 1 Court.

The huge TV audience and press interest didn't faze her and she achieved a monumental feat. She was the youngest competitor at Wimbledon, has gone on to a pro-career and her success continues to generate interest.

In an interview with the BBC, aired before the winner was announced, Laura gave her fans the biggest insight yet into her personality off the court.

She was shy and softly spoken – speaking with the same perfect diction she had used in post-match interviews.

But she didn't stick to tennis talk.

Instead, she giggled childishly as she admitted to knowing all the words and dance steps to the popular *High School Musical* films. She explained how she never missed an episode of American teen drama *Gossip Girl*, revealed her desire to be able to draw better and told how her latest hobby was learning how to juggle.

She loved shopping, hated spiders and bugs and thought her worst habit was biting her nails. She also said she was grateful that the publicity surrounding her Wimbledon win had died down, and she could go shopping again without really being noticed.

Her favourite music to play before a competition was 'Eye of the Tiger' – the famous Rocky theme tune – and the albums on her iPod currently included Rihanna and the Kings of Leon. She said that the biggest sacrifice she had made for her sport was the constant travelling, but added: 'I don't really miss home all that much, so I'm fine with it.'

It could have been an interview with any 14-year-old in the country, and it was an important glimpse into the 'girl behind the racket'. And, after hearing so many warnings about the importance of maintaining a real childhood in such an adult world, it was a relief to discover that Laura was a perfectly normal teenager, and had succeeded in separating her personal from her professional life.

But what set her apart from the other giggling schoolgirls her age was the small fire that burned continuously inside her. And even in the BBC's light-hearted interview, she couldn't disguise her serious ambition.

When asked why she wanted to win Young Personality of the Year, she wrote her answer down on a board before turning it to face the camera. It read: *Because I don't like losing...*

This time she had to lose – because the award went to 13-year-old paralympian Eleanor Simmonds, who had been Britain's youngest individual paralympic gold medallist at the

Beijing Olympics. With it being an Olympics year, there had been stiff competition – in other circumstances, it seems obvious that Laura would have been a shoe-in for the prestigious award.

As 2008 was drawing to a close, Laura had a few more tournaments to play before she would fly to Australia for a good old-fashioned family Christmas with her grandparents. Her relations 'Down Under' must have been keen to celebrate the end of an incredible year with their beautiful and talented export.

And she was planning to warm up in some junior events in Oz before going after her next Grand Slam – the Australian Open.

But first Laura was off to Florida, where she hoped to claim her third Eddie Herr trophy and her first Orange Bowl. Returning to Eddie Herr was like a homecoming – she had won twice before, and, after her explosive year of success, spectators were hoping to see some great tennis from the youngster.

However, it quickly became apparent that something was wrong.

In the second round, she faced Nicole Bartnik, a 17-year-old Bollettieri student whom she had beaten in the spring at the ITF Italian Junior Open.

Despite being the top seed at the under 18s event, Laura struggled from the outset. She couldn't find her rhythm and played poorly. Down 4-0 in the third set, when yet another of her shots caught the tape, she yelled out: 'I can't play any worse!'

The disappointed crowd silently agreed.

After pulling back just one game from her opponent, Laura

lost 5-7; 6-3; 1-6 and was out of the tournament. Commentators called it the 'Junior Tennis Upset of the Year' and everyone wondered if she was overtired, jetlagged, or worse. But, with the Orange Bowl tournament just days away, there was no time to dwell on her defeat.

With such strict limits in place on how many senior events the younger players could play to protect them from injury, it struck some fans as odd that Eddie Herr and the Orange Bowl were played out on consecutive weeks. Nonetheless, Laura progressed through the first two rounds of her next tournament, dropping just six games along the way. Her serve was noticeably slow in her second-round match, displaying none of the intense power it was known for.

In her third-round match, she finally admitted she had a problem. She had pulled a stomach muscle and, despite having bravely attempted to play through the pain, it had now got too much for her. She retired from the tournament. Laura had to watch the rest of the action from the sidelines, with a huge bag of ice strapped around her waist.

Though it had started so morosely, 2008 had eventually turned into a vintage year for British sport. Nineteen gold medals had meant glory at the Beijing Olympics and Paralympics, Formula One success had come for Lewis Hamilton, Joe Calzaghe had punched his weight in the boxing ring and Andy Murray had risen to a career best No. 4 in the world tennis rankings.

And, of course, Britain had met and fallen in love with little Laura Robson, their new heroine of tennis.

Britain finally had something to celebrate and, on New Year's Eve, people raised their glasses with a little more enthusiasm than they had done the year before.

CHAPTER 9

GROWING
PAINS

After her stomach injury in December, Laura was advised to rest, which must have been hard for the ambitious youngster.

She took it extra easy over Christmas, shunning her usual rigorous training regime in favour of relaxing with her family in the glorious southern hemisphere sunshine. In early January, she slowly began training again, her eye firmly on her next prize.

Laura Robson celebrated her 15th birthday in Melbourne, the city of her birth, while making her final preparations for her first Australian Open. As she opened her birthday cards, she grew flushed with joy at the sight of one particular signature – Marat Safin's. Still nursing a crush on the handsome player, her heart must have skipped a beat when she read the few words he had penned on a scrap of paper and slipped inside the card: 'Happy birthday and all the best.'

It was hardly a declaration of love, but it was a welcome distraction from the task ahead.

Robson was fully aware that this was a hugely important tournament – not just for her, but for British tennis in general. The high-profile player Anne Keothavong had got through to the main draw of the senior event without the need of a wildcard. Laura had achieved the same in the junior event.

It was the first time since Jo Durie and Clare Wood had got through to the US Open in 1993 that two British women had simultaneously accomplished this feat, and it was also Laura's first Grand Slam since Wimbledon.

But it was the start of a tough period for Robson, who had shockingly grown a massive two inches since her Wimbledon win, putting her body under immense strain and making her vulnerable to injury. She was now 5ft 9in and still growing in height.

She had to be careful.

Five days after her birthday, Laura marked her return to junior Grand Slam tennis by beating her first-round opponent, top American Christina McHale, 7-5; 6-3.

But it hadn't been easy.

Dressed in a bright-yellow vest and black shorts, with a white visor protecting her eyes from the blinding Melbourne sunshine, Laura had found herself in trouble early on in the match. After 45 minutes she was trailing 5-3, but held her nerve and rallied to take four straight games and win the set. Her serve was broken early on in the second set, but once again she fought back, breaking twice and taking the next four games. McHale tried to stage a comeback, but Robson wasn't having any of it; however, she looked visibly relieved to be through to the next round.

The young American McHale had been touted as one of the best players of the draw and Robson told reporters: 'She's a very good player so I knew it was going to be tough and I'm pleased to have come through it.'

Laura's win had boosted her confidence, but in her next match she had more to worry about than just her opponent. Walking out on court, it felt like someone had just opened an oven door in her face. It was shaping up to be the hottest Australian January in over 40 years, and was stunning the country, which definitely already knew a thing or two about handling warm weather.

For Laura, the developing heatwave took her breath away.

But, as the soaring temperature hit 40 degrees Celsius, she knuckled down to play Thailand's Kanyapat Narattana, a stocky tomboy in shorts, wearing dark glasses.

It was a tough match, as both girls struggled with the weather. Robson took the first set 6-3, before flagging in the second. But her determination pulled her back from the brink, and she managed to force a tiebreak, which she won 7-0.

'I just said to myself that I wasn't focused,' Robson said after escaping the intense heat of the court. 'I was beginning to get concerned about the heat and I knew I didn't really want to stay out there for another set. It was simply time to get my act together and that's what I did.'

She celebrated by going for an ice-bath to cool down – an unpleasant experience but one that her tennis coach and trainers believed to be necessary after an intense match. Submersing herself in the ice-cold water must have been a shock to the system, but the benefits were supposed to include less muscle pain, less muscle stiffness, injury prevention and a speedy recovery time – all essential when playing in a tournament, which leaves little time for body recovery between matches. Along with massages and warm-down sessions, ice-baths were a necessary evil.

Besides, it must have been a relief to temporarily escape the heatwave, which was causing the city to practically melt. Bushfires were sweeping close to Melbourne, carrying acrid air across the beautiful blue sky. Train tracks buckled; power grids crashed.

The wheelchairs being used by the disabled players in the tennis tournament were becoming literally too hot to handle. Burns and blisters from red-hot metal rims and molten tyres had been making play almost impossible – some tyres had even burst in the heat.

And, although her next match, against Croatia's Silvia Njiric, was played in the early morning – before the worst of the heat could descend – Laura still suffered terribly as she played. She frequently stopped for water, drinking about 12 bottles of the stuff during the match, which was mercifully short.

She won 6-4; 6-2 to go through to the final eight.

After yet another ice-bath, she made her way to the outdoor courts, where her friend and fellow Brit Heather Watson was also playing in the junior tournament. Heather had appeared for support during Laura's match, before leaving to prepare for her own. Laura now returned the favour, trying to find some shade as the temperatures climbed.

The tournament's extreme heat policy was finally put into play in the afternoon and both roofs were closed on the two main show courts. Play was stopped on the outside courts, but Watson's match was still going on while the decision was being made, and she had to complete the torturously long match in the intense heat.

There was no respite, not even through drinking, as Watson's water had become unpalatably hot in between games. At one point Laura winced in pity, as she watched Watson lean on her racket for support: her feet had got so hot they were physically hurting. Thankfully, she beat her opponent, Japan's Miyabi Inoue, and both Heather and Laura could celebrate reaching the final eight together.

'It was so, so hot,' 16-year-old Watson said after the match. 'Thank God I came out on top. I've never played in such high temperatures. Straight afterwards I got into the shower, ate, and then had an ice-bath. Even by the second set I was feeling dizzy.'

Watson had played in two junior slams the previous year, losing in the first round at Wimbledon when Robson won the title, and then reaching the second round at the US Open, in which Laura didn't compete.

'We are both trying really hard to get the best out of our games, and it's fun,' she said. 'We push each other along and get on really well.'

'I felt really sorry for Heather in that heat,' said Robson. 'I found it easier to cope when I was playing rather than sitting down, when you just get hit by a wave of heat.'

Both young women steeled their nerves before walking out to play their quarterfinal matches, and tried to prepare themselves for their opponents.

It was difficult to decide which foe was worse: the girl on the other side of the net or the sun that was beating down on them all relentlessly. Both matches had been pulled forward to a 10am start, but even then the gauge was hovering at around the 37⁰C mark.

Watson sadly lost to Russian third seed Ksenia Pervak, while Robson's match was a far more dramatic affair.

She had won the first set 6-3 against Romania's Elena Bogdan, but was 2-5 down in the second, when Bogdan had cried out in pain. She had heavily rolled her ankle and play was halted while a doctor strapped it up. Nobody was happy about her continuing, since she was clearly still in pain. But she battled on, against a hesitant Robson, who obviously didn't want to see her opponent injure herself even more.

Bogdan winced and limped, playing on for another two points, getting to 30-0. But the doctor was unimpressed and forced her to retire from the match. The heat, the pain and the disappointment caused Bogdan to burst into tears. In the circumstances, Laura felt bad celebrating, but she was through to the semifinal and, putting sympathy aside, she was overjoyed.

Here she was, in the city of her birth, being embraced by not only her British fans, but the Australians too, who were claiming her as their own and backing her all the way.

And so far, the tournament hadn't been all work and no play either. There was that card from dreamy Safin, plus she had watched Federer play and had enjoyed a lively chat with Serena Williams in the locker rooms.

All in all, Robson was very much enjoying her first Australian Open, and she was itching to play her semifinal match – against top seed Noppawan Lertcheewakarn, the Thai player she had beaten to Wimbledon glory seven months before.

Laura was determined to take Lertcheewakarn down again, and pumped her fist as she walked out on court to face her. Fixing her opponent with a steely glare across the net, there was no doubt she meant business.

But the match had been delayed by two hours because temperatures had crept up to an impossible 44 degrees Celsius, and there was no doubt she was tired. When it finally got underway at 5pm, Laura got off to a slow start against her opponent – going 3-0 down before rallying to take the first set. Her momentum steadily built during the second, as she raced to a 4-0 lead by getting a double break on the Thai player.

Lertcheewakarn, desperate not to lose for a second time against the youngster, managed to claw a break back in the next game before dropping her serve for the third time to trail 5-1.

She fought back to take the next two games, but, by that time, the look on Robson's face said she was ready to end things once and for all. Channelling all her lagging energy into the final game, Laura won the match 6-4; 6-3.

Smiling at the cheers from the crowd, she waved as she walked off, only to be surrounded by an enthusiastic group of autograph hunters. She took time to scrawl her signature over various balls and scraps of paper, especially those belonging to the little kids who gazed up at her in awe.

The experience reminded her of the time her exhibition match had been rained off at Wimbledon when she was nine. Alongside eating strawberries and cream, she had spent the day running around with an oversized ball, trying to get people to sign it. Hewitt, Clijsters and Dementieva had all obliged her, and the ball was still one of Laura's prized possessions. Now she was the one doing the signing. She could hardly believe it.

Her mum was back home in London, and Laura was so elated that she forgot to text her with the final score. Her brother Nick had stayed up with his friends to watch the match and got no sleep as he cheered his sister on from afar. But Kathy had been dozing, waiting to hear from her daughter, and hadn't been pleased when she'd had to hear the score from friends.

She could hardly be angry. Her daughter, Laura Robson, was in the final of the Australian Open – but would she have the energy to win it?

'I didn't start so well,' she admitted after her win. 'I felt really out of energy throughout the whole match really, so it was good to get through it. I was just waiting around for so long. So I think that was the problem really.'

Now she would face Russian Ksenia Pervak, the third seed who had knocked Robson's pal Heather Watson out of the Open.

But she was worried about the heat, which, after three consecutive days of being over 44 degrees Celsius, was draining everyone of energy.

'I probably won't get another week like this for a while in terms of weather,' she explained.

'It's been hard dealing with it but I got through it, so that's good. I think, throughout the last couple of days, I've just been getting more and more tired. There's not really much I can do if I'm completely out of energy but I'll just try to prepare as best as I can.'

That night, she had yet another ice-bath, ate pasta for tea and fantasised about winning the Open. She decided she would celebrate by going shopping with her sister, who had moved back to Australia and therefore was close by. But winning would be her main reward. If only she could do it...

Pervak was two years and five months Robson's senior and hadn't even expected to play the junior event when she'd landed in Australia a few weeks before. With a WTA tour ranking of 154, her priority at the Open had been the senior draw, which unfortunately hadn't gone so well for her. But, after making the long journey from Moscow, she had decided to double up in the junior event, which, with her 18th birthday still four months away, she just about still qualified for.

So time and space were the only reasons she'd entered the tournament, which most other juniors could only long to be competing in. Her much stronger physical build and experience had unsurprisingly taken her easily through the junior draw, but she didn't seem grateful in the slightest. When Pervak was asked why she had decided to enter, she said bluntly: 'Because it takes a long way to come here from Russia. That's why.'

Reporters at the tournament all agreed she'd brought an icy Russian blast with her. It all seemed a little unfair, especially since Pervak hadn't played at a junior event for a year. But the rules were the rules and she had made it to the final.

The arena was packed and the temperature was still high when Robson arrived to face her bored-looking opponent in the final. She was hot, tired and nervous and the match didn't start well for the young Brit. She lost her opening two service games, giving momentum to Pervak and forcing her to get angry with herself.

Laura knew she had to keep her rage under control, but, even so, she gave in to a few baseline tantrums. Her frustration was palpable as she sprayed shots long and wide.

Pervak, on the other hand, schemed her way through the match.

When Robson finally started to gain ground, Pervak reached for the towel, disrupting her opponent's fledgling momentum. It was blatantly against the rules, but the umpire said nothing.

The face of Laura's opponent remained expressionless; her movement minimal.

A break to 15 in the fourth game gave Robson a glimmer of hope, and she attacked the ball with renewed enthusiasm. Briefly she rallied, and fired off a series of bullet-quick balls that Pervak didn't even bother to try to return.

As Kevin Garside wrote for the *Daily Telegraph* that night: 'In those moments Robson demonstrated the greater range, the higher peaks. But what she lacked was her opponent's nous.'

Pervak won the junior title 6-3; 6-1.

Laura was graceful in her defeat and smiled for the cameras while clutching her runner-up prize of an engraved silver plate and a cuddly toy.

Pervak didn't really look bothered either way.

Waiting in the obligatory drug-testing room after the match, Laura had time to dwell on her achievements. Her defeat couldn't take away the fact that she had progressed considerably since her shock win at Wimbledon.

It was only her second junior slam and she had once more made the final. She had played six matches in as many days in debilitating heat and had risen to the Australian Open challenge, even beating the top seed along the way.

She had nothing to be ashamed of.

The air-conditioning was cranked up in the room and the wait was unusually long. She was given some comfort by Spanish pin-up Fernando Verdasco, who lent her his jumper to take off the chill.

Later, she faced the press, still cocooned in the oversized jumper. 'It was disappointing to lose but I played as well as I could have,' she said bravely. 'It was really good to overcome the weather we had this week so I feel it was a really good achievement. I have played some senior matches, too, so maybe experience wasn't the key factor but her consistency was,' she added.

Pervak told a different story.

'Experience helped me today,' she said arrogantly. 'I had more confidence than she had. She is much younger than me. She's okay but I was better, so what can I say? I was much better than her.'

Unlike the frosty Russian, Laura was pleasant and charming throughout the interview. She said that she had learned a lot at the event and pledged a quieter response to adversity down the line. 'I need to let go when I don't do so well,' she admitted. 'In three of my matches this week, I didn't get the early break in the second set and it started to affect me more. I need to deal with that.'

And she was downright adorable when she was asked how she'd managed to keep her flagging energy up on the court.

'I upped my dosage of jelly snakes,' she grinned, referring to some sweet jelly treats that her nutritionist had allowed her to have.

She had come so far in such a short space of time, and it was only natural for her to feel disappointed. But Laura's defeat at the hands of the experienced Russian was almost a good thing – it was a gentle reminder that she still had work to do.

For now, she would enjoy the rest of her time Down Under before she had to return to Britain's icy chill. She delighted in bagging two much-coveted Australian Open players' towels, and did indeed go shopping with her sister. Then she took her place in the crowd to watch the men's final, between Rafael Nadal and Roger Federer – two giants of the tennis world.

It was an epic battle, stretching over 4 hours and 22 minutes, and no one had any idea which way it would eventually go.

The momentum swung back and forth between the two friends, but in the end it was Nadal who took the title at the Rod Laver Arena.

Federer struggled to contain his emotions as Nadal celebrated his win – he was the first Spaniard ever to win the Grand Slam, and was clearly overjoyed. But Federer had just missed his first chance to match Pete Sampras's 14 Grand Slam singles titles record, and he was devastated. Accepting the runner-up plate, his whole body was wracked with sobs. 'God, it's killing me,' he just about managed over the deafening cheers, which were coming from a crowd whose hearts were breaking along with his.

But eventually he composed himself enough to congratulate his friend. Wiping away the tracks of his tears, he thanked the crowd, the organisers and Nadal himself for a great match. 'You deserved it,' he told him. 'You played a fantastic final.'

As Rod Laver presented the winner's cup to Nadal, Federer continued to weep and Nadal looked distressed. Throwing his arm around his friend, he told him: 'Roger, sorry for today. I really know how you feel right now. Remember, you're a great champion, you're one of the best in history.'

It was a moving moment and Laura must have felt overwhelmed to be there to witness it. She knew how it felt to lose an important match; she knew how it felt to fall foul of your own emotions.

If one of the greatest tennis players in the world could so publicly fall apart, then surely she could be forgiven for sometimes getting emotional. Maybe she should ease up on herself, she reasoned.

She was doing well. She had plenty of time.

And it was only a game after all.

Oh, but what a game.

CHAPTER 10

SCHOOL VS TENNIS

It had been an intense start to the year for Laura, but, when she flew home from Australia at the end of January, it was to focus on her school studies, not on tennis glory.

She had been in the frame for the 2009 British Fed Cup team, but, after a series of discussions with her mother and coach, team captain Nigel Sears announced she would not be taking part. 'We took a lot of things into consideration,' he said.

Presumably her schoolwork was a significant factor in his decision, but it wasn't the only one: focusing on her studies would also give her growing body some respite from the immense physical strain of continuous training and long and tiring tennis matches. Her long legs had been aching painfully as a result of the growth spurt she was going through, and it was better to give them a break than to risk the stresses and strains associated with training intensively during that delicate time.

Laura's bones were growing faster than her muscles, so she was at a much higher risk of injury. Heavy impact, improper form or even just stretching too far could cause her muscles to disconnect from the bone, a painful experience that would sideline her for weeks. Also, due to her age, Laura was limited to playing in ten tournaments throughout the season, and she wanted to choose their timing wisely.

And besides, who knew when she would again have the luxury of being able to take a few months off?

Once she made the full transition from junior to senior tennis, her life would become a constant stream of matches and travel, only ending when she retired from the game. She might not have wanted to refrain from the continuous tournament play that would up her player ranking, but she could definitely afford to slow down a little.

She had been given a wildcard into the qualifiers at Wimbledon, and was hoping that after her sterling performance in Australia this might be boosted to a wildcard into the main draw.

Only time would tell. But in the interim period she knuckled down to prepare for her GCSEs and finally unpacked the myriad suitcases that she had abandoned in her bedroom after each overseas tournament.

'I never unpack,' Laura has said, citing this habit as one of her biggest weaknesses. 'I take one suitcase to a tournament, and then come home and not unpack it and then go to another one with another suitcase and not unpack it.

'So, in the end, I have about five suitcases in my room until it gets to the point where you can't see the floor anymore.'

And so Laura played with Ella the dog, indulged in some

family time and watched as many tennis matches as possible, including an epic Davis Cup play-off match between Chris Eaton and James Ward, that lasted 6 hours and 40 minutes. Watching from the balcony at the LTA headquarters in Roehampton, she was joined by her friend Anne Keothavong, and must have been glad for the opportunity to have a girly catch-up.

In February, she discovered that she had won the MCC 'Young Sportswoman of the Year' award, but missed the star-studded ceremony put on by *The Sunday Times* because she was studying. This clash was somewhat ironic: she'd often had to miss out on studying because of her tennis commitments, and now she was missing out on some tennis-related fun because of her studies.

But it wasn't all bad: she went rock climbing and kayaking and revelled in her newfound freedom from training.

Eventually, well into the spring, it was time for Laura to put down her books and finally lace up her trainers again. She flew first to Barcelona, specifically to train on a clay-surfaced court, and then to Amsterdam because of their exceptional facilities. She even made it as far as Las Vegas, where she attended Gil Reyes's legendary training camp to improve her fitness.

Spurred on in April by the news that she had climbed up in the rankings to world junior No. 1, she approached her return to full-time training with a renewed vigour, excited about getting back on the tournament circuit. At the end of May, she made her return to the professional game – three-and-a-half months after her last competitive match at the Australian Open.

She packed her suitcase and flew to Milan for a high-level

ITF junior tournament, where she made it through to the quarterfinals before being knocked out by 16-year-old American Sloane Stephens. Stephens was one of a crop of young tennis hopefuls that the Americans were hoping would change their fortunes in the women's game, and she was very, very good.

Robson struggled throughout both sets before losing 4-6; 0-6. She could see that the exceptionally fit Stephens would prove to be a challenge again in the future, especially with her footwork skills and powerful two-handed backhand.

But good news from the LTA back home at the All England Club took her mind off the loss: the association had added a special clause to their main draw wildcard recommendation policy, stating that in exceptional circumstances junior players could be put forward for privileged entries, whatever their ranking.

The official cut-off point was a ranking of 250, and with Robson currently at 485, without the new rules she would have had to stick with her wildcard for the qualifiers. Now it looked like she would make the cut when the wildcards were handed out after the forthcoming French Open.

Laura was so ecstatic that not even a first-round defeat two days later, on clay in Grado, northern Italy, could bring her down. But heading to Roland Garros three days later for her debut at the French Open, Laura had other things on her mind: she had to find somewhere to sit her English GCSE, and scouted around Paris for a suitable British school for that purpose.

It was very distracting, especially when she wasn't totally comfortable with her chances at the Open.

While her fellow Brits Hannah James, Heather Watson and

Stephanie Cornish lost in the first round, Robson triumphed over her Russian opponent Karina Pimkina.

Congratulated by a posse of British fans, including a group of lads on a stag weekend with whom she posed for photos, she was definitely pleased with the win. However, she wasn't going to get her hopes up. Her form was still suffering from her absence from the circuit, and, despite specifically training for it, she still wasn't at all keen on the clay surface she had to play on.

'I'm a bit iffy on clay,' she admitted. 'I don't like what it does to my socks. I'm getting into it and working on my movement but my expectations aren't high here.'

It was just as well. The following day she hung her head in defeat as she crashed out in the second round.

But it was grass glory she was after. And when it was confirmed that she had indeed been given a wildcard into the senior main draw at Wimbledon, she focused her training on that event.

In the run-up to the summer showdown, the British press renewed their fascination with the tennis starlet, discussing her strengths and weaknesses and reporting on the public's hopes that she would one day become a British Wimbledon women's champion.

Robson would be the youngest Brit ever to appear in the senior draw, which some were taking to be proof positive that she was prepared for the challenge. In reality, it would be a tall order for the then 15-year-old, who should have simply been allowed to be excited about playing at all. But tennis fever had started early, and this year it had a particularly virulent strain...

Laura tried to take the pressure off by publicly throwing

doubt on her own expectations – something which was unusual in itself, as her advisers weren't usually keen on her speaking publicly unless it was for a post-match interview.

She was, after all, only 15.

'I don't know what I'm going to do but all I can do is go on court and try my best,' she said. 'Then, win or lose, if I had tried my best then I cannot be unhappy.'

They were words that sounded as if they originally came from her parents or her coaches. It was as if by repeating them aloud Laura was trying to make them true. Deep down, the pressure on her must have been overwhelming, especially since she still hadn't sat that pesky English GCSE.

She was training, studying and trying to ignore the constant press speculation. Was it all too much?

Other tennis stars began to wade in to try to ease the public pressure. 'It's a great opportunity,' said Tim Henman. 'Whatever happens it's going to be a positive for Laura. She's playing the biggest and the best tournament at home and this is purely about experience so she should enjoy it.'

The Williams sisters told her to 'just go out and enjoy herself', while Jennifer Capriati added: 'She must make certain she treats it as just another court and not let the experience get to her.'

'Perhaps she will win a round or two but, if she doesn't, it shouldn't be regarded as a catastrophe,' said Martina Navratilova. 'This is merely the prologue to her Grand Slam career.'

Andy Murray knew more than most what it was like to feel the weight of British expectations. 'Laura is going to be a great player anyway, regardless what happens this year, so she might as well go out and enjoy herself and learn as much as she can,' he said supportively.

Everyone had something to say about Laura Robson: once again, she was the talk of the town.

Ten days before her first match, Laura finally sat her GCSE English exam – a year earlier than other girls her age. It had been a struggle for the Robsons to find a suitable location for the test, especially with the last-minute training and preparation she also had to somehow fit in.

'It was murder,' said Kathy when it was over. 'Other kids don't have that sort of pressure. I don't think it's really fair but you know we couldn't change it.'

Laura had just over a week to get ready, and during that week there was silence from the Robson camp. They didn't want any hype surrounding Laura's senior debut at Wimbledon, and hoped that by staying quiet they could keep her calm and focused.

While other tennis stars glammed themselves up and partied in Kensington with media mogul Richard Branson, and former Destiny's Child singers Michelle Williams and Kelly Rowland at the official pre-championship party, Laura stayed out of the limelight.

Finally, on the day itself, Laura faced the press.

'I'm really looking forward to being back at Wimbledon,' she said carefully. 'It's going to be an unbelievable experience.'

For her first match, she had been drawn against Daniela Hantuchova, the 26-year-old Slovakian world No. 33. Daniela was an experienced player who was nonetheless often prone to nerves, and there was a chance that Laura could get the upper hand over her. But Robson was mostly keen to emphasise her intention to approach her first senior Grand Slam as simply a learning experience.

'Remember you're out there because you love playing,' mum Kathy had told her that morning before she left the house.

Waiting in the locker room for the match to begin, Laura distracted herself by wondering what the towels on court would be like. The expensive and much-coveted towels, which at Wimbledon were designed and produced by iconic British firm Christy, were different at every Slam, and Laura was trying to collect as many as possible. Both players and spectators always yearned for these towels, which were seen as trophies from the tournament, and as such were hard to keep hold of.

Then, taking a deep breath, Laura pulled her brown hair securely back into a ponytail and walked out to face the 4,000 spectators who had already taken their seats. Among them were Virginia Wade, Ann Jones and several members of the All England Tennis Club, who had decamped from their familiar ground of Centre Court and Court One to watch Laura play. Kathy, Andrew and 17-year-old Nick Robson were there too, ready to show their support.

Laura showed no sign of nerves as the match began at noon, under a depressingly cloudy sky. There was tension in the air, both from the weather and the court atmosphere. The seconds slowly ticked by.

Laura took the first set, earning only a discreet round of applause. She was 15 and had just won her first senior set against a seeded player: it was an achievement in itself but no one dared get excited.

After a break up in the second, Laura's confidence started

to waver. 'Come on,' she muttered to herself as she was about to serve. The points were elusive, and as the tough match went on Laura looked more and more like she was about to cry. She hit a ball on the ground in frustration, prompting her mum to shout out: 'Come on, Laura, focus!'

Nick made little barking noises – emulating Laura's beloved dog Ella – to cheer her on.

Despite her nerves, Laura was playing well. She was hitting the ball like an adult, outserving her opponent in terms of power, and she managed to dispatch ten aces to fox her foe.

But, when Hantuchova began displaying the same sort of tactics that had given Pervak the edge in Australia, Laura was thrown off her stride completely.

Hantuchova fiddled around at the back of the court, keeping Laura waiting and stalling the play. Players with her experience knew all too well how weak most umpires were when enforcing the 20-second rule between points and, on that day, Spanish official Mariana Alves was no exception.

A steady stream of double faults – 14 in all – made it clear the gamesmanship had got to Laura. Hantuchova prevailed in the second and third sets to triumph 3-6; 6-4; 6-2.

Defeated, Laura slumped to her chair with her head in her hands. Moved by her distress, every spectator in the arena rose to give her a standing ovation. She slung a prized pink-and-blue towel over her shoulder, gave a meek wave and bolted off the court – presumably to mourn her loss away from all those sympathetic eyes.

But the crowd kept cheering.

Outside, Kathy blamed the pressure of her exams for her loss, and praised her daughter's efforts: 'She played really well, it was tough out there. It is mentally tough, she is still 15 and she needs to work on that side of her game. She just needs to grow up a bit. I don't think it is that disappointing, I think she played very well, so we are going to focus on the positives.'

Hantuchova was impressed by her opponent's efforts, and said that playing Laura felt like playing a younger version of herself. 'It was so tough, to keep focused and think about my game,' she said. 'But obviously, you know, it didn't feel very good being a set down and a couple games down and getting kicked by a girl 11 years younger than me.'

When Laura finally faced the press, she was honest, but philosophical about the experience. 'I'm just a little bit upset, but I'm pretty proud of myself,' she said. 'I thought I played really, really good for a good part of the match, and then in the end just a couple of things let me down a bit. I just got really nervous. I made a couple more mistakes than I should have.'

However, when the talk turned personal, she politely fielded questions about her favourite TV shows before getting a little exasperated at a question about her social life. 'I do socialise,' she protested. 'What do you want me to say – that I have no friends?'

All in all, Laura had handled her first proper outing at Wimbledon exceptionally well – from the game itself to the inquisitive press. And Laura's Wimbledon dreams weren't all over – she still had her junior title to defend.

In the week that followed, her mood was lightened by Kathy's attempts to get her to work on her timid wave. 'She has this little embarrassed wave and we're trying to get her to wave more enthusiastically,' she told the press. 'But she just rolls her eyes and says, "Mum, no way I'm doing that!"'

The sun made a surprise appearance over Wimbledon and it was hard not to enjoy the jovial atmosphere.

Laura readied herself to defend her girls' title.

Her coach warned that this year Laura could expect a very different experience from her dramatic run to the 2008 final.

'I think Laura could be very proud if she won it again because there are plenty of other good girls out there and it is going to be a real test,' he began. 'Against Hantuchova she showed just how well she can play on grass so I hope that will have given her a lot of confidence.'

But he emphasised that this year's Wimbledon was just one small part of a much longer development plan for Laura, who was having to learn to live with the high expectations that were being placed on her.

'She is still growing and getting used to her body so we need to be careful with her,' he said cautiously. 'Movement around the court is something we will always have to keep working on and it will be possible to do more work when she has stopped growing.'

He was refusing to rush her, and since she was, remarkably, still growing – she was now at 5ft 10in and rising – that could only be a sensible course of action. Plus he knew something that only a few others did – Laura had injured herself again...

While Laura pushed aside the pain and prepared to face Canadian Katerina Pallivets in the first round of the girls' singles, it couldn't have escaped her notice that Melanie Oudin – whom she had beaten as a junior the year before – was now playing in the fourth round of the women's singles, having dispensed with Jelena Jankovic a few days before.

It was a bitter pill to swallow, but Laura used it to fuel her game, and she made it safely through her first junior match. Despite a few nerves in the opening games, when she was broken twice, it was a solid if not spectacular 6-3; 6-2 win.

But the crowd loved her.

Mobbed by autograph hunters, she smiled kindly as she moved swiftly through the throng of fans, clearly not entirely comfortable with the attention.

It was the same after her second-round win over Australia's Sally Peers, where she claimed a second comprehensive win, despite being put off by a wasp on match point.

The headlines once more proclaimed her to be the next British teenage sensation, and Laura was a celebrity once again. It took seven security guards to usher her off court, as the fans swarmed around the flushed and tired teenager. She tried to oblige them as far as possible, but drew the line when a young boy asked her for her towel. There was no way she was giving that baby up...

The next day, Laura was pensive as she waited for her third-round match. She was still hurting, and so she took time out from training to join Andy Murray's army of growing female fans in watching him perform a topless workout during a practice session.

Wearing a baby-pink headband, she cut a lonely figure as she sat on a nearby bench, her brow knitted in concentration. While everyone else was swooning, Laura was studying Andy's form.

Finally, she sloped off to play Holland's Quirine Lemoine.

From the start she was wincing in pain.

She needed three medical time-outs in the first set and, despite a battling display, she lost 6-2; 4-6; 8-6 – crashing out of the girls' singles tournament.

'I'm a bit drained,' she explained afterwards. 'It's just unfortunate it had to end this way.'

Talking about the back pain that had destroyed her dreams, she revealed: 'It started a week-and-a-half ago and gradually got worse so it was difficult for me to play. I felt like I couldn't really hit the ball that hard, especially on my serve.'

It was an anti-climactic end to the fortnight, but it had been exciting nonetheless. And, when she watched her former opponent Noppawan Lertcheewakarn lift the winners' cup, she was gracious about it. 'Congrats to Noppawan for winning the girls,' she tweeted. 'She played really well.'

That night, instead of dressing up and posing for the cameras at the Champions' Ball, she went to see the musical *Billy Elliot*.

Laura was back to being a normal teenage girl once more, and it must have been just a little bit of a relief.

CHAPTER 11

NEW YORK, NEW YORK

As August arrived and Wimbledon became somewhat of a distant memory, Laura continued on her ambitious quest for a higher ranking by playing in two ITF tournaments – one via a wildcard and the second through qualification.

She didn't make it past the first round in either.

But her fellow Brit Andy Murray was still convinced she would one day be able to replicate her junior success in the senior ranks. He had been watching her closely and admired her skill and attitude on the court. 'I think she's very good,' he told journalists. 'I know she's had a few problems here and there with injuries because she's been growing a lot, which is normal around that age. She will get into the top 50. After that, anything can happen.'

For the next month, Laura concentrated on her training, moaning on twitter that she wasn't a fan of sprints and showing a vague concern about her taste in music.

'Is it worrying that I've had "Party in the USA" by Miley Cyrus in my head alllllllll day??!!' she tweeted.

The song obsession was probably subliminal, because, soon after, she hopped on a plane to New York to start her first run at the US Open. She had won a wildcard into the senior qualifiers at Flushing Meadows and was excited about the tournament – and the trip to New York itself.

Her sister, Emily, was also making the journey and it would be a good opportunity for the two young women to spend some time together. Laura hadn't seen much of her older sibling since her move back to Australia almost six years before, so it would be fun to have her around.

She marvelled at the hallowed Arthur Ashe Stadium, recalling all the matches she had watched being played there on TV. A blimp circled above as she explored the Billie Jean King National Tennis Center, and Laura tried not to get nervous in anticipation at what was ahead.

She was momentarily distracted when she received a tweet from young diving superstar Tom Daley, whom she had met when they were both finalists at the Young Sports Personality of the Year awards a year before.

'Hey just thought I'd say good luck for your next tournament ;) you're doing awesome,' he wrote.

Laura didn't quite know what to reply, especially when a week later he tweeted: 'Good luck in your US tournament ;)', adding a kiss for good measure.

It wasn't long before stories began appearing about the pair's 'budding romance' – Daley had apparently been enamoured of Laura since her Wimbledon win. One of his friends was reported to have told the *Daily Mail*: 'Tom has been sending texts and twitter messages to Laura like there is no tomorrow. I think she likes him too.

'He is young and doesn't want any real commitment because his diving comes first. But he fancied Laura the minute he saw her at Wimbledon.

'They are the same age and I think they both have things in common. The two of them are British rising stars and each understands the pressure the other is under.'

But, as much as the press would have delighted in love blossoming between the pair, it didn't seem like anything was really happening – it was just a bit of friendly encouragement. Laura simply replied 'thanks', and went straight back to training, having to fend off a bit of teasing from her new friend Andy Murray.

And when, just a few months later, Daley revealed that he was in a relationship with another man, there were more than a few surprised journalists in London... It was clear they had definitely misread the situation.

Laura's senior qualifying quest got off to a great start when she beat Stephanie Foretz, a player more than 300 places higher than her 460 ranking.

'In the beginning I was a bit overwhelmed,' she admitted when it was over. 'But I soon got into the match. I started to feel more comfortable and realised I could do it.'

Her second qualifier, against Hungary's Aniko Kapros, went the same way, and suddenly Laura was just one match away from reaching the main draw.

But, as she woke on the day of the match, the skies were dark and foreboding: tropical Storm Danny was scheduled to hit the New York area, and rain began lashing down in preparation for its arrival.

Robson's match was delayed.

All she could do was watch as the heavens opened.

It was somewhat ironic. Eight months before, her matches had been delayed by the extreme crushing heat in Melbourne. Now her play was being halted by a fully fledged tropical storm. At 7pm, the match finally got underway, and Laura faced Eva Hrdinova, a Czech woman ranked at 203.

Laura dropped the first set in a tiebreaker, and was down one point in the first game of the second set when the rain began to pour down once more. Play was suspended for the day, leaving Laura both wet and frustrated. It had been a close match so far and Laura knew deep down that she could win it.

The waiting must have been torture. The US Open was a week away and she wanted to reach the main draw so badly. When play resumed the following evening, she used all her pent-up frustration to face her opponent.

She immediately went 3-0 down in the second set, before winning four games in a row and gaining the momentum to win 6-4. She raced into a 4-0 lead in the third set and it looked like she had it in the bag.

But things are never what they seem in tennis, and Hrdinova broke Laura's winning stretch to take five games in a row. Robson's desperation began to show and she racked up 13 double faults in the deciding set.

She won the next game to love, but both players then failed to hold their service games and for those spectators who had braved the gloomy evening weather it must have felt like the match would never end.

Laura was holding her own against the higher-ranking player, she just needed one last push. In the final-set tiebreaker, Hrdinova wasted two match points. But she finally pulled rank and closed out the match.

Laura hadn't made it to the main draw of the seniors.

She had caused two huge upsets, beating players far above her in the rankings and giving Hrdinova a very tough time on court. But for now she would once again have to rely on the junior tournament for any hope of glory. And at least with her sister there and her pal Heather Watson playing in the tournament too, it would be a fun few weeks.

For the next seven days, Laura worked on her training, chatted to Andy Murray and her junior tennis pals, and went sightseeing with her sister. It was violently windy, as the tropical storm kept threatening to announce its arrival, but Laura didn't care. The Empire State Building, the Statue of Liberty, Fifth Avenue... New York was amazing.

When the US Open finally began, Robson was a force of nature to rival Storm Danny. She breezed through to the second round of the junior tournament with a 6-0; 6-0 victory over Tunisia's Ons Janeur, then on to the third by beating American Lauren Embree.

Heather Watson came through beside her and they both then mastered the increasingly strong chilly winds on court to make it into the quarterfinals.

Newsreader Trevor McDonald was part of the considerable crowd who watched Laura dismiss Belgium's 12th seed Tamaryn Hendler 6-2; 6-1. Not even an uncharitable time violation in the second set, which happened while she was waiting for the fierce winds to die down, could halt her impressive form.

Both Heather and Laura were flying the flag for Britain,

and in their demure matching blue-and-purple outfits they were a force to be reckoned with.

The quarterfinals and the semifinals would be played in quick succession on the same day, and, as the two Brits woke up on that Saturday morning in September, they could already see the rain was back with a vengeance.

The games were moved indoors.

Robson beat American wildcard Lauren Davis for a place in the semifinal, while Watson took down Laura's old rival, Noppawan Lertcheewakarn.

So far so good.

But, while 17-year-old Watson was positively thrashing Russia's Daria Gavrilova to secure a place in the final, Robson was struggling against Yana Buchina. After winning the first set against the Russian, it had begun to look like it might be an all-British final – the first in US Open history. But Buchina had fought back and emerged the victor, after narrowly winning the next two sets.

Laura had come so close to the final. But now Heather was there and, instead of being part of it, Robson would be watching from the sidelines.

It was disappointing, but also exciting. She desperately wanted Heather to win. And Laura was among the 300-strong crowd who watched when Watson did exactly that.

Beating Buchina in straight sets, Heather Watson became the first British girl in history to win the junior US Open.

It was an accolade that Laura herself had longed for, but she was happy for her friend and congratulated her enthusiastically.

Suddenly, the papers were full of stories about Guernsey girl Watson, who, like Laura, had been virtually unknown before her big win. The inevitable comparisons were made between the two girls, but Watson made it clear that, professional rivalry aside, the two Brits were great pals.

'Laura and I are very good friends,' she told the *Daily Mail*. 'We're always supporting each other and pushing each other along. It's great she's doing well and I'm doing well too.'

Although Watson may have lifted the US Open trophy, Laura had got her own reward from the tournament: she was going to partner up with Andy Murray for Australia's prestigious invitational event The Hopman Cup.

Murray had been watching Robson closely and had seen her obvious potential. Despite her US loss, there was just something about her that screamed 'Champion', and out of all the female players in Britain he wanted her to be by his side for the famous Perth event.

For Murray, it would be a gentle warm-up for the Australian Open, which was always played shortly after the January invitational. 'It's the first time he's chosen to prepare for the Australian Open in Australia, so that's a big statement by Andy,' said Hopman Cup director Paul McNamee.

'He indicated through his management he wanted to do something different this year. They noticed Djokovic and Safin used the Perth route to win the Australian Open so they are giving it a shot.'

For the event's promoters, it would prove to be a huge draw for punters, in a country with an enormous British expat population.

Having the British duo compete in the Cup would be very lucrative for them.

For Robson, it would be an exciting and important

experience – her first mixed doubles with the great Andy Murray.

'It's going to be great to learn from him and see how he prepares,' she gushed when the news was officially announced.

But, most importantly, it would be Britain's first glimpse into the dream future that the public wanted so desperately to see: Andy Murray and Laura Robson, No. 1 British male and female respectively, dominating the tennis landscape together... Seeing them play side by side for Britain would give people hope that this dream could one day become a reality.

For the rest of the year, Robson continued to gain experience by dipping her toes in the shallows of the professional game. In October, she went out in the first round of two ITF tournaments, one in Barnstaple and another in Joue-Les-Tours, France. Then she entered the qualifying draw at the Luxembourg Open, and made it to the final round before losing to 27-year-old Italian Maria Elena Camerin.

To get even that far she had done exceptionally well, beating world No. 180 Zuzana Ondraskova and No. 79 Julia Gorges – both of them older and more experienced players.

In November, she went out in the first round of another ITF tournament, this time in Nantes, before making the quarterfinals in Minsk by beating both 26-year-old Ukrainian Yuliya Beygelzimer and 28-year-old Tetyana Arefyeva in straight sets.

She ended the tennis year ranked 403, with her friend Heather Watson behind her at 561. The pair had decided to team up at the forthcoming Australian Open as doubles partners, and Laura was excited at the prospect.

'It's going to be great to have two British girls with a

chance of winning junior Slams next year,' she said enthusiastically.

In the meantime, she sought out the services of a sports psychologist to help with her nerves, before packing her summer clothes into a suitcase and jumping on yet another flight – this time to the paradise island of Mauritius.

While the rest of Britain wrapped up warm to open their advent calendars, Laura swam in the turquoise waters of the Indian Ocean, with dolphins jumping and playing on the horizon. But this was no holiday – well, not really, anyway.

She was in training for Australia 2010, and, aside from the occasional hour spent lying on the perfect sandy beaches, she was there to get up close and personal with the island's towering mountain range.

After spending a week climbing the peaks to work on her fitness, she posted pictures on twitter of her burned nose and icicle earrings.

'Guess my factor SPF75 didn't do the trick,' she joked.

She'd need much more of the stuff in Melbourne.

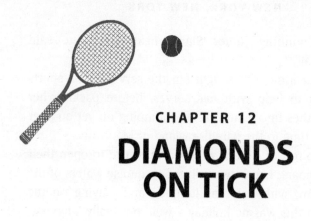

CHAPTER 12

DIAMONDS
ON TICK

After a low-key Christmas spent training in Miami, Andy Murray flew to Perth to keep his Hopman Cup date with Laura Robson.

He was nursing a broken heart, after splitting from his long-term love Kim – the daughter of the head of British women's tennis Nigel Sears – and had been training mercilessly to take his mind off his failed romance.

Alongside track sessions of 200m, 400m and 800m sprints in the Floridian heat, he'd been pushing himself with back-breaking workouts in Miami University's weights room. Now he was hoping his tie-up with Laura would enable him to do what he had so far failed to: survive deep into the second week of the scorching marathon that was otherwise known as the Australian Open.

He had been a casualty on three of his four appearances at the tournament and was hoping that the warm-up

Hopman Cup event would acclimatise him to the intense heat of an Australian summer, giving him the edge he had previously lacked.

But Australian Lleyton Hewitt, who was partnered in the Cup with Sam Stosur, was dubious about the British pair's chances.

'Andy Murray is such a quality player but he's playing with a young girl, so how they fare is up in the air,' he said.

Hewitt was right: it was a big gamble. But Robson wasn't just any young girl. Murray had an inkling she would actually turn out to be his secret weapon...

Robson had flown straight to Perth from her training in Mauritius, and was excited about the Cup, which would feature eight nations in two groups of four, playing against each other in a format of women's singles, men's singles and a mixed doubles. Perth was her mother's home city, and the crowds inside the Burswood Dome would be the biggest she had yet faced in her career. It was going to be an epic event – and image-conscious Laura wanted to make sure that she and Andy looked their very best.

On the day of their first match, Robson bravely fired off a text to her doubles partner, asking him what colours he was planning on wearing. When he replied with 'blue, green and white', Laura was pretty horrified: she was planning on purple, which would clash terribly, and she told him so. He must have stifled a giggle at the demanding tone of her text – but he made sure he changed to blue and white to keep her happy. She continued to dictate their outfits all week.

The first country the British duo faced was Kazakhstan. Murray comfortably beat Andrey Golubev, while Laura lost to

Yaroslava Shvedova, forcing a tiebreak that would be decided in the mixed doubles. Watched by a crowd of nearly 9,000, both Murray and Robson were buoyant as the match began.

Smiling and laughing at each other, it was clear they were thoroughly enjoying themselves in Perth. Andy's demeanour especially was unusually bright – he was not usually known for his beaming smiles on court.

But Laura's excitement and quick wit had seemingly sweetened his usually serious mood. They played well as a pair, naturally falling into a good rhythm and easily outclassing their opponents. Together they won the match, making it through to the next round and putting on a great show for the crowd at the same time. Facing the media after their win, they were still in high spirits.

When asked about a momentary lapse in form during the second set, Murray said lightly: 'I'm going to blame it slightly on my partner. She started asking me if I moisturise my hands and I think maybe she lost her concentration just a little bit. But she's only 15 so I'll let her off.'

Robson jumped in: 'Have you seen his hands? They are pretty disgusting. It was a good question though.'

'It was fun,' said Murray, with a wicked glint in his eye. 'She hit me on the back at one point with her racket – I don't think I deserved that... it was sore already because I was carrying her!'

As her mouth opened in mock shock, Murray put his arm around her and Laura grinned. They made a fine double act and teased each other continuously. Laura even mocked his dedication later that night over dinner, where he was downing Recovery Shakes – specially prepared refreshment drinks for athletes.

'I'll pass on that,' she told him, wrinkling up her nose at the gloopy liquid.

Up next was Germany, and while Robson eventually fell prey to Sabine Lisicki – after a closely fought match – Murray comfortably beat Philipp Kohlschreiber in less than an hour. They then combined impressively once more to face the Germans together, racing into a 5-0 lead after just 14 minutes.

Robson took the lead role during the match, perhaps feeling she had a little something to prove after Andy's teasing the day before. Murray felt confident enough to let her do so, and they took the German duo down cleanly and quickly in straight sets.

After the match, Laura wryly joked: 'I think I carried him today.'

It was obvious their fledgling partnership was blossoming quickly. Murray was gently paternal towards his younger partner, displaying a softer side to his character that was rarely seen.

In return, Robson treated him like a big brother whom she was secretly in awe of – bossing him around, taking his teasing and watching his every move closely, hungry to learn from his wisdom and experience.

Their showdown against Russia went the same way as their previous matches – Robson lost, Murray won, and together they rained down a special kind of hell on their Eastern European opponents.

Having made it to the final, Murray was smug in the knowledge that he had made the right choice in choosing feisty Laura to be by his side. She may not have won any of her matches in the group stages, but playing with Andy had boosted her confidence considerably, and she was saving the best for last.

With no more matches to play after being knocked out by Spain, the British pair's critic, Lleyton Hewitt, might have kept himself busy by eating his words...

Laura was glowing with excitement as she walked on court for her first match of the final rubber. Relaxed and cheerful, her sunny disposition was a winner with the crowds, who cheered her on loudly.

For so long she had played under the intense pressure of ranking points and title matches – sometimes it must have been easy to forget how much she actually loved playing the game.

Partnering Andy in the low-pressure Hopman Cup had lifted her spirits, and made her remember just how much fun tennis could be. And, with her troublesome nerves a distant memory, she claimed the greatest scalp of her career so far.

Laura's opponent, Spain's Maria Jose Martinez Sanchez, was the world No. 26 and had been on top form so far during the Hopman Cup – she hadn't yet dropped a single set. So there must have been a few open mouths in the crowd when the fearless Brit began to take Martinez Sanchez apart, game by game.

Unhinging the Spaniard's trusted serve-and-volley game with a series of pinpoint passing strokes, Laura visibly grew in confidence on court. She broke twice with backhand winners in the first set before serving it out with an ace. Her focus was mesmerising.

The second set was admittedly a far tighter contest, as Martinez Sanchez fought back against the teenager, loudly grunting with the effort. Robson drew on all her resolve to save a set point and pull back a break to force a tiebreak. It was intense viewing. But Laura finally secured glory with a backhand cross-court winner that Martinez Sanchez had no hope of returning.

As the crowd cheered, she punched the air with excitement. Kathy, who had been watching nervously from the sidelines, jumped up and screamed, excitedly hugging everyone around her.

'I completely dominated!' Laura squealed in her live courtside interview, making the presenter chuckle. 'I just hope Andy can go out there and win.'

But Andy did not go out there and win. Instead, he lost to Martinez Sanchez's partner, Tommy Robredo. It would all come down to which dynamic duo could win in the doubles.

Despite being 6-3 ahead in the opening-set tiebreak, the British pair somehow lost the initiative in their final match. Robson fought hard, playing valiantly to keep them in contention, but for once Andy didn't exactly match her.

The Spaniards just clinched it.

Receiving her runner-up award, Laura was happy with how the week had gone. She'd won the biggest cheque of her career (£43,000), boosted her confidence by playing against a variety of high-ranking quality players, and forged a great partnership with Andy Murray.

She was on good form to play the Australian Open qualifiers, had gained valuable experience at playing in front of huge crowds and, most importantly, she had really enjoyed herself.

But she did admit to being a little bit envious when she saw the winner's trophy: it was a tennis ball encrusted with tiny, sparkling diamonds.

Andy felt bad for his new sidekick.

'I kind of let her down today so I feel bad about that,' he said later. 'She is perhaps a little more disappointed than me because of the diamonds, but I told her she can buy them with the prize money.'

He was obviously proud of his young doubles partner, who had done just as great a job at making him smile during a tough personal time in his life as she had done wielding her tennis racket on court.

'I'm sure Laura can speak for herself, but this week was a great experience for her,' he said, beaming at his doubles partner. 'She did great today, beating a girl who is ranked 26 in the world. At her age that is amazing. She has the potential. I know what it's like at that age and she is only going to get better.'

Although the money went straight into her strictly controlled bank account, Laura did treat herself to one of her greatest indulgences with some of it – gambling. While she was not legally old enough to place bets herself, Laura loved a flutter on the horses, or a spin of the roulette table.

Feeling flush as she passed the bright lights of an Australian casino one evening, she begged one of her cousins to pop in and play roulette on her behalf.

'I wanted to go myself but I couldn't,' she said later. 'I love gambling. He placed $100 on red. I doubled my money.'

In hindsight, Laura agreed it was probably wise that the bulk of her career winnings – which were racking up – was, for now, untouchable.

While Laura celebrated, news of her on-court prowess quickly arrived at her next destination, Melbourne, and also reached the ears of Australian Open tournament director

Craig Tiley, who gave her a wildcard into the women's singles as a reward for her Hopman Cup efforts.

Adding his name to the growing list of her fan-club members, he said: 'Laura has had a quick rise on the international scene and deserves her wildcard. We're excited that we can recognise her success and look forward to seeing her in Melbourne.'

Laura's coach, Martijn Bok, was equally pleased with her performance. 'Laura needs more attention on the physical side of her development rather than the tennis side,' he said.

'This is going to be an interesting year – but I don't care about her results at all. This is about developing her game.'

Bok was also impressed with Murray's attitude towards Robson during the invitational.

'In the first two mixed doubles matches, Andy did really well to keep Laura calm, and had time to have a joke with her, to give her confidence,' he had observed.

'Even here, we've seen other times when the male players look away when the woman makes a mistake, as if she does not belong out there. Andy did it just right.'

He certainly did. And his own pleasure at their effective teamwork had planted a gold-plated seed in his head...

'I'll play mixed at the Olympics for sure,' Andy said in an interview with the pair soon after. 'I'd definitely play if Laura's up for it?'

He looked at her encouragingly.

'I'll have to think about it,' she replied nonchalantly, before laughing.

'Do you think you'll get a better offer?' asked the interviewer with a wry smile.

Laura thought for a moment. 'Well, no, probably not...'

CHAPTER 13

BABY STEPS

'Just arrived in Melbourne!' Laura tweeted, when she got to the city of her birth. 'Had a great week in Perth, I definitely carried @andy_murray in the final.'

Still feeling pleased about her great start to 2010, she now had to focus on the task of qualifying for the Australian Open – a challenge that had frustratingly eluded her a year previously, and had continued to do so during subsequent Opens in the USA and Luxembourg.

In the first round, she faced Australian Sophie Ferguson, a 23-year-old who was over 250 places higher than her in the world rankings. The match went to three sets and lasted an exhausting 2 hours and 11 minutes. Laura didn't play her best, and had to overcome 44 unforced errors to eventually beat her opponent.

Sadly, in the second round, Robson fell foul of Holland's Michaella Krajicek, losing in straight sets to the 20-year-old.

She was understandably disappointed, but shrugged it off quickly. There would be other chances for success during her next few weeks at the Australian Open: she'd also received a wildcard into the women's doubles and she was competing in the junior singles and doubles – in which she would team up with Heather Watson for the first time.

Waking up on her sweet-sixteenth birthday, Laura was excited. She would be playing in the first round of the women's doubles with Australian Sally Peers, and she had a party to look forward to in the evening.

Whatever happened, it would be a great day.

Australia had taken the teenager warmly into their hearts and the outdoor Court 5 was packed with fans as she and Sally shook the hands of their opponents, the Americans Jill Craybas and Abigail Spears. They cheered on the Australian/British duo appreciatively, making up chants for the change of ends and yelling at every point they scored.

Her first match as a 16-year-old ended with a win in straight sets over the Americans. Walking off to thunderous applause, Laura was swamped by fans wanting to congratulate her. They showered her with praise and hearty pats on the back. One fan handed her a flower, while another thrust a mock certificate in her hands, promising a great birthday present if she signed it.

When she read it, Laura laughed. The document purported to be an application to change her nationality to Australian, and all it needed was her signature. Flattered, she nevertheless left the space blank. She was a Brit and proud of it.

That night, she went out for dinner with her family and friends, including Heather Watson, Eugenie Bouchard and Andy Murray.

American band The Foo Fighters were on the next table and Watson spent the meal trying to keep calm in the presence of the rock stars. '@mizwatson92 almost had a heart attack,' Laura teased on twitter.

Laura had received a brand-new iPod from her parents for her birthday, and she kindly donated her old one to Murray.

'It has a game on it called Doodle Jump, which I showed Andy how to play,' she told a journalist. 'I had a best score of 42,000 points. Andy took it and played it until he had 48,000. But I have seen him choke big time when he gets close to a big score,' she said cheekily.

The next day, she teamed up with Peers again for their second-round doubles clash on Court 7. Laura proved her team-playing skills were no fluke when she and Sally once more secured a straight-sets win, this time against 12th seeded pair Chia-Jung Chuang and Kveta Peschke.

They did it again in the third round, beating Vera Dushevina and Anastasia Rodionova, to advance to the quarterfinals without losing a game.

Laura was on a roll.

She had quickly progressed through the first two rounds of the junior tournament too, and would be facing Romania's Cristina Dinu for a place in the last eight. But, due to ghastly scheduling, both her next matches would be held on the same day – along with the first round of the junior doubles with Heather Watson.

It was too much for Laura. Something had to give, and, unfortunately for Watson, it would be the pair's chance at junior doubles' success.

Laura pulled out, leaving Heather with no partner and, consequently, no chance.

'We all thought that it would be too much,' Laura explained to the press. 'I didn't say it to Heather, I felt so bad, so my coach did it. It was his decision more than anyone else's so I'm going to put the blame on him. I felt really bad for Heather.'

It must have been terrible for both the girls – there was nothing either of them could do. Heather would have done exactly the same. It was professional, not personal.

The day would be tough enough for Laura as it was, but she didn't like letting her friend down.

In the morning, Laura faced Cristina Dinu in her third-round junior singles match, and easily toppled the Romanian in just 67 minutes. But hours later she was back on court for her doubles quarterfinal, against the notoriously tough Agnieszka Radwanska and Maria Kirilenko.

It was past 10pm when the match began, and spectators were few and far between. Laura was tired, but ready for a fight. Neither she nor Sally had expected to get this far – it was their first tournament together and it had only been a last-minute decision to team up. This was because, on the eve of the tournament, Sally's original partner, Isabella Holland, had withdrawn due to injury and Laura had stepped up to the challenge in her place.

Now they were flying together in a fairytale run that felt almost magical. The dream continued as they stormed to a 4-0 lead in the opening set, leaving their opponents looking more than a little confused.

But then the spell began to fade...

Robson was broken in a very long sixth game, and Kirilenko and Radwanska, ranked 21 and 48 in doubles respectively, slowly found their rhythm. They broke Peers to draw level and then took over the match completely.

Just before midnight, Laura's carriage turned back into a pumpkin: the British/Australian duo lost 4-6; 1-6. With £15,400 to add to her untouchable bank account and the junior singles title still to go after, Laura tried not to be too upset.

As she flopped into bed that night, knowing she had just a few hours to prepare for her next match, she must have felt grateful for the series of incredible experiences she'd had over the past few weeks: partnering with Murray and then Peers, playing and winning so many tough matches one after another – her confidence had rocketed and she knew she was more than capable of going far in the juniors.

The previous year, she had suffered so terribly with nerves when she had faced Ksenia Pervak in the final. This year, things were very different. It was all left to play for – she just had to get a good night's sleep.

The next morning, she got up and annihilated her next opponent, Ester Goldfeld, who was from the USA; Laura beat her 6-1; 6-0 in 43 minutes. The American didn't have a chance as the British player smashed the ball out of her reach over and over again.

Robson was aware that she had been on the receiving end of extremely unlucky scheduling, but she didn't complain. Instead, she was almost grateful for it. 'One of the reasons I played good is that I knew I was tired from last night and I had to be extra focused,' she said. 'The scheduling is what it is, I was never going to complain about it. It's good that I got the win today.'

In the semifinal, Robson was still going strong. Beating Czech Kristyna Pliskova, again in straight sets, she converted 5 of her 13 break opportunities and dropped her own serve just once. She was in the final again and this time she hoped she had progressed enough to win.

'Last year, I was really nervous going into it,' she said.' I didn't feel comfortable playing against the girl that I did. Hopefully, this year I will be more comfortable going into the match. I will be playing the identical twin sister of the girl I beat today, so that should hopefully help me.'

That evening, Laura's father told her to pack her suitcases. She would be leaving straight after her finals match, and would sadly miss the men's singles final.

Andy's tactic of playing in the Hopman Cup with Laura before the Open had paid off, and he was facing Federer for the title. It would have been an amazing match to watch and Laura dearly wanted to cheer Murray on, but it was not to be.

In the Rod Laver Arena the next day, it seemed like Laura's mind was already homeward bound. She showed signs of fatigue and tetchiness, getting angry at herself during the final's first set, which she eventually lost. She overcame her anger issues for the second set, but Karolina Pliskova, her heart set on avenging her sister, outplayed Robson, even when the Brit staged a plucky revival to force a tiebreak.

Robson served a double fault to concede the championship.

Standing next to Pliskova, once more holding the runner-up plate, Robson looked longingly at the winner's trophy in her opponent's arms.

She found it hard to force a smile.

'I'm just a bit exhausted with everything,' she said, following the match. 'I was a bit disappointed with the way I played in the first set anyway. And then second set, she served really well the whole match.'

Reflecting on her stay in Australia, she was pleased overall. But, though it had been an exciting month, it had also been very tiring, and Laura's energy was well and truly spent.

'Starting with Perth, getting to the final there, then the quarters of the doubles, then getting to the final here. I've played a lot of matches. I can go home happy,' she said. 'I think now it's just good to go home.'

She flew at midnight, and was still in the air when Federer beat Murray to the men's singles title.

CHAPTER 14

LAURA'S IN VOGUE

For the next two months, Laura recovered from her loss by keeping herself to herself and staying off the pro circuit. After such a sustained period of match playing, it was time to return to a pattern of intensive training to further improve her skills.

With that in mind, she flew to Paris to train at the famed Mouratoglou Tennis Academy, where she met up with her best friend Eugenie Bouchard. In the company of Eugenie and lots of girls her age, there were plenty of opportunities to get distracted from the task at hand, but Robson was ultra focused.

She was in bed by 10pm every night and preferred to stay in during the evenings with Eugenie, where they danced and sang along to Miley Cyrus songs with Adidas pants on their heads, instead of sneaking out to nightclubs in Paris.

Laura knew that many of her friends back home were partying and experimenting with drinking and smoking, or dating boys, but she wasn't interested. Wasn't it just a little bit childish to run around in secret doing all those predictable things?

Robson was adamant she was more of an adult than that and was focused fully on the future, not the present. She knew what she wanted out of her life and booze and parties wasn't it. She wanted to be a tennis star and she would happily give up those typical teenage experiences to get there.

It wasn't that Laura didn't have fun: she got along well with the girls at the centre and was known as the official 'gossip queen' of the group. The crux of it was that she preferred to enjoy herself by having cosy nights in and catch-ups with her mates, rather than rebelling at the expense of her health and training.

She loved flicking through fashion mags and shopping for coveted designer pieces. Favouring Burberry and Balenciaga, she definitely had expensive taste. Laura had become a Burberry fan the year before, when she'd been invited to visit that top brand's headquarters, and had fallen in love with everything she'd seen.

From then on, her love of fashion had snowballed. She eagerly awaited the twice-weekly emails she received from online store Net-a-Porter, which informed her what was currently in vogue.

Laura was 16 – halfway between being a child and an adult – and she was trying her best to move forward fast. It was understandable. After all, she'd had to make mature decisions even before she'd hit her teens, and had worked on her career from the age of nine. Psychologically, glamorous grown-up clothes must have felt like the first step to not only looking, but really *feeling* like a proper adult.

Well-tailored, expensive clothes suited her tall frame and made her feel older and sophisticated, and, as anyone with teenage girls knows, that's exactly how they all want to feel – no matter who they are.

She still wasn't allowed to touch her growing pot of winnings, which had by now reached nearly £80,000, but she had an allowance and she liked to spend it on quality clothing. Laura also got designer items as gifts from her parents – even if she often had to exchange them to get the things she really wanted.

Robson had been given a pink Marc Jacobs bag for Christmas, and though at the time she'd told Kathy and Andrew that she wanted something different – something that 'went with more things' – she obviously thought the colour was too young for her and wanted a hue that was more edgy.

So she swapped it for a slate-grey Balenciaga satchel.

Her interest in sophisticated adult clothes may have seemed at odds with her preference for pyjama parties and sleepovers, but it was all part of the strange dichotomy of being half-child half-adult.

But while trying to be more grown up was a natural part of being a teenager, so was the smidgen of arrogance, the little bit of smugness and the first signs of a know-it-all attitude that were starting to show themselves in her character.

Laura Robson was changing from a shy youth into a confident woman and it would take some time for her to feel her way successfully across the boundaries of adulthood. A little 'flexing the ego' at her age was normal, but for someone in the public eye it had the potential to get her into trouble – and it soon would.

Robson returned to the ITF circuit in April, flying to the

USA for tournaments in Jackson, Osprey, Dothan and Charlottesville. After a rusty start, not getting past the first round in Jackson or the second in Osprey, she found her stride.

At Dothan, she got to the semifinals in singles and the quarterfinals in doubles, causing her to move up in the doubles' rankings to a career high of 102. In singles, she was now placed 262 in the world rankings. She followed up these achievements by reaching the quarterfinals in Charlottesville. All in all, it was a good start, considering her two-month hiatus.

That year, Robson had decided to avoid the clay shenanigans at Roland Garros completely and would instead focus on her grass playing in anticipation of Wimbledon. And with a break in her schedule she could finally start courting the press, by agreeing to her first ever interview – with style bible British *Vogue*.

Laura knew that her image would be vitally important to her adult career. Although she was sort of 'reluctant' to make herself so visible, she knew she had to start having a solid media presence off the court, and that meant photo shoots and interviews.

Women's tennis was becoming increasingly more glamorous, and, aside from having to compete against rivals like Maria Sharapova and Ana Ivanovic on court, she needed to begin competing against them for column inches in the press too.

There was money to be made through endorsements and brand associations, and that would all happen if she raised her public profile. The fact that this would all start in *Vogue* made it an exciting prospect. On the day of the interview,

Laura took charge of proceedings – another sign that the teenager was starting to assert her burgeoning independence.

Her agent had originally suggested that she meet the magazine's journalist, Vassi Chamberlain, near her home in Wimbledon Village, take her dog Ella for a walk on the Common, have lunch at a local eaterie, Carluccio's, and then drop in at fashionable clothes shop Matches Spy for a quick look around.

But after the photo shoot, where she was visited on set by her family – and the dog Ella – Laura had apparently decided on a new plan. 'You've done the dog,' Chamberlain reported her as saying, before detailing her own venue ideas.

The shoot itself went extremely well. Laura's long legs, tanned skin and slender frame were perfect for the high-end fashions the stylist brought out for her to wear. She recognised all the items and was particularly excited about the Burberry mini and Isabel Marant jacket she was given to pose in.

As the photographer clicked away, Laura no longer looked like the child star everyone had fallen in love with just two years earlier. She was turning into a woman, and this shoot would show the world just that. She reclined in an elegant grey one-shoulder Alexandra Wang dress and towering Lanvin heels, with her hair styled naturally and her make-up minimal but beautiful.

She stood statuesque on a green lawn in the Burberry mini, a gentle breeze ruffling her now smoothed-out hair.

The interview took place in a posh Chelsea café of Laura's choosing on the fashionable Kings Road – but only after she had taken the journalist on a tour of The Shop at Bluebird, a high-end concept store stocking the best in designer clothes and beauty.

Laura appeared to be keen to show off her fashion knowledge as she confidently walked around, picking out various items for her new friend's approval. At lunch, Laura ordered a poached chicken salad and, when Chamberlain asked for her own salad dressing to be delivered on the side, Laura asked for the same.

It is said that imitation is the sincerest form of flattery and it certainly seemed like Laura was simultaneously learning from the elegant and knowledgeable older woman, while also trying to impress her.

In hindsight, her behaviour could go some way to explaining what happened next.

At first, Laura spoke about more obvious subjects, like her training in Paris. 'My coach knows I'm sensible,' she said, sitting poised in her chair. 'I don't like the taste of alcohol and I hate smoke. Some go to nightclubs but I'm not interested.'

She revealed that she had a penchant for older men and still had a crush on Marat Safin, but admitted he was too old for her at 30. She told Chamberlain how gossip in the pro locker rooms was usually very boring, and mostly focused on the famous Wimbledon towels that everyone loved.

And she insisted that there was no infighting among the female competitors, whom she described as 'unbelievably strong women'. What's more, she acknowledged the fact that image was becoming increasingly important to a player's career.

'It's changing – everyone's doing photo shoots. It's more glamorous,' she said knowledgeably.

She showed the reporter a prized photo of her with her 'date' Andy Murray, taken at the end-of-tournament dinner for the Australian Hopman Cup, and quipped: 'The winning trophy had 52 diamonds on it. We would have got it if only he'd won his singles match, so we can blame Andy for that – now he owes me diamonds.'

So far so good: Laura was being both charming and interesting. But then her 16-year-old mouth began to run away with her, and some of the things she said next weren't quite so charming.

Laura spoke about growing up in Singapore, when a coach had first singled out her brother as having tennis potential. 'He was obviously an idiot,' she said of the coach. 'But after that I took the game seriously. I just wanted to be better than my brother. I beat my family one by one.'

Ouch.

She then crowed about her B in GCSE English, gloating at her academic prowess over other tennis players. 'Can you believe it,' she said. 'One of the Russian players didn't even know who Shakespeare was.'

Double ouch.

Talking about her bad temper, which she was finally getting under control, she revealed more details of the Polish trophy-smashing incident that had taken place a few years before.

'I came runner-up,' she said. 'I was so angry I threw it on the floor and smashed it. I was so annoyed losing to this girl who I didn't think was good.'

Triple ouch.

But, although these little nuggets were a bit cocky and childish, they were forgivable and only really put herself in a bad light.

It was her next damning remark that would ultimately define the whole interview.

'Some of the tennis girls, they're sluts,' she said, in response to what has since been described as a particularly probing line of enquiry.

'They go with every guy and make such a bad name for themselves – and you don't want to be known for stuff like that. You want to be more discreet.'

It was a shame Laura hadn't taken her own advice.

Before the piece had even been published in *Vogue*, the British media eagerly pounced on the interview, zeroing in on the remark she'd made about her tennis colleagues.

'Slutgate' was born.

Most papers reproduced the quote and some, like the *Daily Mail*, even wryly suggested that she might have some explaining to do in the dressing room from now on.

Reading those 37 words in the tabloids, everyone must have winced – from her management and family to her tennis pals and fans. It was hardly the best way to endear herself to the WTA, especially when she was still flitting around the fringes of the senior circuit.

'Really enjoyed the photo shoot and looking forward to seeing the full piece,' tweeted Laura. 'Shame some quotes were taken out of context today though.'

Taken out of context or not, Laura didn't deny she'd said those things. And the quote itself was not well received.

The usually glowing chatter on tennis message boards instantly turned sour and disapproving. 'I don't think I like her very much. Seems ultra spoiled,' wrote one fan. 'Welcome to the tennisforum shitlist, Laura,' remarked another.

In the eyes of the public, Robson had gone from tennis darling to egotistical teen in just two sentences.

It couldn't have come at a worse time, either.

Laura had a week left of training before she attempted to qualify for a WTA tour level event in Birmingham. And any day now she would learn whether she had been awarded a wildcard to Wimbledon.

The British player received word that the WTA were not impressed. They requested a transcript of the interview so that they could review her comments and decide whether she had breached any of the rules of the women's tour.

It was a disaster for the young star.

She wasn't really the snooty arrogant girl who had shockingly appeared from the pages of the *Vogue* spread. All of her previous press interviews, strictly conducted after and about tennis matches, had gone down well – with Robson even having made a name for herself among the sports reporters as a bit of a joker.

Maybe she was trying to impress the glamorous *Vogue* reporter. Maybe she was trying to appear more grown up. Maybe her words had been twisted a little... Whatever the case, Laura was mortified. It was her first proper moment in the media spotlight and she had been burned.

It was hard to see how a professional fashion magazine could even attribute a quote so offensive to a 16-year-old girl without thinking of the consequences she would face. But they had, and Laura could now see how bad it looked.

Desperate to apologise publicly, she released a statement to the press. It read: 'Firstly, I would just like to say a big sorry to anyone that I may have offended in an interview published recently. I made a totally inappropriate, throw-away comment without considering the consequences.

'I still have a lot to learn both on and off the court, and

clearly I need to be a lot more careful about how silly remarks may come across when taken out of context.

'I live for tennis, have many good friends in the game and I would never want to do anything that could hurt the reputation of a game I love. I will learn a lot from this and now just want to focus on my tennis.'

The WTA Tour took pity on the inexperienced youngster, releasing a statement of their own in due course. 'Laura did the right thing by apologising and we're glad she showed the maturity and good judgment to do so,' it read. 'She is a 16-year-old girl and this was her first major interview with the press. It's never easy for a 16-year-old girl to answer questions about her private life and the lives of other players.

'The WTA Tour is confident that Laura has dealt with this properly and that she'll successfully move beyond it. We look forward to seeing her back on the tour.'

She must have felt relieved that her career wouldn't be affected, but it was still both upsetting and embarrassing for the poor girl.

It was Tim Henman who led the charge to defend Robson, speaking out to say she was still just a teenager.

'I haven't read the article but I've obviously heard about it,' he said. 'It's a steep learning curve. She's young, she's probably said something that she didn't mean to say and she'll learn from it.'

It was the perfect antidote to the furore, which growing in momentum and needed to end before Laura's next tournament.

'I was a million miles away from Wimbledon at Laura's age,' he added. 'I think that's where it's harder for the girls, because they do mature so much younger and they're thrown into that spotlight so early.

'But the most important thing is she keeps developing as a player and a person and, if she does that, she can have a lot of bigger and better results in the future and she'll be a big asset to the game in this country. She's got massive potential to be a really, really great player.'

Elena Baltacha, then British No. 1, followed suit, saying that most female tennis players would just laugh when they read Laura's quote.

'She is 16. I remember when I was 16, and I did and said some really silly things, and I was glad there were no journalists around at the time,' said Baltacha. 'We've all done that, it's part of developing as a professional and I think the other players will just laugh about it because of Laura's age.'

The pair of them had thrown Laura a lifeline, and she would do as Henman said – learn from the experience. Besides, Laura wasn't the first British teenager to find herself at the wrong end of a media storm. In 2006, the tabloids had a field day when Andy Murray joked he would be supporting 'anyone but England' at the World Cup.

It's precisely this kind of situation that can force players to close themselves off from the press, who actually shoot themselves in the foot by making such mountains out of molehills.

Laura had learned a valuable lesson. Now she had to put it behind her and focus on the WTA Tour.

CHAPTER 15

PUPPIES AND PUPPY FAT

Robson had missed the French Open to focus on her grass-court preparations, and as part of this she travelled to Birmingham for the Aegon Classic, a WTA Tour event taking place in June. She had received a wildcard to the qualifiers, and, putting the drama of the previous few weeks behind her, she set out to make it to the main draw.

First up was Nina Bratchikova, a 25-year-old Russian-born Portuguese player. Laura lost the first set but won the next two to make it to round two. There she faced Vitalia Diatchenko, a Russian girl three years her senior who retired in the second set while Laura was winning 6-3; 4-0.

In the first round of the main draw, she was up against Swiss No. 78 Stefanie Voegele, and played excellently, matching her opponent comfortably and hitting some huge serves. When Laura was 6-4; 0-1 up, Voegele retired due to an injury. It may not have been ideal, but it was a win, and for Laura it was her first victory on the WTA tour. It was a landmark moment, but when she faced the press it was with none of her usual spirit and gusto.

Instead, she stuck to talking about the game and smiled politely, with a newfound wariness of the media that was evident in her cautious demeanour. 'I wasn't really surprised that I won because I feel I always play really well in practice,' she said. 'But I can still keep improving. I thought my serve went really well and, even though she could read it, it didn't make much difference because there was a lot of slice on it.'

She was obviously nervous, but she kept her cool when she was asked if she felt happier than she had over the past few weeks: a question designed to probe her about Slutgate.

'Yeah, I'm really happy with the way I'm playing at the moment,' she said, ignoring the real question. 'It's good to be in the next round. It's been really, really nice. Everyone has been very nice.'

Laura would now face a top 20 player for the first time, in the form of Yanina Wickmayer, a Belgian who *Time* magazine would soon name as one of the future legends of women's tennis. But any hopes she had of measuring her ability against the pro were well and truly dashed by the damp and windy conditions she faced on the day of the match.

Unfortunately, the turf was greasy and slippery, and hampered both players' game, but Robson was clearly more uncomfortable with the situation, which fellow Brit Anne Keothavong described as 'dangerous'. Eventually, Robson asked the tournament ref to inspect the surface, and slumped in her chair for the next ten minutes to await the results.

Wickmayer stayed on her feet.

The ref decided that play should resume, and Robson was

very unhappy. Despite this, she was close to taking the first set to a tiebreak, and even broke her opponent early in the second set to lead 3-1. But the powerful Belgian was too much for Robson, and won in straight sets.

Laura was philosophical about the situation. 'It was slippery but it's the same for both of us so I can't complain,' she said. 'I asked for the lady to come on and check it again and she decided it was OK to keep playing. It didn't really seem like either of us were moving that much. I think we were both a bit wary of it. I could have accepted the conditions a bit more but at the end of the day she just played more solid.'

A week later, Laura flew to the Netherlands for the Unicef Open in Rosmalen, as part of her final preparations for Wimbledon. She lost in the first round to Dominika Cibulkova.

Flying back home to London, there was a new addition to the family for her to look forward to – her name was Kiri and she was a black Labrador puppy, just eight weeks old.

Laura was overjoyed. She was back home for the whole month because of Wimbledon and that meant she could come home at the end of each day to the love and attention of two dogs – one her faithful Ella, and the other the cutest puppy ever.

Having gained a wildcard into the main draw at Wimbledon, Laura knew that the tournament would be tough – but, when she was drawn against No. 4 seed Jelena Jankovic for her first-round match, her heart must have sunk. It was a tough break so early in the tournament, especially as it meant she would be thrust onto Centre Court for the occasion.

It was a lot of pressure. She had never met a top 10 player before and, to top it all off, the Queen was coming. For the first time in 33 years, the monarch had decided to grace the Royal Box on Centre Court, which meant she could end up watching Robson's match.

Opinion was divided as to whether Laura could rise to the challenge. Martina Hingis was particularly negative. Remarkably, she believed that, at 16, Laura was already too old and lacking in experience to learn how to be a superstar.

'I've been following her career, she needs to establish herself, she needs more matches,' said Hingis. 'I was 16 years and 9 months old when I won Wimbledon,' she explained. 'We were allowed to play on the Tour at 14. I broke a lot of records and I'm proud of that. I was on the Tour pretty much full-time by 15.

'Now they have all these restrictions on how many events you can play at a certain age. I don't agree with all that.'

Former coach Alan Jones was more optimistic about Robson's future. Jankovic was known to be highly strung on court and couldn't blast the ball as well as Robson, so there would undoubtedly be openings for the youngster during the match. As for her future, Jones said it would all come down to how well her movement on the court would develop over time. 'That's the one question I would have because in terms of delivering a ball strike she is outstanding,' he said.

'She is young and at a delicate age, but the great thing is you know she will work hard at it. Because of that I think Laura will succeed at whatever she ends up doing in life.'

On the first day of Wimbledon, a steady stream of tennis fans woke up in their tents outside the All England Club, having camped for three nights in the hope of getting tickets to see a match. They were nervous, but not as nervous as Laura, who woke up just a few minutes' walk away, feeling excited in anticipation of the day ahead.

It would be her first experience of playing on Centre Court, a moment she had dreamed of since she was a child. After giving the dogs a quick last-minute cuddle, she went on her way.

Stepping onto the famous court later that afternoon, Laura was relieved to discover it wasn't quite as big or intimidating as it looked on TV.

Mervyn King, the Governor of the Bank of England, was watching from the Royal Box and was looking forward to the match. Near him was Nick Bollettieri, who had been mentoring Jankovic of late. The first few games saw a series of mishits from Robson, causing her to go down 2-0 and leaving her under the threat of a proper spanking. But she forced break points for 3-3 and slowly her power grew, causing murmurs of appreciation to rise from the crowd, including from Bollettieri himself.

Taking the ball early and powering it low and hard over the net, she displayed exceptional timing, and with her serve thumping down a phenomenal number of aces she made Jankovic relieved to reach the second set ahead at 6-3.

It was a tough match for both girls, with the momentum swinging wildly between them both. Whenever she got in trouble, Laura hauled herself back with an ace or service winner, and Jankovic began to look very hot and bothered.

At one point, Robson's opponent gazed despairingly at her supporter's box, concerned that she was going to lose at the hands of the ferocious wonderteen.

The atmosphere was tense in the crowd, as Laura's fans

willed the Brit to win and go through to the next round. At times, it really felt like it was possible – a dream moment on Centre Court that they would all bear witness to. The set went to a tiebreak, and Jankovic was relieved when Laura missed a forehand with the court wide open. In the end, Jankovic just edged a win.

As Robson smiled wearily for the crowd, they rose to a standing ovation in appreciation of her valiant efforts, which had severely tested the Serbian No. 3.

'It's really amazing because she's very young and she really has a great serve, especially her first serve,' said a clearly surprised Jankovic. 'When it goes in, it's very hard to return, especially on grass courts.'

As a first-round loser, Laura walked away with £11,250, and she still had the doubles to play, in which she would be teaming up with her Australian Open pal Sally Peers.

Facing the press, she vowed to one day win Wimbledon. 'Ideally, I would have liked to have won it this year, but that's obviously not going to happen,' she said.

She was still cautious in front of the media, but had relaxed enough to banter a little when she was asked when she thought it might be. 'Why don't you give me a year,' she joked.

Elsewhere at Wimbledon, Laura's fellow Brits were being defeated one by one. After just two days of strawberries and Pimms, Andy Murray was once again the only Brit left in the tournament.

It was the worst performance by British female players since 1968 when the Open era had begun. Along with Laura, Anne Keothavong, Elena Baltacha, Melanie South, Heather Watson and Katie O'Brien, all suffered first-round defeats.

From the men's side, Jamie Baker joined the women's whitewash, leaving Andy to fly the flag alone by teatime on day two.

Nigel Sears was disappointed. He had hoped to showcase Britain's steady year-round female progress at the tournament, but instead he would attend one of the most depressing events on the sporting calendar – the post-mortem for British players at Wimbledon.

'I'm very disappointed and I'm most disappointed for the girls – they are not chokers,' Sears insisted. 'I have seen them be very brave and come through tough matches on other stages.'

Sears was joined at the 'inquest' by his colleague Leon Smith – in charge of the men – who tried not to dwell on the fact that he'd had just two Brits in the main draw (and now had just one left).

Instead, he attempted to blame negativity in the press for affecting the players. But the media was not impressed, and questioned how British tennis could have received a staggering half a billion in profits from Wimbledon alone since 1990, and still not have produced a Wimbledon winner?

Why were they still cosseting players who show elite potential and neglecting the grass roots of the game?

Why wouldn't the governing body shift more resources away from elite performance and into making it easier for more kids to play tennis?

The £40 million National Tennis Centre (NTC) in Roehampton was called a 'monument' to the LTA's 'folly', with journalists citing its state-of-the-art facilities but empty courts. And they spoke of tennis's brightest hopefuls –

Robson, Watson and Murray – as having reached their potential without being mollycoddled by the LTA.

It was a pretty damning assessment of the state of British tennis. The LTA would just have to hope that players like Robson and Murray started to produce results soon, to spare them this consistent hammering at the hands of the press.

What is more, it was a shame for the competitors, and not just because of their rankings. The winner of each singles title stood to receive £1 million each, more money than ever before. Laura could have bought a heck of a lot of diamonds with that.

On day five of Wimbledon, there was more disappointment for Robson. She had teamed up with Andy's brother Jamie Murray for the doubles, but the pair didn't have the golden touch together and went out in the first round.

But she did get to meet the Queen, and had a brief chat with the monarch before she took her place in the Royal Box to see Andy Murray beat Finland's Jarkko Nieminen.

Kim Sears, Andy's not-so-erstwhile girlfriend, also watched Murray's victory. The pair had recently reconciled, much to the crowd's delight.

Laura had initially not intended to enter the junior tournament in 2010, as she wanted to concentrate on the senior event instead. But with her early departure she had time on her hands and filled it by attempting to win back her junior title.

As eighth seed, she breezed past Rita Ozaki from Japan to claim a 6-0; 6-1 victory in the first round. Next she clinched a 6-0; 6-4 win over American Krista Hardebeck, to reach the final 16.

And, to the relief of the LTA, Robson was not alone. Five other British players had also stormed their way through – more than any other country. James Marsalek, Oliver Golding, Tara Moore and a 14-year-old named Eleanor Dean had all won their matches, lifting some of the gloom that had descended over the All England Club.

But, while Robson celebrated, she was completely unaware at the huge row that had been sparked about her while she played Hardebeck.

During the match, BBC commentator David Mercer had been filling the airtime with the constant chatter demanded of a sports reporter. But then his mind wandered to a subject that was strictly off-limits to every man the world over: a woman's weight.

'I suppose the one thing that I have at the back of my mind at the moment,' he began – in retrospect he should have left it there – 'Is Laura mobile enough around the court? Perhaps a little puppy fat at the moment, the sort of thing you'd expect her to lose as she concentrates on tennis full time...'

It was an outrageous thing to say about a fit and healthy young girl who was at a vulnerable age. No one could see what on earth he was even talking about – Laura was slender and well built, and comments like that could have caused her and other teenagers to question their appearance in a manner that could ultimately be very damaging.

Tweets of disgust began to flood the social networking site, and Laura's mum was incredulous when she heard what Mercer had said. 'She doesn't have any fat to lose,' Kathy said firmly. 'She is still growing. You can't touch her weight at that age!'

The Women's Sport and Fitness Foundation immediately

waded in on the argument, with CEO Sue Tibballs saying: 'Fit, healthy and even athletic women come in many shapes and sizes. These types of comments are particularly unhealthy in a society in which more young women say they would rather be thin than healthy.'

As the storm grew, a spokesman for Beat, the eating disorders charity, also got involved, condemning Mercer's attitude.

'Any comment about a person's appearance can cause distress and problems, regardless of their age or size,' read the statement they released to the press. 'The body goes through many changes during the teenage years. Laura Robson is clearly fit and healthy and has no need to lose weight.'

BBC bosses started to sweat – they made Mercer apologise, both to Laura in person and also live on air. A fellow commentator revealed: 'David's comments could obviously be construed in a terrible way so he was made to apologise. People were not happy about it, especially with all the problems girls at her age have with their weight issues.'

But Mercer, who some people snidely commented was hardly slender himself, didn't seem too fussed when he was approached the next day for a statement. Chomping away at a huge baguette, he said: 'I wouldn't call it a debacle at all. We are all sitting down later and going through the transcript so that I can see exactly what I said and I can then take a view on it.'

It wasn't the first time a commentator had tried to inject a bit of personality into a report and subsequently landed themselves in hot water. After jockey Liam Treadwell won the Grand National in 2009, Clare Balding, the BBC presenter, asked him to give a big grin for the cameras. He smiled with his lips closed, obviously self-conscious about his teeth.

'No, no, let's see your teeth,' she pressed. 'He hasn't got the best teeth in the world but you can afford to go and get them done now if you like.'

She later apologised profusely.

Before an interview with swimmer Ian Thorpe in 2002, Australian reporter Nicki Voss made a comment about his size 17 feet, asking whether it was true what they say about men with big feet. She was instantly dismissed from her job on the *Today Tonight* programme on Channel 7.

Laura was probably just relieved that the media had moved on from Slutgate and appeared relaxed about the whole affair.

'I've spoken to the guy who said it. It's not a big deal. It doesn't bother me at all,' she said. 'It's his opinion. You know, I don't really care.'

In the third round, Laura beat Germany's An-Sophie Mestach, before dispatching her fellow Brit Tara Moore in the quarterfinals.

Incredibly, yet another commentator decided it would be appropriate to talk about a teenager's weight, when Barry Davies honed in on Tara Moore's physique during the match: 'I gather, perhaps I shouldn't say this,' he said, before completely ignoring his own advice. 'But part of the problem was that she needs not get too heavy. I mean, she went into tennis saying that she wanted to do it for the exercise,' he mused, sounding more like a fashion mag intern than a sports reporter.

'She's chunkily built and only 5ft 5in and she packs a bit of a wallop and there's a balance there that will be watched I'm sure.'

There was a lot of head shaking and sighing that evening at the BBC. A weary spokesman later said: 'We will be speaking to all of our commentators regarding their phraseology.'

Back on court, moving to within sight of the crown she had so dramatically won two years previously, Laura was visibly elated. In reaching the semifinal of the girls' tournament, she joined Andy Murray, who had made it to the semis of the men's singles, and Oliver Golding, who had reached the same stage in the boys' singles, in gunning for British glory.

'Hopefully, we will have a champion before the weekend is out,' she said, grinning. 'I'd like to think so anyway. We all have good opportunities. It's going to be a really tough match for Andy but he has a good chance with how he's playing. I'll try to watch it.

'I don't know who Olly is up against but he is doing extremely well. As for me, it's quite a way off still. I'm up against a Japanese girl who has done really well so far.'

But sadly the semis were far enough for all three Brits.

In her match against Japan's Sachie Ishizu, Laura struggled to gain control over her opponent and eventually her bad temper got the better of her: at one point, she crunched her racket into the grass in frustration, while at another she flung it down completely, clearly frustrated at her below-par play.

'Be positive,' coaxed Kathy. 'Use those legs. Smile.'

But Laura wasn't having any of it.

'Jesus, I can't seem to get any first serves in,' she screamed, forcing her mother to finally shout: 'Grow up, Laura!'

When she finally lost in straight sets, she picked up her

things and stormed off court before Ishizu had a chance to sit down.

Elsewhere, Golding couldn't find his way past Australian Ben Mitchell, while Murray pushed himself to the limit against the Matador, Rafael Nadal, only to lose in straight sets.

'I'm upset, which is understandable I think,' he said afterwards.

It was a sentiment that was echoed by Golding, Robson and every British tennis fan in the country.

CHAPTER 16
ALL CHANGE

Laura may have missed the French Open in 2010, but she certainly wasn't going to miss out on a trip to New York and Flushing Meadows in August.

After her tantrum at Wimbledon, she had composed herself enough to enter an Aegon GB Pro-Series event, where she was seeded seventh – her first senior seeding ever.

She'd got as far as the quarterfinals.

Now she was all geared up for the US Open qualifiers and, hopefully, a couple of days off to explore the Big Apple. She arrived early to get over the jetlag, and spent her time training and hanging out with Heather Watson, who was also at the Open, along with Andy Murray, Elena Baltacha, Anne Keothavong and a host of other British challengers.

Having risen to 219 in the rankings, Laura was itching for a senior win. But when she was drawn to face former Wimbledon semifinalist Jelena Dokic – daughter of crazed tennis dad Damir – she couldn't have much fancied her chances.

On court, she kept admirable control of her emotions and was focused and determined throughout the match. As a result, she crushed her opponent 6-1; 6-4, in the finest win of her fledgling professional career.

'I am very happy with the way I performed today,' said Robson. 'Jelena is a great player and a good friend of mine so I'm very pleased to get through.'

It was a cautious statement, perhaps made with Jelena's father's infamous temper in mind. She celebrated afterwards by eating at one of her favourite restaurants, Chipotle.

In the next round of the qualifiers, she stunned the crowd again with a similarly thumping win over Vesna Dolonc, a Serbian beauty known for her love of hot-pink tennis-wear. She had just one more match to go to qualify for a place in the US Open, and it would be against Spaniard Nuria Llagostera Vives, a canny pro nearly twice her age.

The Spanish star took the first set. Robson stayed calm and took the second before quickly going 3-1 up in the decider. She was more than matching her opponent's racket skills. But it would take more than that to win, and Laura's lack of experience soon showed itself, with devastating consequences.

Deciding that Robson's phenomenal rhythm and momentum needed to be broken for her to have a chance, Llagostera Vives decided to stall. Repeatedly.

Each time Laura was ready to serve, she tried a new tactic. She fiddled with her cap.

She played with her towel.

She played with her sunglasses.

It was the sort of gamesmanship that Laura had struggled

with before, and she still didn't quite know how to cope with it. She lost her edge, and, with it, five games in a row, to relinquish her chance at becoming the youngest British qualifier in Grand Slam history. This was unfair, but it was just another thing Laura would have to learn to deal with on the senior circuit.

For now, she was out of the senior qualifiers and back to the safety net of the juniors again – a move that had been her back-up plan for nearly two years now.

At first she did well, comfortably winning in the first two rounds without dropping a set. But she lost her third-round match to American qualifier Robin Anderson, who saw her out of the tournament and onto a flight home to London.

Nearing the end of the 2010 season, Laura had some serious thinking to do. She was making progress, but it was starting to slow and become unspectacular. She was heading for a stall in her career and needed to make some major changes if she was going to survive the leap from juniors to seniors.

When the new season began in January, she would be 17 and eligible to play more WTA tournaments – up to 20 in fact. She knew she would have to ramp up her playing schedule, leaving the juniors fully behind and throwing herself as far as possible into the tough world of the WTA.

She had discussions with her family, her management and her coaches. And, sadly, one of them wouldn't be continuing with her on her journey.

It was time for Laura to say goodbye to her faithful coach Martijn Bok, the Dutchman who had so carefully guided her to Wimbledon glory. He couldn't commit to her proposed busier schedule.

He agreed to stay with her till the end of the season but, after that, Laura would have to find a new man to guide her through the next stage of her career.

Heading to Asia to wrap up the 2010 season, she now had a new plan in place and approached her final games with a burst of extra enthusiasm.

At the Toray Pan Pacific in Tokyo, a Tier 1, $2 million WTA tournament, she entered the qualifiers where she first faced World No. 57 Anastasija Sevastova, a Latvian player who had recently claimed her first WTA title.

In an ambitious performance, astonishingly she overcame her nerves to beat the No. 6 seed in 1 hour and 33 minutes. All she had to do now, to reach the main draw of a WTA Tour event on foreign soil for the first time, was beat Romania's Simona Halep.

Halep was a talented player who was best known for her bouncing assets – and I'm not referring to her tennis balls!

At the 2008 French Open, her 34DD breasts had attracted an obscene amount of attention and caused her an equally obscene amount of pain. As a result, she'd recently had them reduced in size, hoping it would enhance her game. But her smaller bosom didn't help her beat Robson, who, after losing the first set, came back with a vengeance to monopolise the rest of the match.

Laura was in the main draw and ecstatic about it.

'I am happy. And sweaty. But mostly happy,' she tweeted.

Waiting for the main draw to begin, Laura spent her free time settling into the scene at the WTA Tour. She 'bedazzled' her phone, decorating it with sparkly crystals, and learned how to make sushi in a special class organised by the Tour.

Then she prepared for her first-round match against

Hungary's Greta Arn. She had done exceptionally well just to qualify – to win even one round would be a fitting way to end her partnership with Bok. Sadly, it was not meant to be. She lost in straight sets to the experienced 31-year-old Hungarian, and was out of the tournament.

She stayed in Tokyo to compete in two more Japanese tournaments, but exhaustion was setting in, and Laura was struggling to maintain her form. She won her first-round ITF match against Christina McHale, but retired from the second after complaining of a sore throat and dehydration.

Robson did then pick up some steam and managed to get through the qualifiers at the subsequent HP Open in Osaka, but she once again fell at the first hurdle by losing in the first round.

It was time to go home.

Laura finished 2010 ranked 206. She had jumped up more than 200 places over the course of an exciting year that had seen both huge highs and devastating lows.

Back in Wimbledon, she was glad to be reunited with her beloved dogs Kiri and Ella, and got back into a regular routine at home.

She recommenced her training at the National Tennis Centre, where she hit a few balls with tennis beauty Ana Ivanovic, who was also practising there. Laura noticed an unusual amount of men loitering on the balcony as they played...

Robson then had a low-key and cosy few weeks of family downtime, during which she saw the new Harry Potter film at the cinema and showed off her newfound culinary skills by cooking for her parents. Maybe she was planning to show off her kitchen talents to Andy Murray in January, as she had agreed to once more compete in the Hopman Cup with him to kick off her 2011 season.

Murray was looking forward to teaming up with the teenager again after their previous year's success together. He told the press: 'For me, it was a good start to the year and we went pretty close to winning. I look forward to playing with Laura once again.'

Laura also made time to travel to the Mouratoglou Academy in Paris, to discuss her 2011 training schedule with owner Patrick Mouratoglou. After having trained there regularly for nearly a year, she was now well used to the comprehensive facilities at the Parisian academy and particularly trusted the renowned trainer to advise her on who should coach her next.

Together, they decided she should move her training base full-time to Paris, and work with one of his staff in preparation for the 2011 season. But as her training progressed he began to take a keener interest in her development, and just after Christmas Laura made an interesting announcement: she had hired Mouratoglou himself as her coach.

The permanently tanned Frenchman had a sterling track record of coaching up-and-coming tennis players, having guided Marcos Baghdatis to World Junior No. 1, Aravane Rezai to the world's top 20 and Yanina Wickmayer to the No. 12 spot.

Laura was hoping he would take her to the next level of her career and dramatically improve both her playing and her ranking. With Mouratoglou guiding her, Laura felt she was well placed to finally make the full transition from junior to senior.

'We have worked with her for the best part of a year, so

the understanding is already a little bit special,' Mouratoglou told *The Times*.

'She had been with our physical and medical staff but she was not involved with our coaches because she had her own.

'Now that situation has changed and I took the decision to work with her because I regard her as a very interesting player.'

At the end of the year, Laura flew to Australia to spend Christmas with her family there. On New Year's Day, Andy Murray joined her from his winter base in Miami – 13 times zones away.

It was time for Hopman Round Two.

CHAPTER 17

ANNUS HORRIBILIS

Laura was suffering from a cold when she played her first match in Perth for the Hopman Cup. Andy was struggling with jetlag – a major enemy of the international tennis scene, even for those who turn left into first class when boarding their planes.

The indoor stadium was hot and stuffy as they walked out on court and neither player was feeling too great. As a result, Robson and Murray were both sweating and gasping as they faced their first-round Italian singles opponents.

Robson was up first, playing Francesca Schiavone, the previous year's French Open champion. The British player showcased a cleanly hit serve and pummelling ground-strokes, often taking her agile Italian opponent by surprise. She played remarkably well, considering the frequency with which she had to stop and blow her nose, and admirably showed off her abundant potential.

But after breaking to lead 5-3 in the opening set she began to complain of dizziness and earache, and eventually a doctor was called on court.

She bravely agreed to continue with the match ten minutes later, and subsequently gave it everything she had – even though she often looked confused and in pain. Schiavone definitely found the match a challenge, but in the end she beat Laura 7-5; 6-3.

Andy won his match against Potito Starace, but didn't look comfortable at all on court. Breathing heavily in the humidity of the Burswood Dome, he clearly hadn't acclimatised to the stifling indoor conditions and suffered to get his win.

In the tiebreak doubles match, Robson impressively held her own, but she was still struggling. Andy was occasionally sloppy, clearly still feeling foggy from the jetlag, but the pair played well together and it was a close match.

However, they lost, giving the overall win to Italy.

Andy acknowledged his below-par play, and said he needed a couple of days to right himself. When asked what he thought of his partner's performance, Laura displayed her great comic timing by interjecting: 'Rubbish.'

Side by side, both players laughed. But it was a brief moment of light-heartedness – the constant teasing and high spirits that had so defined their last outing together was in short supply. They had to beat France if they were going to progress to the next round of the invitational.

Robson faced Kristina Mladenovic, a teenager of a similar standard to herself, who had a little more experience on the senior circuit.

It showed.

Robson started brightly, going straight into a 2-0 lead,

before her slightly older opponent fired back with some powerful serves. Mladenovic also employed some of the tactics she had picked up on the senior circuit for stalling, breaking Laura's stride with a stream of fist pumps, calling her own lines, toilet breaks and glances towards her own box for instructions on challenges.

The umpire finally warned her for taking too long between points, but the scolding came far too late.

Laura was defeated once again.

Andy won his match against Nicolas Mahut to level the field, but in the deciding doubles the French duo were tight and on the ball, while Laura looked in pain and Murray fell short of his vintage best.

They were out of the Cup.

The pair still had America to face in the group stages, which would quite frankly be a waste of energy. Having lost to two countries, even if they beat America, they couldn't have progressed to the next round. Andy rose to the redundant challenge, beating American tennis giant John Isner to end on a high note.

Laura faced the eccentric Bethanie Mattek-Sands, a friendly player whose wacky dress sense often livened up her matches. Robson was cheered on by the 8,000-strong crowd in her mother's home town and fought well against the world No. 58. But she was wincing in pain and had to call the doctor out yet again, this time for some kind of strain in her thigh.

Lying on the floor while she was examined, Laura looked crestfallen. She had been suffering all through the tournament with a cold and just as it was starting to clear she had now sustained an injury. She decided to play on but her movement was severely restricted and she lost in straight sets.

The duo had one more match to play – the doubles tiebreaker – but Laura had to pull out. She was in too much pain, even after icing the injury, and needed a scan to find out what was wrong.

It was bad news.

She had torn her hamstring and would be out for three weeks. There would be no Australian Open for Laura in 2011. And, while all her tennis friends travelled to Melbourne for another chance at glory, Laura flew to Paris for treatment.

'Good luck to all the British girls in Melbourne for Australian Open!' she tweeted, mustering up as much enthusiasm as possible. 'Gutted I won't be there.'

'If she had played qualifiers, it would have been very dangerous,' said Mouratoglou. 'She's upset but she's OK. She's going to play many other Grand Slams in future.'

It was a disastrous start to the year.

Laura was supposed to fly to Israel after the Australian Open to play in the Fed Cup – her first time on the British team. Her friends Elena Baltacha, Anne Keothavong and Heather Watson would now have to welcome her replacement instead: Jocelyn Rae from Scotland.

The injured player was frustrated.

She had to concentrate on getting fit again, but it would be months before her next tournament and it was a setback she really could have done without. Laura had seen in the new season raring to go and now, through no fault of her own, she was stalling, stuck in that horrible limbo between juniors and seniors, and there was literally nothing she could do to move on.

Robson turned 17 and, instead of celebrating in Australia with her friends, she had to console herself with birthday wishes from her twitter followers. 'I can drive now', she tweeted. 'Look out for me tearing up the roads.'

But what she really wanted was to be tearing up the courts.

The weeks passed.

She tried to alleviate her boredom by having a fish pedicure, and watching the whole first season of *The Vampire Diaries*, but it was an insanely dull period for Laura. When in March she was discovered amusing herself by cramming her long body into a washing machine, her coach must have been relieved that she was finally ready to begin working on her comeback. It was clear that bored teenagers are not easy patients.

While Laura was getting herself back in shape, her pal Heather Watson had been rocketing ahead in the rankings and the public eye. She had reached the quarterfinals at the WTA Auckland Open in January and after an impressive run was now 149 in the rankings, the youngest player in the top 150.

The British press were going crazy for her. Every day a new interview or photo shoot with the young starlet appeared in the papers. It must have been hard for Robson. She was happy for her friend but she wanted so badly to get back out there and emulate Watson's success.

It was decided that Laura would stage her comeback at a series of low-profile events in the Far East. The priority was to get plenty of matches under her belt ahead of the more high-profile European tournaments later in the year.

For the next four months, she toiled away on the ITF circuit, honing her form under her new coach and gaining

A star is born: Holding the Wimbledon Junior trophy aloft in triumph in 2008.

Above left: Think pink: Attending the Wimbledon Champions Dinner in glamorous high heels as the newly crowned Wimbledon Junior Champion in 2008.

Above right: Early fame: A young Laura in 2009, celebrating her sponsorship deal with soft drinks supplier Robinson's.

Below: By Royal Approval: Meeting Her Majesty at Wimbledon in 2010, alongside Heather Watson and Billie Jean King.

Above: Downtime: Having a laugh with her friend and rival Heather Watson during the 2012 Fed Cup in Israel.

Below left: Happiness: Emerging victorious from a match against Spain's Maria Jose Martinez Sanchez at the 2010 Hopman Cup in Australia.

Below right: Celebrity: Taking time out from all her intense on court action by mingling with fellow athlete Denise Lewis at a 2011 London Burberry show.

Above left: Defeat: Learning another hard lesson by losing to Karolina Pliskova during a 2012 qualifying match for the French Open.

Above right: Determined: Laura's powerful forehand giving opponent Lucie Safarova a hard time on Day 3 of the London 2012 Olympics.

Below left: New deals: Posing with Sir Richard Branson to celebrate becoming the new face of Virgin Active in February 2013.

Below right: Matchpoint: Laura unable to contain her excitement as she retires Kim Clijsters from their historic 2012 US Open clash.

Above: Here come the girls: Laura and her Fed Cup teammates glam up for the official team dinner in Israel in 2013. From left to right: Laura Robson, Elena Baltacha, Judy Murray, Johanna Konta, Anne Keothavong and Heather Watson.

Below left: Taking a break: Chatting to Gabby Logan at The Henley Festival on a glorious summer's day in 2013.

Below right: Determined: Laura bravely serving against Belgium's Kirsten Flipkens at the 2014 Australian Open, despite not being in peak condition. Unfortunately, she lost the match.

Above: History repeating: Signing autographs on oversized tennis balls for her fans – when Laura was young she would ask the same of her own tennis idols.

Below: Clay woes: Tackling the French 'devil dirt' at Roland Garros during a singles match against pal Caroline Wozniacki.

Stunner: Looking elegant and grown-up in green Burberry lace at the 2013 pre-Wimbledon party – at London's famous Kensington Roof Gardens.

Above: On their way to glory: Murray and Robson congratulating each other after defeating Germany in the 2012 Olympic Mixed Doubles semi-final.

Below: History in the making: Proudly displaying her London 2012 Olympic Games silver medal, alongside mixed doubles partner Andy Murray.

All pictures © Getty Images

some much-needed experience of senior matches. In Kunming, China, she lost in the second round. In nearby Wenshan, she reached the quarterfinals.

Over in America, she only reached the second round on the clay courts in Charlottesville, while she fared much better at a $50,000 tournament in Indian Harbour Beach – getting to the semifinals before losing to Alison Riske.

She even won a candlelit meal for two in the players' raffle.

However, some observers had begun to get seriously concerned.

After beating Maria Alvarez Teran 6-4; 7-5, Laura looked to be in bad shape. She limped to the net to shake her opponent's hand, limped back to her chair to get her things, then limped off alone to the locker room.

It wasn't good news.

After suffering from such bad growing pains following her Wimbledon win as a 14-year-old, Laura had thought that she was fully grown at last, and all those agonies were over.

But, despite her already towering height, her body apparently wasn't done punishing her yet. A late growth spurt now quickly took her to nearly six foot and left her once more suffering from swollen knees and throbbing legs.

Back on home soil, she played poorly. In Nottingham in early June, she didn't even reach the second round. Soon after, in Holland, she served 13 double faults against Spain's Arantxa Parra Santonja, spectacularly crashing out of the 's-Hertogenbosch tournament in the first round.

While she was amused to discover she had been included as a character in a PS3 game – *Virtual Tennis 2* – her form wasn't amusing anyone.

It had been the toughest season of her career. She'd been dogged by repeated injuries and as a result she had struggled to maintain a full training schedule.

There had been few wins to boost her confidence, and her hopes of Mouratoglou coaching her to glory in 2011 had so far come to nothing. She had even dropped in the rankings to 257.

Now, Wimbledon was barely a week away and her prospects at the tournament – in which she was in the main draw – honestly weren't looking great.

So it was a shock to everyone when Laura announced she was parting ways with her coach – four days before Wimbledon was due to start.

'We are parting ways by mutual agreement and I really appreciate all Patrick and his team have done,' she said in a formal statement. 'We both felt the time was right to make a change.'

After just six months, their partnership was over, and no one could believe it. Wimbledon? Without a coach? It was madness.

Rumours began to fly that Robson had actually sacked the Frenchman and his team, after he had failed to lead her to glory. But he'd not really had a chance to work his magic, as Laura had hardly been fit enough to play at all.

Others mused as to whether Mouratoglou had lost confidence in the youngster, whose progression had been so terribly set back all year. She'd been practically living in Paris and had admitted to missing her dogs and her family – did she just want to come home?

But, whatever the reason, Paris would no longer be her base for training, and she'd need to secure herself a new coach pretty quickly.

'After Wimbledon, identifying a new coach will be important but right now I want to concentrate on getting ready for Wimbledon,' she said.

As part of her contract with Adidas, Laura had access to their tennis coaches, and it was to them she now turned.

Sven Groeneveld, an Adidas player development coach who had spotted Laura's talent at the tender age of 11, was only too happy to temporarily take over Laura's training. It was a tumultuous time, and Laura had lots to do to get her head straight for her first appearance at the All England Club.

But it wasn't all bad news. With the media focused on Heather Watson's winning court exploits, Laura could compete at Wimbledon fairly under the radar, which would take some pressure off her.

She began to feel more confident.

Having accepted that injuries and growth spurts were things that were beyond her control, she had put her recent losses into perspective.

'I'm really tall now. I've grown a lot in the last few months, it's not anything I've got any control over,' she told the press. 'I just have to accept the problems that come with it. I'm pretty happy with my height now. Fingers crossed I don't keep growing.'

Laura Robson had tasted both success and defeat during her career and with her body now healing she could focus on the future.

It had been a bad season. But she wouldn't let it ruin her favourite time of the year – Wimbledon.

At the WTA's pre-Wimbledon party, held at the Kensington Roof Gardens, Laura was relaxed and chatty.

Wearing a classy black knee-length Alexander McQueen dress with a gently plunging neckline, she looked elegant and grown up, even if she did struggle to sit down in the tight dress.

She'd shunned expensive jewellery, letting her bronzed skin and clear complexion speak for themselves, perfectly set off by the slick of pink lipstick that graced her lips. She looked beautiful, and happy, and ready to face whatever was coming next.

Rain lashed down on the day of Robson's first match – against Angelique Kerber, a German titan of a tennis player placed 77 in the world rankings. Play came to a halt early in the day, and as organisers rushed to reschedule all the matches Laura grew restless.

Laura didn't find out till much later that her match had been officially cancelled.

'Bit of a shambles this evening,' she tweeted. 'Had to wait until at least 8pm before they could cancel my match. Oh well! Looking forward to tomorrow :)'

She amused herself by indulging in a 'plank off' with Anne Keothavong – a competitive game that involved being photographed lying down in the strangest places.

Robson went one up in the competition when she 'planked' in the players' restaurant overlooking the lush, green Wimbledon courts. But she pretty much won when she was pictured lying down on the BBC commentator's desk, as Sue Barker grinned next to her, giving a thumbs-up to the camera. It was planking gold.

The next day, Laura faced her third attempt at a senior first-round Wimbledon match. She had lost twice before, despite the spirit she'd shown during those previous first-round matches, and it must have begun to feel like her own personal 'white whale'.

Laura was calm and composed as she strode out to face Kerber on that grey day in late June. No one expected her to win. But that was just the kind of situation she thrived on.

Robson peppered the first set with errors, letting Kerber comfortably win 6-4. But she persisted in the second set and scrapped her way back into contention. She played with authority, thumping down shots that had her German opponent hurtling across the court to reach the ball.

Her decisive strokes left Kerber frequently stranded, and, having evened the stakes by taking the second set, it was clear that Laura had found her rhythm.

She was determined.

Not even a tactical time-out on Kerber's part for a 'shoulder rub' could break her stride for long.

Immediately after the injury delay, Kerber came back to 4-3 in the decider. But, as the sun finally broke through the clouds to shine on the court, Laura broke back with a sublime cross-court forehand. She served out for the match without dropping a point and sealed the greatest win of her career so far.

It was a triumph and the crowd went ballistic. It was her first Grand Slam win. She was Britain's darling of tennis once more.

'I'm so happy! Absolutely amaaaazing atmosphere on court. Thank you all!' she tweeted from the locker room.

Heather Watson hadn't been so lucky. She had struggled through her first-round match against France's Mathilde Johannsson, and had succumbed to an injury in the second set. With her elbow strapped up, she had continued to play, but she was clearly still in pain and lost soon after.

While Laura celebrated by trying on Bethanie Mattek-Sands's odd white pom pom jacket – her latest wacky outfit – poor Watson was sobbing in her post-match conference.

'I just feel like there's no excuses now. I know how to play tennis,' she said through her tears. 'This is what I prepare for. This is why I play tennis every day, so I should be ready. I feel like I should be winning these matches.

'It's so frustrating and I was just disappointed that I lost.'

It was a feeling that Laura understood and would no doubt herself struggle with again. But for now she was riding high.

Facing Maria Sharapova would make any tennis player nervous. But Laura was actually excited. She had nothing to lose. She'd bagged herself a guaranteed £20,125 just by reaching the second round, and playing against Sharapova would be great experience if nothing else.

She was back on familiar territory: the plucky Brit, the brave underdog, fighting the odds, giving it her all.

Win or lose, it didn't matter.

The nation would love her either way.

The crowd were obviously behind Laura the following day as she stepped out on court to face the Russian champion. And as the match got underway Robson immediately began causing problems for 'Super Sharapova'.

Her serve repeatedly flummoxed the 24-year-old, and Laura looked comfortable as she raced to a 4-1 first-set lead on Court One. It was good to see her smiling again, a sign that she felt in control and was enjoying herself. Sharapova fought back, as everyone knew she would: the Russian wouldn't be going down without a fight. But there was little between them as they battled each other for points, neck and neck most of the way.

One reporter's 'gruntometer' recorded Sharapova at 116.9 decibels as she struggled during the match – breaking her previous record of 105. At 85 decibels, a Harley Davison makes less noise.

Robson played cleverly, outfoxing her opponent with aggression and variety and bringing her fans regularly to their feet in celebration. And, even though she eventually lost 7-6; 6-3, it had been one heck of a game and Sharapova knew it.

'Laura started off the match so well, going for her shots and serving well,' she told BBC Sport. 'I couldn't get too many looks at her first serve. I think she has great potential. It's a really long road – there will be many tournaments, many losses and many wins. She'll get that experience behind her and she'll be a better player.'

Laura had proved to herself that she could definitely play with the big girls. It was a closer match than anyone could have imagined and at some points it had even looked like the crowd would witness one of the greatest shocks in the tournament's history. So, even while she was admitting to a little disappointment at the loss, Laura could feel her confidence returning.

She would need to continue grinding it out on the ITF challenger circuit, while attempting to qualify for the Holy Grail – WTA Tour events – but she didn't mind.

'I can improve on everything,' she told the BBC humbly, acknowledging that the hard work would really start now. 'It's really easy to play well on a day like this where you've got a big stage, a big crowd, lots of support, you're playing against a top 10 player, especially someone like Maria,' she explained. 'It's going to be hard going back to the lower tournaments, but you've got to do to earn the right to play on such a big court again.'

The press rejoiced in what they saw as a huge success for the young player. But a few journalists had a less excitable view on the match. 'A straight sets, second-round defeat, met with a standing ovation. Only in Britain, one might say,' wrote Martin Samuel for the *Daily Mail*.

'And yet, as dizzying as it all was,' his piece continued, 'there remains an inescapable truth gnawing away in the minds of those who have charted the rise and fall of a hundred battling Brits in the environs of the All England Club: when Sharapova was Robson's age, she too was playing against seeded opposition in the second round of Grand Slam tournaments. And winning.'

This was a fair point, as was his next claim that Robson needed to work on her fitness. 'The gulf between the physical prowess of the players was plain, and must be addressed if Robson is not to suffer a lifetime of similar frustrations,' he wrote.

'It is the reason all talk of her potential comes with caveats. The best tennis players are also supreme athletes and, as talented as Robson is, she may never achieve the success of inferior technicians if she fails to address this flaw.'

But, while these were valid comments, neither of his points was new to Laura. And the game had changed in the seven years that divided Sharapova and Robson.

Careers were now starting later and lasting longer – the result of many factors, not least the strict restrictions that were now placed on the amount of senior tournaments younger players could play.

This was bound to slow progress, but it did save on the

heartbreaking possibility of burnout. While ten years ago, it seemed fashionable for the younger women to prosper on court – Hingis, the Williams sisters and Sharapova all won Grand Slam titles before they were 21 – it was now the relatively older players who were taking all the titles.

Laura needed to work on her fitness, and she knew it.

But the rest would hopefully come down to experience, and Laura had years to go in the game to get that.

Right now, no one could deny that Laura had turned her fortunes around. Sharapova was right – Laura needed to continue grinding away on the circuit and that's exactly what she intended to do.

CHAPTER 18

THE ITF GRIND

In July 2011, Laura was spurred on by discovering that she had leapt into the world top 200 for the first time.

Now at a career-high ranking of 184, she entered the ITF Aegon GB Pro Series at Foxhills in Surrey, a hard-court competition with prize money of £15,500. She had reached the quarterfinals at Foxhills the previous year, and had been handed a wildcard to this year's event after her performance at Wimbledon. Tournament director Richard Joyner was so pleased Robson would be attending that he sent out a press release singling her out for attention.

Laura was firmly back in the public eye.

She swept through the first two rounds to come face to face with her compatriot Tara Moore in the quarterfinals. She'd overcome Tara at Sunderland in 2008 and she now beat her again, 6-1; 6-1, to surpass her previous performance at Foxhills and reach the semis.

Robson was steamrollering her way through the event, and, after flattening her next opponent, Lina Stanciute, she found herself in the final of an ITF event for only the second time in her career. Facing Australia's Johanna Konta, who at the time was trying to emulate Laura by becoming a fellow British citizen, Laura began well.

But in an unlucky set of circumstances she had to retire from the match in the second set with an injured arm. It was a shame, but Laura had been motivated by her successful string of wins and wouldn't let it affect her morale.

She wasn't seriously hurt and would heal quickly. It certainly wasn't painful enough to stop her donning her Harry Potter specs and Griffindor scarf to watch the final Harry Potter film as soon as it was released – *Deathly Hallows Part II* came out on 15 July.

Nor did it hinder her ability to 'owl'.

A brand-new craze, 'owling' involved crouching – like an owl – for photographs in odd locations. After chef Gordon Ramsey had posted pictures of himself 'planking' in June, trend-watchers had declared the craze officially dead and 'owling' had sprung up to replace it. As a socially conscious teenager, Laura obviously liked to be on trend with her Internet crazes as well as her clothes.

In August, Laura, along with Anne Keothavong, flew to Vancouver for a $100,000 ITF tournament. Accepting that she needed to work on her fitness, she had added a dedicated fitness trainer to her retinue, who accompanied her on her overseas trip. Laura stayed with a host family and discovered, much to her delight, that they were dog owners.

Taking the canines for a relaxing ramble through some nearby woods, she was told that scenes from one of her favourite movies, *Twilight*, had been filmed right there. The excitement of the trip more than made up for the fact that she lost in the first round to Aleksandra Wozniak.

Next she travelled to Cincinnati, where she trialled the new fashion of high-waisted shorts on its city streets, before facing Maria Martinez Sanchez, the Spaniard she had beaten in her Hopman Cup escapades of 2010.

This time, Martinez Sanchez evened the score, beating her 6-4; 4-6; 6-1 in another closely contested match. Laura consoled herself by having feathers put in her hair and posing next to the most talked-about thing at the event – the rafamobile. A bright-yellow Aston Martin had been spotted in and around the city, with the words 'Vamos Rafa' emblazoned on the side and a Spanish flag painted on the roof.

Its owners, who unsurprisingly were huge Nadal fans, had given the £130,000 car a makeover just for the event. The personalised vehicle didn't give Nadal any extra luck though – he burned his hand at dinner one night and bowed out in the quarters.

This was a star-studded tournament and Laura must have felt lucky to experience it. Seven of the top eight ATP players were taking part on just one day – including Sharapova, Jankovic, Djokovic and Serena Williams.

Williams raised a few eyebrows at the event when she retired from the tournament after winning her first-round match, citing a 'sore toe'.

'If anything this might be a blessing in disguise,' she told the press humbly. 'I might get some more rest and prepare for the rest of the season.'

It must have been a coincidence, then, that one of her

close friends, reality star Kim Kardashian, was marrying her basketball-playing beau Kris Humphries a few days later in California. Now that she was out she could attend, couldn't she?

'I hadn't thought about it,' Serena said when a journalist pointed out the lucky twist of fate. 'I mean, now that I have the time... I probably will. I hadn't thought about it so...'

Her story wasn't helped when just hours later she was pictured riding the diamondback rollercoaster at King's Island, an amusement park nearby. Or that the next day she was out and about in her trademark skyscraper heels in the Californian city of Los Angeles...

Apparently, if you were as big as Serena, you could afford to choose your battles.

Annoyingly, the unseasonably cool temperatures did mean a definite lack of hot shirtless player shots that year. Given that Cincinnati is known for its hot practice photos, many fans were a little disappointed at the overcast skies. But for Laura the tournament was one of the highlights of the year – because Andy Murray won the men's singles.

Finally, after an eventful few weeks in the American state of Ohio, it was time to head to the US Open and the New York courts of Flushing Meadows. Laura had never made it to the main draw in the Big Apple. But, during a whirlwind two days of wet and windy weather, she focused on her three qualifying matches one at a time, and won them all.

It was a sweet moment for Robson, who was steadily proving all her critics wrong. 'I'm a mixture of happy and exhausted,' she told the waiting press. 'In the past two years I said after my third-round matches that I can only learn from those experiences.

'You've always got to think positively so in my third-round match today I just thought, "I've been in this situation before, I've got nothing to lose, and I'll just go for it".'

Her more relaxed attitude to the tournament, along with her dedication to training and a renewed fire in her belly, had finally pushed her forward in her career. But, before she could play her first-round match against Japanese No. 1 Ayumi Morita, Hurricane Irene decided to storm the New York courts.

Serena Williams, fresh from her LA trip, took it as an opportunity to have Manhattan's Park Avenue all to herself for a day. The beautiful street had been emptied of tourists due to the storm, and Williams shunned her usual love of shopping to dance alone there in the powerful downpour.

Laura watched as the hurricane tore down branches and flooded the areas surrounding the tennis site. She was practising on an indoor court on the 39th floor of her hotel, and every time she went to pick up the ball she was struck by the foreboding view from the floor-to-ceiling windows.

But, after a weekend of rain and thunderous noise, Irene passed and the US Open began. The sun shone down on Laura's new pink tennis dress as she took on Morita, who was 127 places higher than Laura in the world rankings.

It was a match that saw a varied performance from the teenager. Moments of spectacular play saw Laura break her opponent's serve four times, while at times a slew of unforgiveable errors crept in to spoil her consistency. She held her nerve and displayed considerably better movement on court than usual. When Morita called for her trainer after the first game of the second set, Robson was up 7-6; 1-0.

And that was as far as it went: Morita retired from the

game with a shoulder injury that gave Laura her second Grand Slam win. 'I just kept trying to refocus and hang in there and stick to the game plan I had, and that worked out in the end,' she said after her victory.

Robson's run ended in the second round when she faced Anabel Medina Garrigues, a speedy Spaniard who had won 11 titles on the WTA Tour.

Laura started solidly, powering a series of thumping serves and powerful forehands past her experienced opponent. She hit 20 clear winners to Medina's 9, but her ambitious series of shots resulted in 32 unforced errors, many of which were miscued rather than ill-conceived.

High-risk cross-court forehands ended up buried in the net.

Overcooked shots strayed into the tramlines.

The steadier Spaniard stroked the ball with infinitely more patience, and her consistency paid off: she won 6-2; 6-3, pushing Robson out of the Open.

It was yet another learning curve for the British teenager.

Back home in London, Laura took a break from playing ITF matches to indulge in her second great love: fashion.

She had been invited to the Burberry Prorsum Spring/ Summer 2012 catwalk show, which was taking place at the Kensington Roof Gardens as part of fashion week.

The young tennis star took the opportunity to debut the newest addition to her wardrobe, a cream military-style Burberry mac embellished with jewelled shoulders, and posed in it for the paparazzi with a huge grin on her face. She enjoyed the show from a prime front-row position, joined by a host of celebrities including Andy Murray, Sienna Miller, Kanye West and Paul Weller.

Her excitement was obvious as she watched Cara Delevingne, the season's hottest new model, strut her stuff on the catwalk. It was clear that Laura was now very much a part of the British celebrity world, and pictures of her at the event appeared in newspapers and magazines all over the country.

Days later, and ranked 146 in the world, she got on a flight to Tokyo for the Toray Pan Pacific Open. Having arrived a few days early, she spent some time sightseeing and was amazed when she stumbled across a traditional Japanese wedding taking place at a central Tokyo shrine.

Laura posted an impressive first-round win against Romanian Alexandra Dulgheru, knocking out the world No. 53 in straight sets to set up a battle with her friend Ana Ivanovic in the second round. She certainly gave her pal a scare as she equalled her point for point nearly the whole way through the match. It was a tight game, but Ivanovic had the edge and beat Laura 7-5; 6-4.

'You win some, you lose some,' she tweeted.

Robson was quickly whisked to Beijing to compete in the WTA Tour's China Open. Settling down to lunch when she arrived, she was amused to discover that the meal would be accompanied by 'a delicate fragrant love plum'. Laura had travelled and seen an awful lot for one so young, but she could still have a bit of a giggle at new cultural discoveries. It must have been a let-down to discover that the 'love plum' was just a prune.

On the drive to her hotel, she passed some of the Olympic stadiums that had hosted the 2008 Beijing extravaganza, and began to get excited about London 2012. It was less than a year away, and, although Laura still didn't know for sure whether she would be competing, it promised to be a spectacular event.

Laura won twice to get through the qualifiers to the main draw – another epic achievement aided by her increased fitness and focus. But she lost in the first round to Slovenia's Polona Hercog.

After a long flight back home, the British player went back to the National Tennis Centre for more rigorous training. It was good to be back, and Laura settled into the stability of a London routine. She literally wept with laughter in the Roehampton gym when she filmed fellow players Luke Bainbridge and Jack Carpenter competing in a dance-off on the gym floor.

'1-0 Bainbridge,' she tweeted.

After all, he did show off some pretty special moves.

Training also included playing football with Olly Golding. Both scored in the mini match. It was just unfortunate for Golding that his was an own goal. She had a night out at the Hammersmith Apollo, where she watched American indie folk band Bon Iver weave their magic over the crowd.

Then, in October, she travelled to Devon for the Aegon Pro-Series event in Barnstaple – her last tournament of the season. After defeating Johanna Konta in the first round, she took a refreshing walk on one of Devon's many stunning beaches and felt at peace with how her year was finally turning out.

But her next match would be a clash she must have been dreading for years: it was time to play her friend Heather Watson.

Laura had always known it would have to happen someday – they were both too good not to have to face each other eventually. And they both knew that, whatever happened, it would only be the first of many such battles between them. It couldn't be helped. They were friends and rivals. They would just have to make it work.

If Federer and Nadal could take it in turns to beat each other and then go out for dinner together to celebrate, surely so could Robson and Watson. But until that moment arrived – a moment when one would triumph over the other – who knew how they would both react?

Maybe they both expected the location for their first clash to be more glamorous than an indoor tennis centre in Barnstaple, but neither of them disappointed on court. Robson was ranked 135, Watson 87.

Most tennis aficionados had backed Watson to win, prioritising her greater consistency over Robson's 'something special'. But Laura had Heather on the back foot from the very beginning of the match, racing through the opening set 6-1 and grabbing an early break in the second.

Watson finally recovered, working up a sweat to level matters at a set all. But Laura simply wouldn't give in. She broke in the third to lead 4-2 and served out the win in style. Laura was pleased to have won, but mostly she was just glad it was over. She hadn't enjoyed the match at all.

'It was really tough and I'm just glad to have got through it,' she said after it was all over. 'Heather and I are really good friends but I know how much winning that match meant to both of us – it was difficult to play under those circumstances but it's something that happens all the time. You just have to deal with it as best you can.'

Heather took the defeat with surprising humour, congratulating her younger friend and admitting she hadn't played her best.

'I just wasn't on form at all,' she said. 'Laura was better than me today and that's how it goes. I'm certainly looking forward to playing her again and hopefully getting my revenge.'

And Laura didn't doubt for a minute that she would try.

After vanquishing her friend for a place in the quarterfinals, Laura lost her next match against Ekaterina Bychkova. And, with that, the season was over.

Despite a terrible start to the year, Laura had pulled back her fortunes – rising from No. 206 to No. 131. She was now the highest-ranking 17-year-old in the world, but was still far removed from the elevated status that previous holders of that title had achieved in the past.

'Breaking into the top 100 is something I'll aim to do next season,' she told the press.

She had overcome a veritable plague of injuries and the loss of both her coach and the public's confidence to pull off some of the most astonishing wins of her career so far. Her junior days were now behind her. Laura Robson had two months to train before the New Year would bring her another crack at the Australian Open, along with her 18th birthday.

The last few months of the year were a good mixture of work and play. She spent some precious time with her dogs and filmed little Ella bounding around the common near her home in Wimbledon.

Her tennis training was mixed up with even more fitness work, and began to include hip-hop and salsa classes, which Laura absolutely loved. She even took up bikram yoga to help with her focus and agility – an intense yoga class that takes place in a room as hot as a sauna.

In November, she had a ridiculously enjoyable time being

dressed by a stylist – so that she could attend the London premiere of the new *Twilight* film, *Breaking Dawn Part I*. With her hair casually swept up at the sides to reveal her clear skin and fresh face, she looked effortlessly beautiful. Her outfit truly flew the flag for British designers: she wore a short black Alice Temperley dress, which had a delicate long sleeved sheer overlay that sparkled with diamanté detailing. To add colour, she used red lipstick and carried a gold Mulberry Fox Lily bag.

The young tennis celebrity looked at ease on the carpet, posing like a pro for the cameras before going inside to watch the latest instalment of one of her favourite film series. She was due to fly to Vegas to spend three weeks on the Adidas Player Development Programme, but had to cancel at the last minute because of the beginnings of a stress fracture in her left shin. She had a scan to determine the extent of the damage and was horrified to discover that her growth plates were still wide open – Laura was still growing.

It was a huge blow. Growing pains had caused her so many problems for so long, and it didn't look like they would cease any time soon. But she tried to take the news in her stride, and was determined that it wouldn't affect her any more.

Hobbling around on crutches in November, Laura wasn't taking any chances. She had the time to rest up and she was determined to do so. It didn't prevent her from going to the National Training Centre though. Most of her friends were training there and the Roehampton site had all the facilities she needed to rehabilitate.

Plus it had a big kitchen.

She might not have been able to challenge her friends to

a tennis match, but she could certainly take them down in a bake-off. Things definitely got messy in the kitchens at the NTC.

As December arrived and Laura counted down the days to Christmas, she was pleased to hear that Judy Murray had been appointed the new captain of the British Fed Cup team. The position had actually been vacant since Nigel Sears had given it up to coach Ana Ivanovic in the summer, and Judy was well known to have one of the sharpest tennis brains around.

She was the country's best-known sporting mother, having coached both Andy and Jamie to world-class status. Having her guiding the players would definitely be a bonus for the lucky women whom she picked to be on next year's team.

And Laura was one of them.

She'd missed out on being part of that year's British contingent because of her injury at the Hopman Cup, so Laura was overjoyed to be joining Heather Watson, Elena Baltacha and Anne Keothavong in the elite team.

In late December, she flew out to Australia for her annual Christmas family reunion. She wouldn't see Britain again until 2011 had ended and 2012 was well underway.

Robson was glad her annus horribilis was over. Her 2011 season may have eventually ended well career-wise, but Laura never wanted to go through all that pain and frustration again. Yes, she had learned a lot and she had gained valuable experience. But, boy, it had been tough.

Looking ahead, Laura hoped that 2012 would be an exciting year. She would legally become an adult, she would have another crack at all the tournaments she so desperately wanted to win, she would play in the Fed Cup and, of course, there was the Olympics: the greatest sporting event in the calendar was coming to her hometown of London and there was a chance she could be trying for a medal or two.

There was no time to dwell on the past when the future had so much to offer.

CHAPTER 19

RAINBOWS AND RIGHTS

Over Christmas, while other girls her age were helping themselves to another round of roast potatoes, Laura was training for the Australian Open.

'Swam in a 50m pool today. Felt like it never ended,' she tweeted, just days after the family festivities. 'As Dory from *Finding Nemo* once said "just keep swimming, just keep swimming." Wise fish.'

Wise fish indeed. Laura had a lot in common with little Nemo: the tenacious youngster who never gave up. Now not needing to use the crutches, she was busy building up her strength without jeopardising her still delicate body.

Melbourne was both busy and hot as the city prepared for its annual wave of tennis fever. Laura had never before reached the main draw of the tournament, but she was hoping it would be third time lucky as she began the gruelling qualifying process.

Her first opponent was Melanie Oudin, a player she had both beaten and lost to during her career.

Rain had delayed the match, providing a little relief from the heat of the day. It also meant the stands were practically empty when the qualifier eventually began, and thus there was hardly anyone to witness Laura's victory, or her cute new pink-and-blue tennis outfit. She was in high spirits as she was driven back from the match, and entertained her driver by singing One Direction's 'One Thing' very loudly from the back seat.

One down, two to go.

Next up was Italy's Anna Floris, and Laura took no time in dispatching the seasoned 29-year-old: Anna was pushed out of the Open in just 56 hot and sweaty minutes.

Finally, Laura had to face Olga Savchuk, a Ukrainian with a powerful two-handed backhand. After Laura beat Savchuk 6-1 in the first set, the 23-year-old fought back to make the second set one heck of a close call. But Robson just edged it and, with a small fist pump to celebrate, she was into the main draw without dropping a set.

'It's the second time I've come through qualifiers, which is very good,' she told the press. 'And the last two Grand Slams I have played I have won the first round in the main draw and I hope I can do that again here,' she added.

It was a remarkable return to form, especially since she had been hobbling around on crutches for two weeks in November.

'I came into the tournament with no expectations as I had only been playing points in practice five days before my first match,' she said, 'so I am very happy with how I am playing and hopefully my form will continue to get better throughout the tournament.'

Laura joined fellow Brits James Ward, Andy Murray, Elena Baltacha, Anne Keothavong and Heather Watson in the main draw. It was an impressive result: not since 1992 had there been so many British players in an overseas Grand Slam, and the British fans swelled with pride at the achievement.

As the Open began, there was a lot of talk about the female youngsters of the group, Robson and Watson, who were being heralded as the two most exciting prospects for British tennis for many years. So many hopes were being invested in their blossoming rivalry, including those of the new Fed Cup captain, Judy Murray.

'They are very exciting – Heather is a solid counter-puncher and an excellent athlete, Laura can hit lots of winners and has great natural timing,' claimed Murray, keen to praise them both. 'They are quite different sorts of players but both have talent. They are both lovely-looking girls, fresh personalities and fun characters, and they can both still improve a lot.'

The competition the girls were now providing was also keeping the more established Baltacha and Keothavong on their toes, especially as the race was now on to secure one of the limited singles berths in the forthcoming Olympics...

Day one of the tournament finally arrived. But, as the sun eventually disappeared beyond the horizon, Andy Murray was the sole survivor of a series of matches that saw five Brits wiped from the competition.

First to fall was James Ward, who was knocked out by Slovenian Blaz Kavcic.

Next to crumble was Baltacha, whose game was unusually error strewn. She struggled to hold back tears after her defeat, which came at the hands of French veteran Stephanie Foretz Gacon.

Heather Watson found herself overpowered by third seed Victoria Azarenka, while Anne Keothavong, hobbled by food poisoning, retired 6-0 down against Mona Barthel.

Robson's hammering came from Jelena Jankovic. In the warm evening sunshine that lit up the Margaret Court Arena, the crowd was definitely on Laura's side as she faced her Serbian opponent. However, she didn't showcase her best skills on the court, and lost nine games in a row to lose 6-2; 6-0.

Once more, it was a case of 'over to you, Andy', and was particularly bad news for Judy Murray, who would soon fly the four girls to Israel for their Fed Cup matches.

Baltacha tried to stay positive, saying: 'I think everyone is disappointed but it's the third week of the year, it's just the start.

'It's been hard for all of us but that's tennis.'

Laura backed her up, stating: 'I am not trying to make excuses for us but I don't think it's a disaster.'

But, though depressing, the British whitewash got surprisingly less coverage than Robson's choice of headwear for the Jankovic match...

The arena where Laura's match had been played had been named after Margaret Court, Australia's most decorated tennis veteran. Regarded as one of the greatest players in tennis history, Court won a record 24 Grand Slams during her career and was still a famous figure, both on the tennis circuit and in the Australian media.

Formerly a Catholic, Ms Court became an evangelical Christian in 1972, a year before winning her last Australian title. She had gone on to found the Victory Life Centre in Perth in 1990, where she was now the senior pastor.

However, Margaret Court had recently spread widespread controversy in the country with her provocative views on homosexuality, which had infuriated gay rights activists and provoked criticism from openly gay tennis champions such as Martina Navratilova and Billie Jean King.

Her comments included accusing gay people of indulging in 'abominable sexual practices', and describing same-sex marriages, which were being promoted by recent legislation introduced by the current Australian Labor government, as 'unhealthy, unnatural unions'.

When challenged, Court was indignant.

'I've nothing against homosexual people,' she had told national newspaper *The West Australian*, just a few weeks before Robson's match. 'I help them to overcome. We have people at the centre who have been homosexual who are now married.'

Her incendiary comments just kept coming.

'Politically correct education has masterfully escorted homosexuality out from behind closed doors, into the community openly and now is aggressively demanding marriage rights that are not theirs to take,' she stated firmly. 'The fact that the homosexual cry is, "We can't help it, as we were born this way", as the cause behind their own personal choice is cause for concern.'

As the Australian Open had approached, the storm against Margaret Court's views threatened to overshadow the tournament with protests and marches.

'A lot of people have evolved, as has the Bible. Unfortunately, Margaret Court has not,' said Navratilova, weighing in on the argument. Open about her own sexuality for many years, she felt it her place to counter Court's claims, which reflected badly on the tennis industry as a whole. She went on to say: 'Her myopic view is truly frightening as well as damaging to the thousands of children already living in same-gender families.'

Tennis Australia, the sport's governing body in the country, was quick to distance Court from the game she was so closely linked to. 'Her personal views are her own and are definitely not shared by Tennis Australia,' they said, in a statement released to the media. 'We concur wholeheartedly with the WTA who state that all human beings, regardless of gender, race, ethnicity, sexual orientation or otherwise, should be treated equally.'

Their emphatic rejection of Ms Court's views did some-what soothe the restless mood in the city, but gay rights campaigners were still discussing whether to protest against these sentiments by taking rainbow flags – a recognised symbol of diversity and acceptance – onto the Margaret Court arena during Laura's first-round match.

A few flags had appeared in the crowd, but not enough to really make any impact – until Laura walked on to the court.

Laura had read about the controversy, and wanted to show her support for equal rights, so she had gathered her hair up into a rainbow-coloured headband. She hadn't read about the rainbow flag plan, and was simply independently making a gesture of solidarity. But pictures of her wearing the headband instantly appeared on the protest's Facebook page, where she was praised for making a stand.

Robson was completely unprepared for the media onslaught that followed her match. Feeling dejected after her loss, she was completely overwhelmed by the reporters who crowded round her to question her political stance on gay and lesbian rights. They saw her hair accessory as having been part of the planned protest, and were eager to print her views as an LGBT (Lesbian, Gay, Bisexual and Transgender) advocate.

'It was just a rainbow-coloured headband,' she said nervously. 'I didn't see anything about a protest today, I wore it because I believe in equal rights for everyone, that's it.'

But her simple gesture of solidarity had walked her unwittingly into a huge political row, and subsequently reignited the media uproar surrounding the situation.

Protesters even began calling for the arena – Melbourne Park's third biggest – to be renamed, and Laura was repeatedly asked to expound her views.

'I just have a lot of headbands and they get sweaty,' she remarked meekly a few days later. 'My intention was purely to tell people what my beliefs are – equal rights for all – but there isn't much more to say.'

Back in the UK, sports journalist Mike Dickson was acerbic in his summary of the teenager's fashion choice, writing: 'Those around Robson would be better off dissuading her from making statements like yesterday's rainbow-coloured hairband until she is sufficiently confident in her opinions to back them up when asked.'

Now keen to keep a low profile, Laura wore a plain hairband for her first doubles match a few days later. Laura, partnering with Australian prodigy Ashleigh Barty, failed to advance to the second round.

Her Australian dreams were over for yet another year, but it was only the first tournament of the season, and Laura had many more matches to play.

She had picked up more winnings to add to her war chest – $29,600Aus in total – so there was certainly enough money to blow a little on her 18th birthday celebrations. Her one wish for this auspicious event was that she wouldn't have to be on an aeroplane when the day came.

Sadly, she would be, as now that she was out of the Open she had Israel to prepare for. Instead, never one to party hard, Laura went out for a low-key dinner on the eve of her 18th with Sally Peers, her birthday twin. It was a landmark birthday, made all the more exceptional for its tranquil celebrations.

Despite it being four years since the British newspapers had gone nuts over Laura, crowning her the country's new princess of tennis, she had managed to pass her teenage years relatively untouched by the media.

The 18-year-old had normal friendships and interests, loved *Twilight* and shopping like most girls her age and preferred being at home with her dogs to attending celebrity parties and boozing in nightclubs.

She would undoubtedly change as time passed, but, thanks to a solid family background and careful parenting and management, Laura would rise to whatever heady heights she was destined for as a friendly, down-to-earth young woman.

And the public would love her in return.

CHAPTER 20

FED CUP
DEBUT

Being part of the British Fed Cup team was set to be both an honour and an experience for Watson, Keothavong, Baltacha and Robson. It was a chance for the talented four-some, headed up by Judy Murray, to join forces and put aside their competitiveness for the good of their country.

Whatever the outcome, they were in it together and that would transform the often-cited lonely sport into a fun team venture. Whether celebrating or commiserating, they would have each other to rely on and – somewhat bizarrely – to play darts with.

Laura, like Judy Murray, was a huge fan of darts and decided to take a roll-up board out to Israel so that the team could enjoy a spot of tungsten tickling. Judy even joked that her first major captaincy decision was to OK the dartboard being installed in the team room.

Robson would be the first to admit she wasn't exactly a

darts pro, leading *Telegraph* reporter Ian Chadband to jokily compare her to darts legend Phil 'The Power' Taylor, by calling her Laura 'The Power Cut' Robson.

But she was adamant that watching Phil Taylor and his rivals was a good way of learning how to cope with sporting pressure. 'You can learn a lot from a darts player,' she insisted.

What impressed her the most was how the best players handled their key moments on stage despite the roaring, beer-fuelled crowd. 'I find it amazing the amount of pressure they're under to just make exactly the right shot at the right time,' she explained in an interview with Chadband. 'You can see that they start to shake sometimes and, hopefully, we don't do that when we're playing.'

Despite the huge difference between darts and tennis, Laura recognised a similar intensity in player concentration, which helped her to reflect on her own ability to overcome crushing on-court nerves. 'Dealing with that pressure, I think, is something that comes with experience. I've had some horrible matches in the last few years when I've been leading and then lost concentration. But it's definitely something that's improving.'

Soon after arriving in Israel, Laura was given a dare to mark her rookie Fed Cup status. It involved rapping in front of a room full of people to Sir Mix-A-Lot's 'Baby Got Back' – a song that featured the classic lines '*I like big butts and I can not lie, you other brothers can't deny, that when a girl walks in with an itty bitty waist and a round thing in your face: you get sprung...*'

She rose to the challenge, firmly cementing her place in the team. The dare was part of a concerted effort on Murray's part to engender team spirit, an often elusive feeling at such a serious level of the game, which she was convinced would help her new team.

The next day, Robson joined Heather Watson in cheering on her teammates Baltacha and Keothavong in their pools stages singles matches against Portugal. Grinning from the sidelines at each game, the two friends made a perfect cheerleading double-act, and their excitement at being at the event was plain to see. At one point they even stood draped in Union flags to sing a little song they'd made up for Baltacha.

Each posting straight sets over their opponents – Maria Joao Koehler and Michelle Larcher de Brito – the older players gave new coach Murray a winning start to life as captain of the team. It was a solid opening to the Europe/Africa Group I Pool C campaign, and gave everyone something to celebrate. After the team had languished for so long in the lower group, the victories gave them hope that maybe this would be the year Britain would rise up in the ranks.

Next, Heather and Laura teamed up against Portugal for the doubles round. It was great for them to be side by side rather than facing each other, and the firm friends worked well together. Heather's more relaxed attitude was balanced by Laura's ferocious competitiveness. Concentrating hard, neither youngster wanted to let their teammates down and, despite stiff opposition from the Portuguese players, they also won their match.

Amazingly, Britain had hammered Portugal into submission, and now faced Holland's Kiki Bertens and Bibiane Schoofs.

Keothavong was first up against Schoofs, playing under

such windy conditions that she could hardly hear the shouts of support coming from Robson and Watson. The girls had wrapped up in huge jackets to watch the game, and regularly jumped up and down to keep warm for their own match, which would be later in the day. Keothavong lost, but Baltacha won her match against Bertens to even the score. It was down to the new dynamic duo to secure a win, which they did that afternoon.

Judy was stunned. 'Our kids went straight in there against an experienced Dutch pair who play very good doubles and they whooped them,' she said.

The GB gang had got off to an amazing start in the Fed Cup, and now only had to face the home team to set up a Euro/Africa Zone Group I play-off against Austria. In fact, their spot in the play-off was secured before their matches even began, thanks to Portugal's defeat over Holland, but the team wanted to finish off the round-robin stage in style – and they certainly did.

Keothavong beat Julia Glushko in straight sets, followed by Baltacha doing the same in her match with world No. 37 Shahar Peer.

Robson and Watson then completed their run of doubles wins by stomping all over their Israeli opponents to win 6-2; 6-1.

Judy cried with joy at the way her team had performed, exhilarated by the whole experience.

'All our girls have played every day and they've proved now that they're a winning team,' said the proud coach. 'Again today they showed some fantastic competitive spirit and have done tremendously well to get through as group winners.'

The shock streak of success must have felt like a dream for everyone, and it continued when they faced Austria.

Keothavong and Baltacha did all the work, both winning their singles matches to give Great Britain their place at the top of the group. As Baltacha scored her final winning point, Watson and Robson screamed – there was no need for a doubles game, so they could relax for the duration of their stay in Eliat.

All four girls ran to their captain, who threw her arms around them to celebrate. For Keothavong, it was particularly emotional. 'Since I made my debut for the team 11 years ago we have finally managed to get out of this group,' she grinned. 'I'm so delighted for the team, it's absolutely brilliant.'

The victory was a winning start to Murray's tenure as captain. She had used both her coaching skills and her motherly instinct to support her team, making sure that they had a good balance between work and play for the five-day stint.

Now, the team had the opportunity to take a significant step forward for the women's game in Britain by finally reaching a stage where the likes of the United States, Japan, France and Australia competed.

And it had all happened when Robson had joined the superteam. She had been the missing link for success, and couldn't wait for the April promotion play-offs, where the fab four could take Great Britain into World Group II.

Returning home, Laura fell ill with a virus and the virulence of it knocked her sideways. Back in Wimbledon, she felt frustrated, with little choice but to let Kathy 'mother' her back to full health. It would be three weeks before she could get back on a court, causing yet more costly delays to her training. Back in the familiar surroundings of her bedroom, there was nothing she could do but accept the setback. She relaxed into the cosiness of family life, smiling when she occasionally heard her mother singing a lullaby to the dogs Kiri and Ella in the kitchen.

When she was feeling a bit better, she flew to Las Vegas for coaching on the Adidas Player Development Programme.

It was March, and Laura still hadn't employed the long-term services of any particular coach. She had been mainly working with the LTA's Luke Milligan, who had been acting as a sort of caretaker for the teenager. In Vegas, she hooked up with Sven Groeneveld again, so as to have a change in training.

She was in awe of the size of everything in the city, especially her hotel. 'The walk from the lift to my room at the hotel in Vegas takes 2 minutes 3 seconds using a fast paced walk,' she tweeted.

Yes, she did time it.

As well as training, she took part in some promotional activities as part of her role as an Adidas ambassador, and briefly played in the BNP Paribas Open in Indian Wells, California.

With her form still suffering somewhat from her sick break, she didn't make it past her first qualifier. She consoled herself by spending a huge amount of time in a local pet shop, gazing longingly at the puppies.

She fell hopelessly in love with one particular ginger spaniel, and spent some time trying to work out how she could engineer taking her back home to be a companion for her two Labradors. But she had to fly to Miami a few weeks later for the Sony Ericsson Open without the cuddly canine.

In the Miami heat, she won two qualifying matches before losing her third, preventing her from making it to the main draw. She stuck around for a few days, taking in a showing of *The Hunger Games* at the cinema and watching *Frozen Planet* in her hotel room.

She also entered a $50,000 tournament in Osprey, where she faced her best friend Eugenie Bouchard in the first round. It was a tough match, and Bouchard eventually emerged triumphant.

Then it was back to Britain to prepare for more Fed Cup action.

'Flying home today!' she tweeted on 1 April. 'Bye America. I will miss your weather. And your puppy stores.'

She wasn't back for long before she was on a plane again, this time to Copenhagen for the e-Boks Open. Laura was accompanied by Groeneveld, who trained her alongside tennis starlet Caroline Wozniacki for the event, to give her some top-class experience.

It was a fun time for Robson, who felt comfortable with the Dutch coach and the Danish player. 'I've known Sven since I was 11 and he has a lot of knowledge about my game,' she told reporters at the event. 'It has been fantastic practising with Caroline. She hardly ever misses a ball and there is so much I can learn from her. Apart from anything else she is a very nice person.'

She enjoyed herself at the players' party dinner, held at MASH, a famous city steakhouse. She was seated with Groeneveld and Wozniacki but had to take it easy because her first match was going to be tough – 'Jelena Jankovic' tough.

Now ranked 121, Laura was edging her way close to the top 100, but facing world No. 20 Jankovic would still pose a significant challenge. Robson had certainly tested her when they had last faced each other, but it would take a little bit of a miracle to beat her – a miracle that this time didn't occur.

Clothed in a cute red-and-peach tennis dress, Robson showed off her sinewy arms, which were taut with effort as she faced the Serbian. She succeeded in breaking her opponent five times during the match, but hit 48 unforced errors and eventually succumbed 6-4; 7-6 (10-8).

It was a valiant effort, but Laura obviously still wasn't ready to beat the powerful player. It had been yet another tough few months for the youngster, but she wouldn't let it break her good mood – especially since she would now be reunited with her Fed Cup teammates in Sweden.

Arriving in Boras in late April for the play-offs, Laura immediately immersed herself in the happy atmosphere engendered by captain Murray. In the two days before their first matches, the girls let their hair down a little. Laura put on her 'happy pants' – a stripey pair of baggy trousers – for a dance competition, and even ate cake with the girls, normally a big no-no before games.

But, while Judy spent some time watching her team have fun, she was also shrewdly analysing the competition in anticipation of their clash against Sweden. She was looking to end 19 years of Brits being outside the World Group, as not since 1993 had Britain been among the top 16 nations in women's tennis.

All they had to do was beat Sweden, and Robson was confident they could do it. 'We're looking forward to kicking Sweden's arse!' she joked.

Judy had more to lose than Britain's world ranking. She had pledged to jump in the freezing cold Viskan river if the girls won, and given that temperatures in Boras were in the single digits it would not be a pleasant experience.

Before the tournament began, the girly gang festooned their team bench at the Borashallen Arena with a stack of Union Jack paraphernalia, including flags and towels.

Another fab four, The Beatles, had played at the 3,000-seater venue nearly 50 years before, and the girls played homage to this by making their official entrance by dancing along to the Beatles' song 'Twist and Shout'.

But, at the end of the first day of play, they left feeling rather more subdued. Baltacha and Keothavong had both lost their matches, the first two of the play-off, leaving them trailing Sweden 2-0 with three matches left to play.

Judy Murray had a long night of thinking ahead of her.

Heather Watson had a slight foot injury so she couldn't play the next singles match, which Britain would need to win to keep the tie alive. And Baltacha had shown she wasn't entirely on form after suffering an ankle injury two weeks before.

That left Judy toying with the idea of sending Laura in as the underdog, relying on her ability to cause surprising upsets in big matches. It would mean the fate of the team would be in Laura's hands – an awful lot of pressure to place on the youngest player.

'I have a big decision to make overnight,' said Murray. 'Laura showed me what she can do when we played group matches in February. I think she has got a big-match mentality.'

When the sun rose, Murray had made her decision – Laura would be the one to face Sweden's experienced Sofia Arvidsson.

Baltacha, Keothavong, Watson and Murray were all

courtside to cheer on their fellow Brit as she tried to stage the team's comeback.

She battled through the first set, showing incredible movement and thumping down numerous winners, before losing 4-6.

Then, in the second set, she came alive, blitzing the Swede 6-1 and causing Murray's heart to soar with hope.

'She made a nonsense of her world ranking of 121,' wrote the *Daily Mail*, 'which will surely be shrunk once she gets a run free of injury.'

It was an incredible match and, with Robson hitting a stonking 47 outright winners, it often looked like she would indeed save the day.

But it was not to be, and Arvidsson took the final set 6-3 to secure a win.

Laura instantly broke down in tears, feeling like she'd let everyone down. It was heartbreaking to see, especially when Judy and the other girls tried to console her by hugging her tightly.

Judy Murray praised her brave efforts, saying: 'She is very exciting. She hits the ball very heavy off both sides. When she is hot, she is red hot.'

However, Robson was not ready to be cheered up. 'Maybe in a few days I might take some pride from this but I'm pretty devastated right now,' she managed to say, her eyes still red from crying.

It had been a deflating weekend. Breaking into the top 16 would have to wait for another year.

CHAPTER 21

EXPEDITIONS FOR EXPERIENCE

As summer 2012 approached, all Laura could really think about was the Olympics. Yet again, the early part of her season had been a trying time, marred by sickness and injury, and she must have wondered if she'd ever get a clear run at glory.

But, if she was going to earn a spot on the Olympic team, she had to train hard and play as many matches as possible to prepare. And to do this she had to once again put her confidence-shattering losses behind her and focus on the future. Though she had hardly been home all year, she flew to Amsterdam to train with Groeneveld at the Tennis Centrum Academy, before heading to Switzerland for the $25,000 ITF Chiasso Challenger in early May.

When the draw was released, she was delighted to discover she was the top seed, and would play qualifier Kateryna Kozlova in the first round. Securing her first win on red clay of the year, she must have felt the surge of a frisson of confidence. Spurred on, she next beat Irina Khromacheva of Russia in straight sets, and definitely was relieved.

It was the first time she had won two matches in a row at a tournament since the Australian Open, which now seemed a very long time ago. Reaching the quarterfinals boosted her confidence no end, even though she then lost to Germany's Tatjana Malek. She had little time to dwell on this upset, because she was whisked off to France for another ITF challenger, this time a $100,000 event in Cagnes-Sur-Mer.

She swept through the qualifiers without dropping a set, but annoyingly had to pull out of her first-round match due to yet another injury, this time to her foot. Laura steeled herself to the challenge of recovering in time for the French Open, which she was determined to qualify for. Back in the UK, she spent some time with her mum, watching *Britain's Got Talent* and the *Eurovision Song Contest* and singing along in the car to the band 5ive's 'Keep On Movin'. It was an appropriate anthem for the way that Laura felt during that long month.

Arriving in Paris at the end of May, she allowed herself to be inspired by the sight of the Eiffel Tower at night – lit up in all its glory. The timeless structure would tower over the city during the times she won or lost on many occasions in the future – and, just like that monument, she needed to stay grounded and realise that the sun could shine on her, or she could be battered with rain, but she would still stay standing, ready to see another day, another match, another tournament.

Laura had not entered the French Open since her second-round junior defeat in 2009, and, as such, this would be her first time in the senior competition – if she made it through the qualifiers.

Robson steamed through the first two matches at Roland Garros, before losing her third qualifier against Karolina Pliskova. She still managed to earn a place in the main draw as a lucky loser, after Silvia Soler-Espinosa pulled out due to injury.

It meant that she had now reached the main draw in four successive Grand Slams, but, if she was honest with herself, she would admit that she had yet to truly capitalise on any of them.

Laura discovered she had been drawn against clay expert Anabel Medina Garrigues, the Spaniard who had been responsible for knocking her out of the US Open the year before. With ten titles won on clay courts, the most of any active player, Anabel was a tough first-round opponent. Robson, more comfortable on grass, was at a distinct disadvantage. Although she had played more matches on clay this season than ever before, she still wasn't exactly used to the awkward surface. And, though her natural power shone through, and it once more tested her older opponent, Medina Garrigues still won the match.

Robson was still not fully over her latest injury, and the French Open had been a valiant effort. She was looking forward to getting back to the UK and the grass surface that transformed her powerful service into a veritable lethal weapon.

'I'm not completely healed but it's getting better,' Laura told reporters in France. 'I'm still going to play all of the grass tournaments I think. I'm a big girl, I can handle a bit of pain.'

Heather Watson was also playing at Roland Garros, and

had reached the second round for the second year running. Like Robson, she had her eye on one particular prize – the 2012 Olympics. 'I'd absolutely love it,' Heather mused. 'Whether it's doubles, singles, just to be involved.'

At that point, mere months before its kick-off, it very much looked like Watson was more of a safe bet...

Back in the UK, as May turned into June, Laura only made it to the second round in her first two tournaments of the grass season: at Nottingham and Birmingham. She allowed herself a few moments of self-pity.

'Hopefully, I've stopped growing now,' she said just after learning that she'd again been given a wildcard for Wimbledon. 'I've had enough of it. Do I think it's affected me? Yes, I think so. Obviously, as a tennis player, it's a good thing to be tall so I can't complain too much. But I've not been able to do as much work, fitness-wise, as I would have liked.'

In Birmingham, she'd taken some time off to do a bit of shopping, and laughed when she ran into a number of other female tennis players who were also indulging in some retail therapy in the prestigious store Harvey Nichols.

'Literally the whole shoe section was only tennis players. Elena Vesnina was trying on four pairs I think,' she told reporters. Laura admitted: 'We all love our shopping. Also, people don't generally recognise me when I'm not sweaty – that's why I dress up.'

Robson had been in Nottingham while the country had celebrated the Queen's Diamond Jubilee and had been sad not to be in London for the event. Her neighbours in Wimbledon had put on a street party, and she'd been especially gutted not to be able to attend.

Instead, she watched it all on TV with Naomi Broady, the British No. 6, and got emotional when Prince Charles made his speech.

'Your Majesty... Mummy,' he'd begun. 'As a nation this is our opportunity to thank you and my father for always being there for us. For inspiring us with your selfless duty and service and for making us proud to be British...'

Laura was proud to be British, and felt roused by his heartfelt words. But she hadn't been impressed by singer Stevie Wonder's efforts though. 'I couldn't understand why he was singing "Happy Birthday",' she fumed. 'It wasn't her birthday. He didn't even call her "Your Majesty" – he said "Your Honour".'

The Queen had valiantly made the day a success, despite the fact that the torrential rain and freezing temperatures must have made the whole thing a bit of an ordeal for the 86-year-old monarch.

The rain was still of biblical proportions when Laura made her way to Eastbourne a few days later for the Aegon International. Like the Queen, Laura was undeterred and qualified for the main draw without dropping a set.

As her foot had finally stopped hurting, she could focus fully on her first-round match – against World No. 49 Maria Jose Martinez Sanchez, the wily Spaniard she had so comprehensively beaten at the 2010 Hopman Cup, before losing to her in Cincinnati a year later.

Had her win been a fluke? She now had the chance to find out.

On Court 2, outdoors, the crowds stood six deep to watch the 18-year-old's match against the Spanish star. She lost the first set 3-6, but by the time the second set began she had worked out Martinez Sanchez's effective mix of spins and slices, and started to take her apart in much the same way she had done two years previously in Perth.

With powerful shots, she pushed the Spaniard to a less comfortable position at the back of the court, thereby avoiding her dangerous volleys. She dominated the next two sets and comfortably won them both 6-2 to take the match. Finally, Laura had a big win to truly lift her spirits – and, with the Olympics imminently close, a victory was definitely needed.

Watson had come through her first-round match too, beating Hungary's Greta Arn, meaning that both girls had made the final 16, six days before Wimbledon.

'For long periods of their [second-round] matches at the Aegon International at Eastbourne, Heather Watson and Laura Robson were equal to their considerable high-ranked opponents,' ran the article in the *Daily Mail*, following their matches. '[But] when it came to the crucial points, neither could quite muster what was needed to cause an upset.'

It was a succinct summary of the day's events.

Watson had started strong before fading in the second set to hand her opponent Lucie Safarova – whom she had beaten before – the victory.

However, it was the opposite for Robson, who had suffered through an error-strewn first set to come back fighting, with groundstrokes that more than matched the quality of her Russian opponent, Ekaterina Makarova. There was the occasional yelp when things went wrong, but she succeeded in looking comfortable throughout the match, despite her loss.

Watson was dejected, telling reporters how she was trying

to control her emotions on court with the help of her mental-conditioning coach. 'He helps me because I'm very emotional on court,' she explained. 'It's because I care so much. I put myself on the line because it's life or death out there.'

Robson was much more positive after her loss. 'I'm feeling confident in my game, so going into Wimbledon I'm really pumped,' she said. 'I don't want to stop at the top 100. I want to be top 50, top 20.'

She was still displaying her sunny disposition when the first day of Wimbledon arrived. 'Wimbledon is looking quite lovely today,' she tweeted.

Part of her happiness may have come from the fact that she had just sneaked inside the top 100, and was ranked 97 going into the tournament – six places ahead of Heather Watson.

As the players readied themselves for their first-round matches, looking around at each other in the locker room there was an opportunity to reflect on the changes in the game that had occurred over time.

From top-end players Serena and Venus Williams, Kim Clijsters, Maria Sharapova and Victoria Azarenka to the young pretenders Heather Watson, Laura Robson and even Petra Kvitova, the defending champion – the title could go to anyone.

Eight different players had claimed the last nine Grand Slams; a marked contrast to the early to mid-1980s, when Chris Evert and Martina Navratilova monopolised 18 out of the 19 majors, and the late 1980s/early 1990s, when Steffi Graf and Monica Seles shared 22 out of the 25 titles.

Competition was now a lot broader; titles more difficult to defend. But this also meant that gaps could open up for determined youngsters to push through to glory. The possibilities for shock defeats and surprise victories were endless, making for much more interesting viewing than in previous decades.

This was quickly exemplified by five-time champ Venus Williams, who crashed out in the first round in straight sets to the Russian Elena Vesnina. And also by Heather Watson, who made it through to the third round before bowing out to Agnieszka Radwanska.

Laura's first-round opponent was Francesca Schiavone, the 2010 French Open champion. Laura was ranked 71 places below the Italian, but you might have been forgiven for thinking it was the other way around as their first game got underway. Schiavone looked positively ordinary in the face of Robson's majestic display of powerful baseline tennis. Spurred on by the crowd on Court 3, she took just 25 minutes to wrap up the first set, taking it 6-2.

But Schiavone, clearly embarrassed by the thrashing, changed strategy and, instead of trying to win by skill alone, she began to use the pedestrian tactics Laura so hated. Between the first and second set, she had 15 minutes' worth of off-court treatment for a back injury, giving time for Laura's energetic momentum to fade.

During the second set, when Laura won her first service game, Francesca began grunting loudly, much to the crowd's dismay. Then she developed a pressing need for her towel between nearly every point, knocking Robson further off her stride. She even called the physio to the court twice more during the set before taking it 6-4.

Strangely, Schiavone didn't need any medical help during the deciding set, when she battled her way to victory over

Robson, whose spirit had clearly been broken. But Laura smiled and waved as she left the court, although it was easy to see that it had been an effort for her to do so.

Later, Schiavone wryly acknowledged her tactics, but defended her conduct by saying she had every right to bide her time.

'She wanted to be fast, and sometimes you have to stop a little bit more,' she said. 'We have a lot of seconds [between points], and it's important to use them. We forget that because we are in a rush, but it's important to play at the best, and not just keep running and running.'

Robson was crestfallen at missing out on an opportunity for claiming another highly prized tennis scalp. But, although she admitted that the 32-year-old's approach had made the match tough, she stopped short of actually criticising her, and instead took responsibility for her own failure. It was an admirable attitude.

'I don't think it affected me because I won my first service game in the second set, and then I was holding serve fairly easily until the one service game that I lost,' she said, referring to Schiavone's medical time-out. 'I just tried to go for a little bit too much on my first serve. I should have just stuck with how I was playing before.'

But she added: 'In general, I think she took a lot of time between points, and that gave me more time to think about what I was doing. I think that's really tough.'

Laura was determined to see the match as a positive experience, and summed it up by saying: 'I'm really disappointed today, but she's a Grand Slam champion and I am definitely closer to winning matches like this than I was a few months ago.'

She may have been feeling dejected, but just hours later her spirits were soaring: Laura was going to the Olympics.

Thanks to the generosity of the ITF, seven British players would be joining Andy Murray on the British Olympic tennis team. Anne Keothavong and Elena Baltacha would play in the women's singles matches, while Laura was set to partner up with Heather Watson in the doubles. The mixed doubles was yet to be announced...

It was an amazing achievement – just to be part of the team meant that she would be at the centre of the huge event. She would represent Britain on home soil and be immortalised in history as part of the British team fighting for medals in London. Laura would be watched by millions of people all over the globe, cheered on by the whole of the country, and would mingle with the top athletes in the world.

With the Olympics now to look forward to, Laura thoroughly enjoyed the rest of Wimbledon 2012. She caught up with her pal Eugenie Bouchard, who was competing in the juniors, and competed in the doubles with Watson. They were knocked out in the first round in straight sets, but it was good practice for London 2012.

On a wildcard, she paired up with Dominic Inglot for the mixed doubles, and stormed past the defending champions Jurgen Melzer and Iveta Benesova to make it to the third round. There they were defeated by fellow Brit Colin Fleming and his partner, Taiwan's Hsieh Su-wei.

Robson mingled with her friends, teasing Heather about her eating habits, which included cold herrings, and screamed for joy when Brit Jonathan Marray won the men's doubles with his partner Frederik Nielsen.

And, although she was happy to be playing in the

women's doubles at the Olympics, she had her eye on the mixed as well – and she wanted her partner to be Andy Murray.

The Scottish player was now unsure, however, and didn't know if he would bother. He was already in the singles and the doubles – he reasoned that playing in the mixed might be more hassle than it was worth.

'Hopefully he'll change his mind,' Laura told reporters. 'I would love to play with him. I think we're just going to see who's doing what that week.'

She had breakfast with Martina Hingis, and followed Murray's progress as he smashed his way through his opponents to reach the final.

When Eugenie Bouchard followed in Robson's footsteps to win the junior championships, Robson was overjoyed for her. The pair celebrated their twin success by posing together with their junior trophies – though it had been four years since Laura won hers.

Robson took time out from watching the matches to go to the Hyde Park Wireless Festival, where she watched acts such as Childish Gambino and let her hair down for a while. But she made sure she was back to watch Andy play in the final, against 'the Sweeper', Roger Federer.

Britain had been waiting for years for Murray – or indeed any Brit – to claim the Wimbledon men's title, and now that he was in the final, the country was collectively holding its breath in anticipation that this could be the year it would finally happen.

Inspired by Fred Perry, the last British male to claim the trophy, way back in 1936, Andy was under a huge amount of pressure as he stepped out onto the sunny court.

It was an epic battle, lasting three-and-a-half hours, watched by a nervous crowd that included the Beckhams, London Mayor Boris Johnson, Pippa Middleton and her sister, the Duchess of Cambridge.

As the *Daily Telegraph* put it, Andy began by playing like he had never played before. He ended by crying like he had never cried before.

He snatched the first set from the six-time Wimbledon champ, but, despite playing his heart out, Murray eventually lost to Federer, leading to a rare emotional outpouring that finally softened the tough Scot's image in the eyes of the public.

Sobbing through his runner-up speech, he finally convinced his many sceptics that he wasn't just a 'granite-faced automaton' or 'incapable of showing any feelings on or off the court', but that he was a magnificent athlete who had focused his whole life on winning an elusive Grand Slam, and who was now openly weeping after a more than narrow defeat.

You could practically hear people's emotions softening towards him all over the country. 'I'm getting closer,' he said, wiping away tears. 'Everyone talks about the pressure of playing at Wimbledon, but it's not the people watching, they make it incredible,' he said. 'There are mixed emotions. Most of them are negative. I felt like I was playing for the nation and couldn't quite do it.'

Federer, who had himself wept just a few years before when Nadal had beaten him in Australia, put his arm around Murray to comfort him. But he couldn't suppress his own joy at the outcome – he'd finally overcome his 'white whale', equalling Pete Sampras's record seven Wimbledon titles, and bettering the American's longstanding record of 286 career weeks as world No. 1.

Focusing on the future, Murray said: 'This fortnight was a step in the right direction. I won't go back on the court until my mind is right and I am over the loss. The Olympics is a special event and I want to make sure I'm ready. If I play like I did this week, I have a good chance of winning a medal.'

Laura was overcome by the match, and tweeted: 'Well I don't know about you guys but I'm crying,' before retweeting Rory McIlroy, who said: '@andy_murray did himself, his family and his nation proud today. Played like a champ. His time will come for sure.'

His moments of glory wouldn't be long coming. And neither would Laura's.

CHAPTER 22

COUNTDOWN TO 2012

As an emotional Wimbledon ended, the Olympics were fast approaching. But before Laura could go after medal glory she had a WTA Tour tournament to compete in.

If the British tennis player was going to convince Andy to go for mixed doubles success, she had to prove her worth, and she travelled to Palermo in Italy to do it. In the blazing heat at the Italiacom Open, Laura's suntan became more and more pronounced as she progressed through the competition.

In the first round, she beat Valentyna Ivakhnenko in straight sets, only dropping one game to the Ukrainian. When she faced second seed Roberta Vinci in the second round, onlookers were astonished when she pushed the Italian out of the competition – again in straight sets.

Laura was finding her stride, and it was just in the nick of time, too. She was in her first quarterfinal on the WTA Tour, just weeks away from the start of the Olympics.

The quarterfinal match, against Spain's Carla Suarez Navarro, started in temperatures in excess of 30 degrees, and the heat climbed relentlessly as the match progressed. Robson broke her opponent early in the first set, and kept the advantage to win it 6-4. But, as the heat grew more oppressive, the more acclimatised Spanish player regained control and dominated the second set to win 6-2.

Robson was struggling with the stifling conditions, and it showed. But, when the start of the third set was delayed by ten minutes due to the weather, she had a chance to cool down and take stock.

Heading back out on court, she finally realised what a break in pace could do for those on the losing side of things. She fought back and once again shocked onlookers – as well as the tennis cognoscenti back home – by winning the match.

Her first semifinal on the WTA Tour... It was a landmark moment in her career, but it had caused her one problem: tan lines.

Relaxing by the pool in her hotel, Laura tried to let her white ankles and feet get as sunburned as her golden brown legs. 'Going to sit...with only my feet in the sun, in the hope that my tan lines won't look so appalling tomorrow,' she tweeted. '#tennisplayerproblems'.

Having lessened the contrast of her skin shades a little, she next faced her semifinal opponent, Barbora Zahlavova Strycov, a player 42 places higher than her in the rankings.

Robson won the first set 6-2, and it almost looked like she may have had the upper hand over the seasoned Czech. But she eventually lost the incredibly close second set and was thrown off track. Strycov won five games in a row, and, although Robson held for 5-2, she was just delaying the inevitable.

After a sensational run, Laura was out, and, although she

was disappointed with the loss, she couldn't have been disappointed at her heroic overall performance in Sicily.

She must have had her fingers crossed that her form could convince Murray to double up with her at the Olympics – but, over in the USA, someone else was also proving themselves worthy of partnership at the eleventh hour: Heather Watson.

At the Bank of the West Classic, in Stanford, California, Watson had just won her first WTA title: and as part of a doubles pairing, no less. Along with New Zealand's Marina Erakovic, she had stomped her way to victory at Stanford University, and held aloft the huge glass winner's bowl to celebrate her triumph.

It was great news for Team GB; but not such great news for Laura.

Would Andy choose Watson – now at No. 67 in the rankings – as his partner over her if he agreed to compete in the mixed doubles? It didn't bear thinking about.

Back in the UK, excitement was rising as the countdown to the games got well and truly underway. The Olympic torch relay had been running since 19 May, when the Olympic Flame had arrived on flight BA2012 from Greece.

The burning emblem was now nearing the end of its 70-day relay, which would eventually include 66 evening events, 6 island visits, and over 8,000 people travelling over 8,000 miles in order to bring it to London.

Britain had been preparing for the Games since its successful bid to be host city in July 2005 – when Laura was just 11. A former industrial site in Stratford had been redeveloped into the 490-acre Olympic Park that Laura would soon be wandering around with her fellow Team GB members, and the park's creation hadn't been without its fair share of controversies.

Bad weather had set back construction of the Olympic Village, and it would be down to the wire whether it would be finished in time for the 27 July Opening Ceremony.

And there were more, wider-ranging problems.

Just weeks before the start of the Games, British giant G4S – the contractor hired to provide the huge security presence that would be needed throughout the event – admitted it was an incredible 3,500 staff members short of requirements.

CEO Nick Buckles was hauled before parliament for an emergency hearing, where he was shamed into agreeing the whole situation was a 'shambles'. Soldiers, sailors, airmen and marines from all over the country had to be drafted in to make up the shortfall.

New Olympic driving lanes, designed to help athletes avoid the nightmarish London traffic on the way to events, had opened amid angry protests from Londoners – and had caused a 30-mile traffic jam on their very first day.

As organisers sweated and scrambled to rectify these last-minute issues, Laura was having a much more serene experience. She had a sophisticated haircut and blow dry at the Jo Hansford salon in Mayfair, in preparation for the hundreds of promotional pictures she would be posing for as part of Team GB.

She also proudly tried on her official kit, taking a few 'selfies' for posterity, before going on a little exploratory trip around the Olympic Village, accompanied by Anne Keothavong, Jamie Murray and Andy.

The quartet posed for a picture under the huge Olympic Rings Sculpture that dominated one of the greens, decked out in their matching kit, with special passes hanging from their necks – all except Andy that is, who mysteriously wasn't wearing his for the picture.

'Dude is like "my face is my pass",' tweeted one of Laura's fans when she posted the shot online.

'Andy hasn't got a pass because he's too cool,' commented another.

Laura posed in her official GB dressing gown for another shot, looking half like a boxer about to get into the ring, and half like the incredibly excited teenager that she was.

'So ready for the Olympics to start!' she tweeted, two days before the Opening Ceremony, alongside a picture of some very patriotic red, white and blue fingernails. While Laura was clearly having the time of her life getting ready for the event, she did manage to focus on her training too.

Practising at the All England Club in the run-up to the event, she worked on her skills and even managed to hit a few balls with Maria Sharapova. On the day of the Opening Ceremony, Laura headed straight back over to Wimbledon for more practice.

London 2012 banners were all over the All England Club, which would be one of the host venues for the Olympic tournament – and, although all was now quiet, the place would soon come alive, filled with spectators from all over the world. It was surreal, especially since Microsoft magnate Bill Gates was on the court next to her while she smashed out her serves.

Laura Robson would not be taking part in the ceremony, and was planning to watch it at home instead – so she couldn't wait to get off court to prepare for a night in watching the televised extravaganza.

But while award-winning director Danny Boyle was

nervously making his final preparations for the ceremony – now just hours away – Laura was receiving some astonishing news.

Croatia's Petra Martic, who was in the main draw for the Olympic singles tournament, had injured herself and had to pull out. As the highest-ranked alternative player on site, at 96, Laura was first in line to take her place.

That meant she was in the draw.

Which also meant that she now had two chances to win a medal, and two chances to represent her country at the London 2012 Olympics.

She could hardly believe it.

Laura must have been bursting with excitement when she finally sat in front of the TV to watch the Games officially begin. A four-hour tribute to Britain, it was watched by over 900 million people in countries all over the world, and involved thousands of volunteers.

It did not disappoint.

Artistic displays representing Britain's history depicted the country's transition from a 'Green and Pleasant Land', through the Industrial Revolution, to the present day, and featured our NHS, literature, pop music and, of course, the great British sense of humour.

This ceremony was a patriotic display that immediately washed away any lingering concerns over the Games, filling the country with an overwhelming sense of pride that brought thousands to tears. Highlights included well-loved character 'Mr Bean', playing a single note on a synthesizer as part of the Philharmonic Orchestra's performance of 'Chariots of Fire' – before getting bored and causing mayhem; plus a short 'James Bond movie' extract that made jaws drop the world over.

In this clip, Daniel Craig played a Bond tasked with escorting the Queen to the ceremony, via a helicopter trip over London. Walking up behind what was expected to be an actress playing the role of Her Majesty, no one could quite believe it when the lady turned around to reveal herself as the real deal!

When the movie then switched to live camera footage of the Queen parachuting out of the helicopter into the stadium, it was clear she'd had a stunt double perform that part. The stunt performer was dressed in the exact same peach dress and pearls that had been worn by Her Majesty.

David Beckham brought the Olympic Flame via motorboat to a nearby dock, where Olympian Steve Redgrave then carried it through an honour guard of 500 of the construction workers who had built the park.

The iconic football hero then passed the flame onto a team of seven sporty youngsters, each nominated by a famous Olympian, a performance intended to symbolise how sporting prowess was inspiring the younger generation.

It was these athletic youngsters who jogged through the stadium to deliver the Olympic Flame to its final resting place – the Olympic Cauldron. Designed by Brit Thomas Heatherwick, this was an awe-inspiring and beautiful piece of metalwork, consisting of 204 individual 'petals', to signify each competing nation.

Moving to fill the arena, each youngster lit a petal, the fires slowly spreading to ignite all the others, one by one. As each flaming petal was raised to the heavens, they came together to form an Olympic Flame like no other before it.

The 30th Olympic Games were officially open.

CHAPTER 23

LAURA BECOMES AN OLYMPIAN

As an athlete, representing your country at the Olympic Games is at once an honour, an achievement and a landmark life moment.

But to be an athlete in your teens, competing in your first Olympic Games, on home soil, must feel almost unreal.

Laura was giddy with excitement, as was Heather Watson, but they didn't have time to soak up any of the atmosphere before their first match, because it was on the very first day of the competition.

Changing into their matching white tennis dresses, the two British youngsters knew they were facing a titanic battle in their first doubles outing, as it was against Germany's Angelique Kerber and Sabine Lisicki, both of whom were recent Wimbledon semifinalists.

Surprisingly, the Germans played abysmally in the first set, faulting over half of their serves and letting the high-fiving

British duo cream them 6-1. Watson's and Robson's play was superb, with the pair managing 76 per cent of their first serves and firing down three aces to their opponents' none.

The second set started in much the same way as the first, with the British duo ruling the court with their impressive footwork and shots. But during an opportunity to break and serve for the match they failed, and it turned out to be a crucial mistake.

Kerber and Lisicki punished them by bringing it back to serve and stealing their momentum, before going on to take the set 6-4. With determination etched on their faces, Watson and Robson overcame their disappointment and started the third set by breaking their more illustrious opponents straight away. But they failed to take advantage, and it wasn't long before the Germans broke back and took command of the court.

This time, the opposing pair kept the upper hand, and won the match by two sets to one. It was a score that didn't reflect the monumental skill that the British duo showed, which was by far over and above their German adversaries. They were out of the doubles tournament. But the British girls had no time to be upset – not only was the atmosphere electric, but they also both had their first singles matches the following day and they had important things to do in the meantime: like seeking out badges.

There were pin badges available to represent each nation, but they were so popular they were like gold dust and not at all easy to obtain. Both Laura and Heather had made it their aim to collect as many of these as possible, by whatever means necessary, and this gave them a good excuse to mingle with the higher-ranking players from other countries – under the pretence of begging for a swap.

By the end of the day, Laura had managed to get St Kitts and Nevis, Aruba and Guinea, and a range of other pins to decorate her player's pass with.

The next day, both young women woke up and prepared to face their first opponents in the singles tournament: Watson was up against Silvia Soler-Espinosa, while Robson would play Lucie Safarova.

After heading over to the All England Club, Laura had time to pin-hunt before her match began, and she managed to beg one off both Andy Murray and Roger Federer. She was doing well off-court, now she just had to do well on-court.

Both matches happened almost simultaneously, so the girls couldn't support each other – but the crowd's loyalty more than made up for this. While Laura was warming up for her match, the spectators gave her a rendition of 'God Save the Queen' to help her on her way. The impromptu singing was rousing, but also terribly out of tune, leaving her in fits of giggles.

Robson revelled in the different court atmosphere being created by the mixed crowd, which was much more energetic – and loud – than the normally sedate tennis spectators she was used to. They chanted her name over and over, which was very distracting for poor Heather, who was playing on the court next door. 'All I could hear was Laura, Laura – it was very tough to focus,' Watson said after it was over.

Laura was in high spirits when her match began, despite the fact that she was facing world No. 23, Lucie Safarova, who was also a 'lefty'.

But she was desperate to impress after the previous day's defeat, and took the match very seriously. She raced to a 5-1 lead in the first set, spurred on by her lively supporters, whom she regularly rewarded with a beaming smile that shone out from under her red visor.

Safarova was no pushover, and fought back to force Robson into a tiebreak. But the Brit's determination won out and she took the set. Lucie was tense during the second set, and double-faulted at a crucial moment, giving Laura another opportunity to take control.

When the Czech sent a wild forehand flying, the massive crowd, which included Judy Murray, went ballistic. To both players' credit, they were neck and neck for the rest of the set, before Robson broke at the perfect time to give her a 5-4 advantage.

It was nerve-wracking, especially when Laura went 15-40 down as she served for the match. But she steeled herself to the challenge, and showed just how much she had progressed in her training, by seeing out the match to win 7-6; 6-4.

This was an emotional moment for the teenager. She had beaten a high-class player, won an Olympic tennis match and was through to the next round.

Leaving the court to a deafening round of applause, Laura immediately ran into Heather Watson, who had just won her own match too. After congratulating each other, they gossiped about their day so far and caught up on their pin-badge action.

'I spoke to Roger this morning,' said Watson, now clearly on first-name terms with Roger Federer. 'He was playing cards. I asked, "Are you winning?" and he just said, "Of course".'

Laura recounted how Federer had promised her a pin badge only that morning, and the pair giggled like schoolgirls. Talking about her match, Laura was quick to praise the crowd. 'Every time the Czechs got loud, they got louder,' she said proudly. 'It was perfect.'

She confided in Watson about how she was feeling deep down, admitting: 'It's really nerve-wracking playing for your country, more so than when it's just me. You do put more pressure on yourself to do well, but the crowd helped me a lot. It's definitely up there with the best wins in my career.'

Watson would next be facing Maria Kirilenko, a Wimbledon quarterfinalist, while Robson was up against Russian titan Maria Sharapova.

It was an interesting prospect for Robson. They had last played each other at Wimbledon the previous year, where Laura had severely tested the glamorous Sharapova, much to the surprise of everyone watching. And, despite eventually losing to the older player, she had definitely proven herself a threat to be taken seriously.

She focused herself as much as she knew how to before she stepped out on court to take on Sharapova. It was day four of the Olympics and excitement was reaching hysterical proportions in Stratford, where thousands of people were streaming off the tube and into the Olympic complex to soak up the atmosphere. On the tennis courts in South London, things were no different.

Robson started the match with her usual all-or-nothing attitude, delivering bruising shots from the back of the net with a bazooka-like strength. Sharapova was equally on form, and for the whole hour that it took to get through the first set, the crowd was transfixed as the pair matched each other nearly shot for shot.

Laura still managed to smile, even when the ball slid under her racket on set point in the first-set tiebreak.

Sharapova rushed to a 3-0 lead in the second set, but Robson was undeterred, and fought back to level the score. And, despite Sharapova eventually winning 7-6; 6-3 – the exact same score as their last encounter – even she had to admit it had been a tough match. 'She has certainly improved since the last time I played her,' the Russian player said, paying tribute to her younger opponent. 'I am sure she has a great future in front of her.'

'Same score,' Robson said. 'But today I felt much closer. And she played a lot better than last time.'

Elsewhere, Watson was also out, having lost to Kirilenko in just 85 minutes.

But, just when it looked like both girls could spend the rest of the Olympics licking their wounds together, the ITF made a surprise announcement: Andy Murray, who was racing through the men's singles tournament, had decided he *would* play in the mixed tournament after all.

And he had the pick of the British women to play alongside him; as well as Robson, Heather Watson had expressed an interest in partnering up for the event. It seemed obvious that, despite his history with Robson, Watson was most likely to be his choice.

What's more, the Murray/Robson Hopman Cup success had been over two years ago and the pair had hardly played together since. And, while Robson was British No. 3 in singles and No. 6 in doubles, Watson was British No. 1 in both, making her the obvious one to choose. After all, Watson had only just returned from winning the doubles at the WTA Tour event in Stanford.

Heather was hopeful.

She'd been upset at losing to Kirilenko, which had ended

her Olympic dreams, and an entry in the mixed doubles would give her another chance at a medal. But Robson was equally anticipating the possibility of being chosen, for exactly the same reasons.

One of them was going to be ecstatic, while the other would be devastated. Murray had a tough choice to make. He spoke to the team coaches, and eventually made up his mind.

Robson was in!

The moment she found out, she was happy to share her joy with the media. 'It should be really fun playing with Andy. We haven't played since the Hopman Cup in 2011, so it's going to be tough. But who knows?' she gushed.

'I think I'm fairly decent at doubles, depending how my serve is doing, and Andy is obviously one of the best returners in the world, so we've definitely got a chance.' She jokingly added: 'And who's boss on the court? I think we're equal!'

But, when her friend Watson faced the press, she broke down in tears, and made no attempt to hide her feelings on the matter. 'It hurts that I have lost because it is my first Olympics and it only comes around once,' she said, visibly crestfallen. 'I think the reason why I'm upset also is I wanted it to carry on, I wanted it to be longer. I'm just disappointed that I let everybody down, but it was tough. I gave it my everything.'

And she must have made Laura wince when she added: 'I was hoping to get in through the mixed draw. I thought I deserved a spot in the mixed draw because of my ranking, because of how well I'm doing. So it's disappointing. I got in the singles by myself, not a wildcard. I got my ranking to where it should be. But there's not much else I can do about it now.'

Watson had every right to be upset, but Andy truly believed in Laura. They had worked well together as a team and sometimes that counts for more than a ranking. Her big hitting would be an asset, while her relative lack of mobility compared to the athletic Watson wouldn't really be an issue on the shared court.

It was a huge test for the girls' friendship, but they had always known that one day they would face this kind of crisis of professional rivalry in some form.

They had been playing 'tennis leapfrog' their entire careers, and had enjoyed the friendly competition. Robson had landed the first blow with her junior Wimbledon titles, then Watson had beat her into the top 100 and to a WTA title. But now it was Robson's turn to jump a little higher.

As mentioned above, they could only hope that this huge blow wouldn't have equally huge repercussions for their friendship. Andy Murray's decision also meant that there was a lot of extra pressure on Laura to perform. Every fault she made would cause a thousand murmurs of 'it should have been Heather'.

Laura had a lot to prove and, with their first match just hours away, she didn't have long to prepare.

Andy was sympathetic to Watson when he made his appearance in front of the press. 'Heather Watson has played some very good doubles this year and is our No. 1 player as well so obviously it's tough for her,' he said. 'But tough decisions have to be made sometimes. It was hard but I listened to what the coaches on the team had to say. The decision was made because that's what we felt was the best to try and win a medal.'

And his was the last word on the matter.

The following day, the controversial pairing began their assault on the mixed doubles title, facing the Czech duo Radek Stepanek and Lucie Hradecka.

Murray had just booked his place in the men's semifinal, and looked grimly determined as he stepped out on Court One.

Laura, now that the initial excitement was over, looked very nervous. It would be a tough match, especially because of the windy conditions. Robson was a little off form at first, mishitting a lot of shots and berating herself often. But, with Andy encouraging her, she soon settled into her stride.

Her serves were as overpowering as everyone had hoped they would be, and they took the first set 7-5 – no small achievement against a duo that were internationally renowned for being excellent doubles players. Hradecka in particular was a formidable foe, because she was already through to the doubles semifinals in the Olympics.

The crowd roared when the Brits broke at the start of the second set, with Robson landing a stunning lob on the baseline. But she wobbled in the eighth game, giving away a costly three double faults and helping the Czechs break back to 4-4.

With the prospect of a match tiebreak looming instead of a third set, the home pair were desperate to wrap it up in two, but they missed a match point and the Czechs levelled, forcing the issue.

It would be the first to 10 points, and things didn't look hopeful when they trailed 5-2. But the British pair fastened their seatbelts and went full throttle, winning seven points in a row before Murray powered away a volley to clinch victory.

The grins on their faces said it all: Robson had proven

herself worthy, while Murray had clearly made the right decision in choosing her.

After the match, Federer made good on his promise to get Laura a pin badge, and it wasn't just any old pin – instead it was an ultra-rare 'Team Federer' pin, emblazoned with the initials RF and complete with its own velvet bag. She posted a picture of it on twitter, calling it the 'crown jewel' of pins, which prompted a stream of envious replies.

In the quarterfinal, Robson and Murray faced their old foes, the formidable Australian duo of Lleyton Hewitt and Sam Stosur. Both Grand Slam champs, they definitely felt they had something to prove after losing to the same two Brits at the Hopman Cup two years before. While British flags waved in the crowd, Murray and Robson got off to a confident start on Centre Court, winning the first set 6-3.

But the Australians refused to go down without a fight and showed their class to level the match. It would once more come down to an excruciating super tiebreak, which was made even more painful when the first point had to be replayed when a ballgirl mistakenly ran across the court after wrongly thinking the point had finished.

Tension mounted.

Murray must have found it particularly difficult to stay focused, as he had made it to the men's final and had the stressful prospect of facing Federer again in a few days' time. It had only been a month since his Wimbledon loss to the tennis leviathan, and with a gold medal at stake he was under a lot of pressure.

Victory looked distant when he and Robson slipped 7-5 down, and Murray let out an agonising howl of frustration.

But once again they pulled it back, securing their spot in the semifinal – taking place that same day.

There was no time for nerves, no time for tiredness. Laura was within one match of at least a silver Olympic medal, what's more a silver Olympic medal at London 2012 – a once-in-a-lifetime opportunity.

She had overcome years of countless injuries, humiliating defeats and a severely tested friendship to get this far, and no amount of exceptional tennis players were going to stand in her way – not even the German pairing of Christopher Kas and Sabine Lisicki.

Back on Centre Court a few hours later, the Brits got off to a promising start, quickly overpowering the Germans and going 3-0 up. Murray had to save two break points in the fifth game, but the duo quickly broke Kas's serve for the second time, allowing Robson to serve out the set. She more than held her own in the match, where she was in very high-quality company, and they quickly broke again to lead 2-1 in the second set.

However, nerves set in, and Robson began to wobble. She conceded her serve for the second time in the match, before double-faulting at just the wrong time to allow the Germans to break back for 4-4.

Murray calmed her down, telling her to take her time. She redeemed herself by saving a point in her next service game to take the set into a tiebreak. The momentum swung back and forth between the opponents, with both sides making mistakes and epic comebacks.

But then Murray missed a crucial volley, slamming his racket to the ground in sheer frustration, and the two Germans took the set.

This was demoralising. For the third time, they would have to go to a super tiebreak. By now, Andy and Laura were exhausted, and no one would have blamed them for losing. The two sides matched each other, point for point, until at 7-6 up Lisicki dumped a volley into the net, giving the duo a mini-break.

Now it was Laura's turn to serve. All eyes were on her and she didn't disappoint: winning both of them to carry the Brits through to victory.

It was an unreal moment.

Whatever happened in the final, Laura had secured a silver medal – for herself and for her country. 'Can't even explain how happy I am right now,' she tweeted, overwhelmed by the turn of events.

That night, she truly saw what amazing company she was in. As twilight fell, Jessica Ennis, Greg Rutherford and Mo Farah all claimed gold medals for Team GB, and, incredibly, Britain was heading for third place in the medals table.

And Laura was helping to make that happen.

But, before she and Andy could stake their claim in the mixed doubles final, Andy had Federer to face. And both matches would take place on the same day – the next day, in fact.

The wait for a Brit to win the Olympic singles title had been even longer than that for a Wimbledon winner. Josiah Ritchie was the last Brit to stand on the top of the podium for men's tennis, and that was way back in 1908.

Most people wouldn't say that playing two intense matches the day before trying to change this situation was the best form of preparation – especially when to do so meant a face-off with one of the greatest tennis players in existence.

But Murray was ready.

Laura took her place in the crowd as Murray and Federer stepped out onto the same court that had seen such sorrow for the Scot just four weeks previously.

Nervous mum Judy was among the spectators, as were Jeremy Clarkson and Virginia Wade.

But, under the bright-blue British sky, Murray became David to Federer's Goliath, crushing him emphatically in a match that shocked everyone who was watching. It was almost embarrassingly one-sided: the newly reinstated world No. 1 was so overpowered by the determined Murray that he went fully an hour without winning a game.

It was more than remarkable, it was magical – the roar of the crowd was nearly constant as Murray edged his way to victory. He took his time with the final shot, bouncing the ball a few times more than normal, accompanied by the cheers of a crowd that knew what was coming.

He served.

Federer missed.

Murray won.

Screwing his eyes shut as if he was trying to wake from an impossible dream, Andy fell to his knees in disbelief.

Seeing that Federer was making his way over to him, he raised himself up on wobbly legs to shake his hand.

In the crowd, Laura enveloped Judy in a huge hug, the excitement on her own face plainly visible. She knew that this win would have a dramatic effect on Andy's morale, which would need to be high for their next match together.

Andy must have been exhausted. But he and Laura would be chasing gold together now in the mixed doubles final, after just a few minutes of rest.

The British duo were all smiles as they walked out on court to face the Belarusians Victoria Azarenka and Max Mirnyi.

Azarenka was world women's singles No. 1, while Mirnyi was men's doubles No. 1. Together they were the mixed world No. 1s as well. They were formidable opponents, also hungry for gold.

Andy had the comforting weight of the gold medal that had just been hung around his neck to ground him, while Laura was happy that, whatever happened next, she would have some kind of medal hung around hers.

Laura's whole family was in the crowd – taking pictures, waving flags and flushing with pride.

In the first set, she played beautifully in support of her gold medal-winning partner, and served out to seal their 6-2 win in just 30 minutes. She was dominant at the net and from the baseline, but Azarenka and Mirnyi managed to take a 3-1 lead in the second, and stayed calm to level the match.

It was neck and neck, and going into the super tiebreak everyone was nervous. The chants from the crowd were loud and supportive, while Murray and Robson bumped fists and whispered strategies together. They were a great team, and no one could now doubt that Andy had made the right decision in choosing her to be his Olympic partner.

But then Laura double-faulted twice, sending her into a panic, while Murray wasted a crucial chance to draw level at 7-7 by hitting a weak second serve from Azarenka into the bottom of the net.

They were playing catch up from then on and, despite saving 2 match points, they eventually succumbed 10-8. It was Laura who hit the last shot out and she ran straight to Andy for comfort after the loss.

They both congratulated their opponents before gathering their things together and making their way to their family and friends for a series of congratulatory hugs.

Before long, they were face to face with Sue Barker and the BBC news cameras. Laura was smiling as she thanked Andy and exclaimed that it had been one of the best weeks of her life to play alongside him.

Andy was quick to praise her in return: 'She played great, she played unbelievable at the start of the match,' he began. But he could hardly finish his sentence, as he was so disappointed he looked like he might cry.

He really felt he'd let Laura down.

Laura stepped in, still beaming, to say: 'They're the top seeds for a reason, but for me I was just happy to be in the final.'

Sue tried to cheer Andy up by reminding him he had a gold and now a silver medal from the Olympics, but Andy wasn't having it. 'It's just annoying, we were so close... but we did well, it was a good game,' he finally conceded.

Both of them were grinning by the time they stepped up to the podium to receive their silver medals.

Laura could hardly keep her excitement contained: she had won a silver Olympic medal at 18 years of age – the third youngest tennis female medallist in Olympic history. When it was placed around her neck, she gazed down at it in awe, before looking up at Andy as if to say: 'Look! I can't believe it!'

She watched proudly as Andy raised his medal to the crowd – the 36th of the Olympic Games for Team GB.

Later, Laura admitted to a well of mixed emotions at the defeat. 'We were so close to a gold medal so I'm just disappointed but to be a silver medallist is pretty cool,' she said in an interview with the *Telegraph*. 'I think we played really well considering this was the only tournament together since the beginning of last year.'

'I put a lot of pressure on myself to be playing for GB and I was more nervous,' she admitted. 'But playing for Andy was great and I said thank you to him because it has been one of the best weeks of my life.'

It must have been hard to think about the near future – the Olympics were still in full swing and there were many events she wanted to watch and fellow Brits she wanted to support.

However, she would have to do it from afar, because she was now set to travel to America to prepare for the US Open by competing in a series of WTA tournaments. 'I think anything will be an anti-climax after this,' she said.

But she was very wrong.

CHAPTER 24

RETIRING CLIJSTERS

'**O**ff to the USA for my next tournaments,' Robson tweeted two days after receiving her Olympic silver medal. 'Huge good luck to all the @teamGB athletes who are still competing! Will be supporting from afar.'

Leaving the excitement of London behind, she flew to Cincinnati – the city where just a year earlier she had asked Murray to partner her in the mixed doubles at the Olympics. Once there, she knuckled down to practising on the hard courts of the American city, in preparation for the qualifying rounds of the WTA Tour tournament that would start there on 13 August.

And by her side was a new figure – a Croatian by the name of Zeljko Krajan. Laura had been without an official coach for over a year, but the time had come for her to appoint someone who would guide her to WTA glory. Krajan was that someone.

A former No. 88 on the ATP Tour, Krajan was 33 years old

and known as a hard taskmaster. For such a young man, he had built up an already impressive coaching CV. He had helped Russian Dinara Safina to world No. 1 before their split in 2010, then followed this up by taking on the diminutive Slovak Dominika Cibulkova, who reached both the US Open and Wimbledon quarterfinals under his guidance, and most recently he had been working with Serbia's Jelena Jankovic. His goal was now to transform Robson's huge potential into success.

They worked together at Cincinnati, where Robson lost in the second round of the qualifiers to Urszula Radwanska.

Next she travelled to New Haven, where she lost in the first round to Marion Bartoli – and was cheered up by a very cute tinfoil silver medal handed to her by a group of youngsters. But it was all good practice for the US Open, which, as the summer turned into autumn, was her ultimate US destination.

Checking into her Manhattan hotel in the middle of August, she was excited to see that *Gossip Girl*, one of her favourite TV shows, was being filmed right outside.

'Gotta love NYC,' she tweeted.

Robson had got into the main draw for the US Open for the first time on her ranking alone, and she was joined by Anne Keothavong and Heather Watson, with whom she was back on good terms, after almost falling out with her at the Olympics.

It would be a momentous US Open – both Andy Roddick and Kim Clijsters had announced they were retiring from tennis after this, their last tournament. Both had triumphed spectacularly during their illustrious careers, and it would be sad to see them go.

Laura was drawn in the first round against a relatively unknown qualifier, Samantha Crawford. It was a lucky break, especially since Watson was facing Li Na and Keothavong would be up against Angelique Kerber.

Playing a delayed match under the night sky at Flushing Meadows, Robson took control of the first round and her opponent's ferocious ball strike. She regularly grinned at three of her supporters, who had come dressed as clowns for the match, and who led singsong chants about her during the changeovers. They were proof of her stateside popularity, which had been steadily growing.

Laura had never before progressed past this point at the US Open and, though Samantha made life difficult for her by giving no sign of any rhythm to her game, Robson triumphed – to take another huge step forward in her career.

But her next opponent wouldn't be anything near so easy – she had won the US Open title three times, most recently in 2010, and was one of the most famous females in tennis history. Not only that, but she had a huge point to prove, as this was her last tournament ever. This was Kim Clijsters.

Kim was not the sort of opponent a young girl with no WTA titles to her name should have any chance of beating. But winning an Olympic silver medal had done something to Laura, perhaps it had broken down some kind of invisible barrier that had previously been keeping her from reaching her full potential.

When she had won the junior girls' title in 2008, the nation had heaped an overwhelming amount of pressure on little Laura Robson. And, although she may not have quite fully realised it, she had been treading water while trying to live up to the country's hopes and dreams, weighed down by nerves, fear and desperation.

But now that she had indeed proved worthy of the nation's lofty predictions, she had made it clear to British people that they were right in exalting her as a future champion. With the burden of failure lifted, she was free to progress in her career at exactly the pace she should.

'She doesn't even know herself how good she is,' remarked her new coach.

Clijsters was about to find out.

On the centrepiece Arthur Ashe court, the crowds were less than packed when Robson and Clijsters began their duel.

Most of the spectators had sloped off to watch the Williams sisters play doubles, confident that there would be more chances to watch Clijsters in action once she had dispatched this young British pretender. As the match got underway, Robson's footwork was much more assured than usual, and her serve had powered up to 112 mph, making it an even more dangerous weapon.

Playing strategically, Laura kept the ball as deep as possible against Clijsters, whose killer angles had been a decisive factor in her domination of the rankings. Both fought like lions for points, edging game by game in equally impressive steps towards the win. Laura held her nerve to take the first set to a tiebreak, which she eventually won.

Her confidence could only grow in the second set, although there were some shaky moments as the long game went on. At 30-all in the 11th game, she smashed a high ball into the net at the end of a rally that she really should have won; but Clijsters couldn't convert the break point and Robson held with an ace.

She was obviously happy with how things were going, because during a changeover she couldn't help but sing along to the Taylor Swift song that was playing. In the 12th game, Robson held two match points, but Clijsters toughed it out to level for a second tiebreak. It was an exhausting slog of a match, which had already lasted over two hours, and now the pressure was back on Robson.

It was an incredible battle, with shots powering back and forth between the two opponents, and nobody knowing who would triumph. But the British player didn't buckle, and instead set up her third match point by sending a miracle shot straight down the line.

Laura took a few deep breaths to calm herself before their next exchange. She served, and when Clijsters returned everyone watched the ball as it arced high and landed... way over the line.

With that, Robson sent the Belgian into retirement.

The stadium rose to applaud both players, but it was Laura who deserved all the glory. 'This is what the fuss has been about,' reported the *Daily Mail*, and everyone agreed.

It was one of the finest moments of her young career, and coming so soon after her Olympic success it seemed that Robson was finally carving her way into the tennis hall of fame. She looked up at the crowd with a disbelieving grin, before running over to Clijsters and throwing her arms around her.

Walking back to her chair, she began to giggle wildly, shrugging her shoulders in disbelief at the enormity of what she had just achieved.

She had put a halt to Clijsters' phenomenal 22-match winning streak – the last time the Belgian had lost at the US

Open was when Robson was only nine. And she was the first player ranked outside the top 10 to beat Clijsters at Flushing Meadows.

Laura's voice wobbled as she spoke to ESPN a few moments later.

'I had to work my butt off,' she admitted. 'I was just trying to play as well as I could because I knew that if I didn't Kim would completely dominate. Thanks to Kim for being such a great role model to me for so many years. It's been an absolute pleasure to finally play against you.'

Clijsters said that she had followed Robson's career since seeing her play An-Sophie Mestach, years before. 'She's a great ball striker,' she mused. 'When she's behind the ball she hits it so clean. She has a very good eye for the ball as well. Laura played extremely well today. I gave it all but I just wasn't good enough at the end.'

Back home in Wimbledon, Laura's family went crazy. Kathy had stayed at home for this US trip, and had been watching it on TV like everyone else.

Andy Murray had been in the crowd for the second set, and was happy to talk to the press about her success. Not wanting to reload her with the pressure that had caused her so many worries, he carefully said: 'It's going to take a bit of time to get the consistency but you saw when she was playing against some of the guys in the Olympics that she was returning the serve with ease sometimes.

'She's got very easy power and great timing, and if you look at how many teenagers there are in the top 100 compared with what there used to be she's right up there with the best in the world.'

It had been another incredible day in the life of Laura

Robson, but, instead of celebrating, she had a little bit of physio, stretched down and went back to the hotel to get some sleep.

She rose once, to make a short trip to Whole Foods for cereal and lactose-free milk, but other than that life carried on as normal. She had made the third round of the US Open, but she had no plans to stop there. Next she would face world No. 7 Li Na, who had beaten Heather Watson in the first round and was also flying through the tournament.

Once more, Laura would be the underdog, but she took it in her stride. Watson passed on any information she could about Li Na's winning tactics and Robson listened intently. On the last day of August, under a clear New York sky, Robson steeled herself for her next challenge.

In the first set, both players struggled to find their rhythm. Distracted by the wind, the incessant chatter of the American crowd – who even walked around in the middle of points – and a large plume of smoke rising above the old press box, it was difficult to concentrate.

Sirens cut through the air as the emergency services attended to a nearby fire, and the result was a mix of repeated breaks of serves, often prompted by double faults, and few rallies of more than six or seven shots. But, gritting her teeth, Robson threw down the gauntlet by taking it 6-4.

The second set contained just one break each, as both girls settled into the fight. It was neck and neck, and, although there were a few moments when Robson was only two points away from snatching it, Na held firm to set up a finely balanced tiebreak and even the match. Na, sensing that she could now win, began to hit the corners with her powerful forehand, sending Laura running all over the place.

Robson could have been forgiven for crumbling, but instead she took her own game up a gear, and wrestled each point into submission. Her serenity was rocked by a couple of flashpoints over line-calls, including one outrageous moment when the umpire demanded the point be replayed because of a judging error. Na had been nowhere near the ball, and, to add insult to injury, the ruling came on a crucial break point.

But Laura stayed rock steady. After another deuce, she converted the break to go 3-2 up, before smashing through the final three games and securing yet another truly unbelievable victory.

She was into the fourth round at the US Open, a feat not managed in any Grand Slam by a British woman since Sam Smith 14 years earlier.

'I couldn't do anything,' conceded Li Na.

Laura was finally blossoming, and everyone everywhere had an opinion on her career. 'Amazingly she is still only 18,' wrote the *Daily Telegraph*'s Simon Briggs. 'In an era when success is coming later and later, in both men's and women's tennis, Robson is something of a throwback to the time when the likes of Martina Hingis and – more recently – Maria Sharapova were winning Grand Slams as teenagers.

'Yet it is easy to forget that – in her words – she is "still the baby of the locker-room" because she seems to have been on the scene for an age.'

Martina Navratilova came forward to claim that Robson was finally achieving her true potential, after being hindered by her early success in winning the junior Wimbledon title: 'She won it a year or two too early. Expectations go up,' she said.

'Teenagers are not meant to make much of an impact in tennis these days but nobody seems to have told Laura Robson,' remarked Mike Dickson for the *Daily Mail*. 'Here is a player destined to... keep Andy Murray company in the spotlight for years to come.'

'Laura is someone that a lot of people expected to do well from an early age,' said Maria Sharapova. 'This is definitely her breakthrough tournament, her breakthrough Grand Slam. She's been playing extremely well.'

Even football star Wayne Rooney sent praise Laura's way by tweeting his admiration for her – even if he did spoil things slightly by calling her Laura Robinson. For her part, Laura was almost confused by her own achievements, jokingly replying, 'no idea!' when she was asked what on earth was going on.

'I've been working on moving my feet and trying to make one extra ball to make it harder for the opponent,' she said. 'I shout at myself a bit. When I got tight in the second set I kept telling myself to go for my shots, keep moving.

'The level has always been there but in the last few weeks I've gained a bit of confidence, worked hard. This summer has been the first I've been injury-free, and that's the big thing.

'I have had lots of tough matches against some very experienced opponents so, the way that I see it, it was time to start winning a few of them,' she laughed.

Although it was too early in the relationship to credit Krajan with much input, Robson was clearly benefiting from the Croatian's tactical know-how.

She said: 'I think the level has always been there. It's just in the last few weeks I have gained a bit of confidence and the work that I have done with him [Krajan] has been very specific in terms of tactical stuff.

'So just in the last few matches I think it's noticeable that, instead of just trying to hit a winner off a tough shot like I have done in the past, I'm trying to make a percentage shot back. That makes all the difference really.

'I have always thought that I can play with the top girls. Whenever I've practised with Caroline [Wozniacki] or Maria [Sharapova], I've always felt that the level was there.'

Laura was proving that it certainly was. Even her next opponent, defending champ Sam Stosur, the Australian who had beaten Serena Williams in the final the year before, was concerned.

'It could be a very tricky match,' Sam told reporters. 'She's probably got nothing to lose. She's had two of the best wins of her career, and she's starting to maybe live up to some of that potential that people have talked about from when she won junior Wimbledon when she was 14.'

The British tennis star was similarly composed, and smiled as she said: 'I have had a fairly tough draw, haven't I? You have to beat who is in front of you. That's what I've managed to do so far.'

Laura's boost in fitness should be credited to Jez Green, Andy Murray's excellent trainer, whom she had approached a few months before for help. Jez had definitely been a huge part of her recent success, and her rise to No. 88 in the world rankings – she was now the youngest player in the top 100. And, although she couldn't quite topple Stosur when they finally faced off in their fourth-round encounter, Laura was now an undisputed tennis star.

Robson had arrived at Flushing Meadows with a mixed

doubles silver and bags of enthusiasm. She left being followed by a trail of news cameras and holding a mobile phone that repeatedly ran out of battery because of all the messages of support she was receiving.

'Yesterday there was a camera crew outside my hotel,' she explained before she caught her flight back to the UK. 'I got really excited because I thought they were waiting for someone really famous. I didn't really think they were for me until they started following me to the car.'

Laura had finally come of age.

CHAPTER 25

ASIA – GANGNAM STYLE

Returning home in September, Laura had just a week before she was set to travel to Asia for the next leg of the WTA Tour.

She focused on her training of course, but she also found the time to go to the Olympic Village to watch the Paralympic Closing Ceremony, and to take part in the parade. Putting on her Olympic kit for the last time, she smiled and waved to the thousands of spectators who lined the streets to see her go by. She must have been so proud to be part of Team GB, who had provided inspiration to a whole generation of young sporting hopefuls.

Then she settled down in front of the TV to watch Andy Murray win his first Grand Slam title, by beating Nojak Djokovic at the US Open. British tennis was enjoying a huge turnaround in fortune and she was a part of it. This was an exciting time for the sport.

Next she flew to China to compete in the Guangzhou International Open – her first outing as world No. 74 and British No. 1.

Laura had finally overtaken Heather Watson in the national rankings.

She passed comfortably through to the second round when her first opponent, Maria-Teresa Torro-Flor, was forced to pull out with a thigh problem. She then beat second seed Jie Zheng to advance to the third round, proving yet again that her talent was no fluke.

It was hot and humid in China when she faced seventh seed Shuai Peng in the quarterfinals, but the floodgates were now open and there was no stopping Laura. She broke her Chinese opponent three times in the tight opening set, before losing an equally tight second set to send the match into a decider. But, after registering three more breaks in a straightforward third set, she finally emerged triumphant, after more than three hours on court.

Laura was on a roll.

She had a massage and an ice-bath to soothe her tired muscles and joints in time for her next match, which would be against Sorana Cirstea in less than 24 hours.

'It's going to be a really tough match because she's a very aggressive player,' she told *The Tennis Space* website. 'She hits a lot of winners so I'm going to have to be ready to run a lot, that's for sure.'

But on the day of the clash Robson was a human steamroller, mowing down her Romanian opponent 6-4; 6-2 to become the first British woman in a final since Jo Durie in

1990. Laura was marking out her place in history with a firm hand, after an impressive run of form that had made this the best summer of her life.

When the day of the final arrived, it was unbearably hot and humid on court. Both Robson and her opponent, Taiwan's Su-Wei Hsieh, were in danger of wilting even before the match began. Robson was pouring with sweat and clearly uncomfortable in the shaky first set, which, despite a classy performance, was won by the experienced Taiwanese player.

Robson saved five match points in the second to take it, causing her opponent to have some kind of mental breakdown on court. The players were granted a ten-minute break to recover from the stifling heat, and both were grateful for the respite.

On their return, Robson took a 3-0 lead in the decider, but then the heat became even more oppressive, and Robson's body simply stopped working.

Hsieh took the final set 6-4, and with it the title.

Laura's bubble had finally burst and, though it wasn't the end of the world, she was very upset. She could hardly hold it together when her opponent lifted the winner's trophy in front of the roaring crowd.

Laura had been so tantalisingly close to success and, though she couldn't be disappointed with her mature performance, she admitted that she was devastated.

'In the end, I just totally ran out of energy, I kept fighting, but I wasn't able to hit the shots as hard,' she said. 'The more matches you play the more experience you get and to play in a really tough final like this is a big experience. Hopefully next time I play in a final I'll be a little more ready for it – and hopefully it won't be so humid.'

Shaking off her disappointment, Laura continued on her tour of the Far East by heading to Beijing for the China Open. She was reunited with her best pal Eugenie Bouchard, and together the pair toured the city sights armed with a video camera, to make a unique version of Psy's cult summer hit song 'Gangnam Style'...

They visited the Great Wall of China and the Beijing Olympic Stadiums and collected some great footage for the film.

Robson qualified easily for the main draw of the Open, and made it to the second round before falling to Spain's Lourdes Dominguez Lino.

Together with Watson and Bouchard, she next travelled to Japan for the HP Osaka Open, where she was seeded eighth – her first ever seeding in a WTA tournament.

The players had a blast together – cake-decorating at the players' party and roping in other players to perform in their music video. Then they posted their film on YouTube, where it became an instant hit. Maria Sharapova introduced the video, which saw Bouchard, Robson and Watson dressed up in various outfits copying the famous dance moves from the original music video.

Jo Wilfred Tsonga had a few lines, along with Fernando Verdasco, while Sharapova uttered the final lyrics.

It was good to see that Watson and Robson were still firm friends, and it was even better to see all the girls enjoying their time in the Far East so much.

'We are both very competitive and when one sees the other do well it makes us want to do better, but we can still be friends,' Watson decisively told an army of inquisitive reporters.

Back on court, Robson beat her first two opponents in straight sets to reach the quarterfinals, followed quickly by Watson. But, while the Guernsey girl made it past her French rival, Pauline Parmentier, to reach the semifinals, Robson was beaten in a tiebreak by Kai-Chen Chang.

She watched with mixed emotions as Watson went on to win in the final, becoming the first British woman to win a main WTA Tour event since Sara Gomer, 24 years before.

This was the record that Robson had so desperately wanted to break herself, but she couldn't help but be happy for her pal, and celebrated with her by singing karaoke and going tenpin bowling.

With the tennis year now over, Robson had risen to No. 52 in the rankings, two places below Watson. Both girls had gained very different but equally impressive achievements, and so it was appropriate that they should share the *Sunday Times* 'Young Sportswoman of the Year' award, which was given to them at a special ceremony when they returned to Britain.

Both girls dressed up for the event, with Laura in angelic white lace and a Burberry trench, and Watson in a colourful sequin dress. They posed with their arms around each other, grinning broadly for pictures that they both posted on Twitter. Robson pushed aside any references to a rivalry with her friend, saying: 'We are both competitive people but we want each other to do well. So far it should be easy staying friends. I don't know if it will be harder as we get older, but I hope it stays the same.'

In an interview with the *Daily Mail*, John McEnroe shared his thoughts on the two girls: 'Heather has done well but it might be a bit tougher for her because of her size,' he explained. 'Robson to me is the one with the bigger upside. She has got a lot of ability and clearly if she is committed and in tip-top shape, I think she could easily be top 10.'

Around the world, the global tennis media agreed, and showed their commitment to her by voting her the 'WTA Newcomer of the Year' in late November, just ahead of Watson. Both Brits then flew to Florida for their winter training – Watson to Tampa and the IMG Academy, while Robson settled into a routine at the Chris Evert Academy in Boca Raton.

For the rest of the year, Laura focused on her punishing training regime, which saw her flopping into bed each night at 9pm, the monotony only occasionally broken by watching one of her favourite horror flicks – if she could stay awake for it.

Returning to Wimbledon for her first Christmas at home in five years, she relaxed with her family and revelled in beating her brother Nicholas at some festive board games. And, as 2013 arrived, she said farewell to a year that had seen her achieve more than she could have ever dreamed of.

CHAPTER 26

BLAZING
AHEAD

Laura started the year by reaching the top 50 spot in the world rankings, just three behind her pal Heather Watson. Together they were making a British assault on the world tennis scene reminiscent of the 1980s, when Jo Durie and Sara Gomer were both nudging their way up from the No. 50 spot.

During the run-up to the Australian Open, Laura was offered an unusual distraction when she joined Caroline Wozniacki and Maria Kirilenko for a practice with a difference – on a mirrored court created by Adidas to promote their first collection by Stella McCartney.

In modelling the new Barricade collection, Laura was finally a designer's muse, fulfilling another one of her many ambitions. She looked beautiful in the photos – the brunette between two blondes, her eyes sultry, her form statuesque.

Built in a warehouse in West Melbourne, just a stone's

throw from the Australian Open, all three of the girls took a turn in the kaleidoscopic court, where they were filmed for an exclusive online movie and posed for fashion photographer Astrid Salomon.

Laura would be wearing the new sportswear when she made her assault on the Open, just a few days later. Before then, she relaxed by visiting Hobart's rescue sanctuary and playing with some koalas, and bonding with baby kangaroos in the players' café – no one could say that being an international tennis player didn't have its perks...

After a brutal first-round loss at last year's Australian Open, Laura was keen to prove herself in her first-round match against Melanie Oudin. During her career, she had both beaten and lost to the American, who was now some distance below her in the rankings at No. 84.

It was sweltering when she finally stepped out on court to face her personal 'white whale': the first round of the Australian Open, which she had never before been able to get past.

Wearing her new Stella McCartney white dress, she looked poised for domination. And she was backed by the crowds, who showed their devotion by singing 'God Save the Queen' and 'Laura Robson's Barmy Army' – an interesting vocal display.

She blazed like the sun that beat down on court, firing off a series of powerful winners and taking the first four games before Oudin could even absorb what was happening. The American steadied herself to win two games but she was unable to stem the tide of Robson rockets and the set was Laura's in just 35 minutes.

In the second set, there was no let-up – from Robson or the

above 35 degree heat – and in another whirlwind of points Laura took the set and the match.

Laura was through to the second round, and she was very happy about it. But her coach, although pleased with the result, ordered her straight to the practice courts to iron out a few problematic groundstrokes.

She was hot and tired, but she did as she was told.

Robson's next opponent was the 2011 Wimbledon champion Petra Kvitova, another titan of the tennis scene.

'I've heard it's going to be 38 degrees,' Laura said nervously. 'I don't really like the heat but I seem to play well in it. I can approach the match with nothing to lose.'

It was a good attitude, and it served her well when, under cover of darkness, she took on the Czech giant. It was a wildly undulating three hours of combat that literally ended the next day – the clock struck midnight half an hour before the match was over.

And, to their credit, Robson's fans stayed up to cheer her on as loudly as ever. Granted, the Australians would have dearly loved to claim her as their own, given her birth there, but that wasn't the only reason for their support – Robson's popularity was beginning to transcend borders, emulating Federer and Sharapova with its international fan base.

It wasn't a beautiful match, with the two left-handed players aggressively and awkwardly clashing to create a mountain of mistakes on both sides. But Laura's bloody-minded determination saw her overpower Kvitova to a 2-6; 6-3; 11-9 win, causing the Czech to throw her racket to the ground in frustration.

'I could definitely hear the crowd,' Robson said, smiling

sweetly. 'I knew it was going to be tough but in the end I got through.'

It was another high-profile win, but an exhausting one and she flopped into bed that night heady with victory.

She was fast getting a reputation as a giant-slayer, and she would need it in her next match, set to be against Sloane Stephens, who was living up to all the expectations that had been placed on Laura in her younger years.

But, as her showdown with Stephens approached, she couldn't shake a niggling pain in her serving shoulder. She would have to grit her teeth and play through it. She played hard and fast as the match commenced, but so did Stephens, and it was the latter who quickly went 4-1 up, putting a dagger through Robson's recent serene composure.

Laura called a time-out for some courtside treatment on her shoulder, which was taking a considerable amount of battering, and spent a full five minutes having it worked on.

Showing admirable willpower and grit, when she returned, she held, trading meaty shots from the baseline that forced Stephens to give up a break point. Robson pushed her deep in an ensuing long rally, rushing the net to punish an underhit return and belting in a pleasing winner to get back on serve. The crowd was overwhelmingly with Robson, stunning Stephens with their booming cries of support.

But Robson was suffering increasing pain, and, although the physio returned to work on her shoulder during the changeover, it was to little effect. The British player struggled to work past it, but as the shadows lengthened on court she could only go down, fighting to the last. Laura took the loss with good grace, smiling and waving to her fans and walking off court with dignity.

Stephens was relieved at the win, mindful of the fact that there was little to choose between them, and tried not to think how different the situation would have been if Laura hadn't been in such shocking pain. She was amazed at the support Laura was garnering, which was worthy of a home crowd.

'It was intense,' Stephens said, clearly amazed. 'I felt like I was playing an Italian player in Italy. It was crazy – who knew that all those people would come?'

She admitted that Robson had more than matched her, and quipped: 'We're turning into the Federer–Nadal rivalry.'

Robson was happy with her performance overall, and said that she was still feeling positive. 'I toughed out the two wins,' she said humbly. 'It was still a pretty good tournament.'

Laura quickly got a doctor to check out her shoulder, mindful of her past form with injuries, but, luckily, there was no lasting damage.

And so she celebrated her 19th birthday in high spirits, going out for dinner with her father and sister, and clutching a sparkly balloon as she blew out the candles on her cake. As a result of her impressive form, she rose to No. 43 in the rankings, edging ever closer to that coveted No. 1 spot...

Flying back to the UK, she was prepared for the snow that she had been told would await her.

'Just landed back in London. Some people on my flight are still wearing shorts and flip flops. #enjoythesnow,' she tweeted.

Robson went straight back into training. She had barely a week before she was set to go to Israel with her Fed Cup teammates, and she was determined to make the most of it.

Flying out to Israel in February with Judy Murray and the girly gang, Laura was excited. She had loved being part of the tight-knit team the year before and couldn't wait to try once again to launch Britain back into the elite World Group for the first time in 20 years.

At the official team dinner in Eliat, all the women put on matching red dresses, and enjoyed a glamorous night out before undertaking the hard work that would leave them sweaty and dishevelled. 'Ladies in Red,' Judy Murray tweeted. 'GB best looking team in Eliat. No question.'

It was hard to disagree.

Judy Murray truly believed that the girls – Robson, Watson, Baltacha, Keothavong and newbie Johanna Konta – had a chance of making an impact in the competition, in which Britain had spent so long in the basement division.

'Laura and Heather have had a very exciting 12 months and I think we are ready to challenge,' she said. 'I think we are in a very strong position in that we have three young players who are very much on the up, while Elena [Baltacha] and Anne [Keothavong] give us a super blend of youth and experience. It's a great opportunity for us to move forward.'

Britain had been drawn in a group with Bosnia, Portugal and Hungary, and would begin their campaign by taking on Bosnia. But, as heavy rain postponed their first rubber for a day, the team amused themselves with a series of team-building board games.

'We've been playing Pictionary and you should see what a talented artist Heather is,' Murray grinned. 'We've got a great team atmosphere.'

Finally, it was time to take on Bosnia, and the Brits did it in style. Keothavong defeated Dea Herdzelas 6-4; 6-2, swiftly followed by Watson claiming a similarly comprehensive victory over Anita Husaric to set up a 2-0 lead. Then Robson teamed up with Konta to whitewash Jelena Simic and Jasmina Katjazovic 6-0; 6-0, giving the team a perfect 3-0 start to their campaign.

After screaming with joy, the girls celebrated that night by playing a dance game on the Wii console in their HQ.

The next day, the team had to work hard at the Municipal Tennis Club against a strong Portuguese side. Robson was up first, facing Margarida Moura in the opening singles rubber, taking her down decisively 6-2; 6-1. But Watson failed to emulate her success, losing to world No. 130 Michelle Larcher de Brito, who was well known for 'screaming' or yelling volubly, during the exertion of play.

They needed a win in the doubles to beat Portugal, and Murray decided that Watson and Robson should partner up for the clash. It was a good decision: in just 55 minutes the duo had seen off their opponents, earning Britain a 2-1 victory in the tie.

They just had Hungary to go in their final round robin – an unbeaten side. Just as with Portugal, it was up to Robson to open the rubber with a singles match against Greta Arn. Laura's shoulder had begun to play up again, and the future looked bleak when she was bageled in her first set, losing 0-6.

But she was treated for the annoying injury, and staged a stunning comeback to take the next two sets 6-2; 6-1, pushing Britain to a 1-0 lead.

Watson made it 2-0 with a win against Timea Babos, making Robson and Konta's subsequent doubles loss irrelevant.

They were through to the play-off, where they would face

Group D winners Bulgaria – the only team standing in the way of the World Group II play-offs in April. The Brits had made it there the year before, where they were beaten by Sweden, and they were determined to at least get there again. 'We are anticipating a tough battle,' said Murray, who was overjoyed at her team's success thus far.

It had been an exciting few days in Israel.

The next morning, it was once more up to Robson to open the rubber. She was up against Dia Evtimova and, in a reversal of fortunes, she bageled her opponent in the first set. But, unlike Robson, Evtimova didn't fight back, and Robson secured Britain a 1-0 lead in less than an hour.

Watson played next, taking on Wimbledon semifinalist Tsvetana Pironkova, and stumbling in the first set. It was looking grim when she lost it 1-6, but Watson battled back to win both the second and the third sets in an astonishing display of determination.

The team were euphoric – they were through.

'We did it!!!' tweeted Robson. 'Heather and I won our singles so we are through to the playoff in April! Very, very happy.'

Judy was proud of her girls, and praised them highly in her BBC online column: 'Thanks to a fabulous effort from the whole team we've earned the chance to win a place in the World Group, and it's a huge opportunity for British women's tennis,' she wrote. 'The structure of the competition means that, if we'd lost to Bulgaria, that would have been the Fed Cup over for us for another 12 months.

'But we've managed to get ourselves a World Group play-off for the second year running, and I think we're now ready to compete at that level.'

She singled out Robson and Watson as her star players, describing their huge leaps forward in the previous 12 months as well as their sweet natures off court.

'They not only play great tennis, but they're also great personalities, lots of fun and good role models who can attract more girls into our sport. Who knows how far they will go but they make tennis look fun, exciting and glamorous. They can keep women's tennis in the public eye.'

It was an insightful observation, and one that surely made the two girls blush with pride. They would have to wait until April to continue their campaign.

In the meantime, they each went back to their own personal quests for glory...

CHAPTER 27

CLASH OF
THE TITANS

After such an impressive run, it seemed unimaginable that Laura could begin to lose again – but, as February turned into March, bizarrely she started to spiral downwards.

Defeats came successively in Doha, Dubai and Indian Wells, where she lost in the first round of all three tournaments.

She had been struggling with a chest infection while she travelled through the Middle East and America, and it had severely hampered her performance. To top it all off, she had her luggage raided while she was in the Middle East, and was saddened to discover that some irreplaceable items of jewellery had been taken.

She seemed unhappy in her matches, troubled by playing. Her fans could only hope it was a temporary blip.

Heading to Florida for the Miami Masters in March, she

badly needed a win to stop her confidence from faltering. Not counting the Fed Cup in early February, she'd not won a match since the Australian Open in January, and was in danger of losing her stride.

As a thunderstorm brewed ominously in the background, she beat Italian player Camila Giorgi in three sets, seeing off the Italian mere moments before torrential rain poured from the sky. But her second-round match against France's Alize Cornet was a bizarre affair, lasting over seven hours and frequently interrupted by power cuts, rain and even a change in court.

Robson started well, capitalising on three of her opponent's double faults to take the first set.

After a rain delay, the match was moved to a floodlit court and, while Robson was competitive, she kept losing her momentum when the lights repeatedly cut out on court. After hours of delays, her concentration deserted her.

Her serve, usually so powerful, was strangely weak, and she lost the last six games in a row. It was a depressing match. Having received a wildcard to the doubles tournament, Robson licked her wounds and teamed up with the American Lisa Raymond to start all over again.

This time, however, glory was quick and remarkable.

She'd only got in because Raymond's original partner, Sam Stosur, had suffered a calf-muscle pull, forcing her to withdraw. But the partnership was fortuitous, and the pair blasted their way to the final of the event, even beating the world No. 1 pairing of Sara Errani and Roberta Vinci in the semifinal.

Robson had stunned everyone with her court performance in the tournament, especially herself. But following the semifinal clash she strangely admitted she felt she didn't really belong when the announcer made his introductions.

'I just felt so inadequate compared to everyone else on court,' she said. 'Errani and Vinci obviously have a couple of Grand Slams, Lisa has too many to count and I was like, "Yeah, I'm fine with a 50k tournament win last year somewhere".'

She was the best performer by far, and her lack of confidence was somewhat out of character. She usually revelled in giant-slaying. Something was definitely wrong with Robson.

Despite the pair eventually losing in the final to Russia's Nadia Petrova and Slovenia's Katarina Srebotnik, Laura appeared happy with the runner-up bowl. She grinned as she held it in her hands, obviously pleased to finally feel success-ful again.

At Charleston for the Family Circle Cup, she cruised past the first round with an easy victory over Spain's Estella Cabeza Candela. But Robson didn't seem as happy as she should have been, and in her next match she still seemed out of character. Perhaps it was because she was facing her best friend, Eugenie Bouchard. There had to be some reason for the slew of errors, including eight double faults, which caused her to lose against the Canadian qualifier.

Bouchard admitted the experience was odd.

'It's definitely tough playing someone you're so close with because you look across the net and see a friendly, familiar face, so it was a bit weird,' Eugenie said after her win. 'We both tried to put it out of our heads. We are both competitive and want to win, but off the court a few hours later we were fine and back to our gossiping ways.'

Laura had other concerns in the friend department too.

Heather Watson had come down with glandular fever, a debilitating illness that saps energy and can often takes months to recover from. Glandular fever is reasonably common in tennis players. Roger Federer, Justine Henin and Andy Roddick have all suffered from it and resumed their careers relatively quickly.

But others have not been so fortunate. Mario Ancic was never the same after contracting the disease, while two-time French Open finalist Robin Soderling credits the illness with ending his career at just 26.

Laura was worried about her friend, especially since she was such an integral part of the Fed Cup team. She would just have to hope that a spell at home in Guernsey would help her overcome the illness.

Robson next flew to Poland to compete in the Katowice Open, a WTA event. She lost in the first round, but consoled herself with the news that she had reached a career-high ranking of 39 – a phenomenal achievement.

Days later, Robson learned that Watson wouldn't be at her side for the Fed Cup play-off in Argentina. Although recent blood tests had shown she was at the tail end of her glandular fever, she still wasn't over it and couldn't make the trip to Buenos Aires. Laura would sorely miss her British friend, who Judy Murray announced would be replaced by the up-and-coming Johanna Konta.

It was a blow to all their hopes and it also meant that it was now up to Robson to lead the team: a huge responsibility for the 19-year-old, who was still out of sorts.

Murray and the tennis quartet flew to Argentina, determined to tackle the play-offs with the Great British spirit of defiance.

They all wore pure white slender Ted Baker dresses to attend the players' dinner at the Pan Americano Hotel, flying the flag for British design as well as for tennis. The young women looked glamorous and athletic in the classically cut knee-length numbers, which showed off their athletic figures and toned arms.

Murray had some serious thinking to do to get her player selection right for the matches. Konta had played well in practice, but had never played a singles match in the Fed Cup. Keothavong had recently won a lower-tiered event but was at her weakest on the 'devil dirt' (red clay), which was the surface they would be playing on. And Baltacha had only played one match since the Olympics because she'd had ankle surgery.

It was pretty much all down to Laura, who really hadn't seemed herself over the past few months. Murray chose Konta for the opening rubber at the Parque Roca Stadium, which was filled with the noise of unruly fans. She played well but in the end was no match for Argentinean No. 1 Paula Ormaechea, who beat her in straight sets.

The World Group II play-offs were a best of five tie, so the Brits weren't out yet, but they needed something to boost their confidence and that something would have to be Laura.

She strode out amid the rumble of the crowd and was ruthless in her taking down of Florencia Molinero. It took all her efforts to ignore the home support hubbub around her, which was so loud that the umpire issued two warnings to the crowd to simmer down.

But Laura didn't let her discomfort show and, a couple of dodgy double faults aside, she steamrollered the lower-ranked player 6-1; 6-1 to even the score.

'We are probably where we expected to be,' said Murray.

'Jo made a very good debut, it's not easy to come out at 10am against a partisan crowd with all that noise and their brass band.

'Then Laura absolutely destroyed Molinero to even things up and we're looking forward to tomorrow, it's all to play for.'

Laura was similarly positive: 'I was very pleased with how I played,' she said. 'I stuck to my game plan and hitting some higher balls to her backhand and, apart from a few double faults, nothing to complain about. It's 1-1 going into tomorrow, it's going to be tough, but we can totally do this.'

Despite her enthusiasm, the next day was an unmitigated disaster. First Robson lost in the reverse singles rubber to Paula Ormaechea, who was a lot better – on clay at least – than her ranking of 143 suggested.

Then Murray drafted in the nearly retired Elena Baltacha to play against 25-year-old Maria Irigoyen, and the team stumbled to a shattering defeat. They huddled together in solace but there was nothing they could do. Britain's Fed Cup dreams were put on hold for yet another year.

Laura was stalling. After a series of disappointing defeats, she was once more struggling to believe in herself, and no one knew what had happened to cause her recent freefall. She had been riding high until just a few months earlier – what on earth had happened?

After flying back to Europe for the Portugal Open, she suffered yet another first-round defeat, this time to Ayumi Morita. Her serve, usually her biggest weapon, was suddenly poor.

Working with her coach, she looked serious and sad. On bended knee during the Morita match, Krajan had been seen sternly trying to talk her round. But his words had no effect. Robson was growing and defining herself as a star player, but she still needed to get a handle on herself mentally, despite all her hard work. She was stumbling through her 2013 season, and after such an amazing 2012 there was simply no reason for it. Or was there?

Next stop was Madrid for the WTA Mutua Open in May. But this time, Krajan wasn't with her, and nor would he be again: the pair had parted their ways. The intense coach had been just too tough for the youngster, and the pressure he was putting on her to perform was threatening to make her crack.

Dominika Cibulkova, who was trained by the Croatian before he moved on to Robson, described him as 'very intense all the time'. Had he unwittingly been the cause of Laura's strange downturn?

When their relationship ended, Cibulkova had said: 'He was just putting too much pressure and with every ball I missed and every match I lost I was putting myself really down because he was very, very tough.'

Krajan was an excellent coach, but perhaps in hindsight the partnership wasn't in the best interests of either party. Laura, despite being a determined and ambitious player, was still a 19-year-old girl, and a fun-loving one at that.

Her family had worked hard to make sure that she was a well-rounded young lady, not just an obsessed tennis brat. Krajan, on the other hand, lived and breathed tennis. He frequently despaired that Laura wasn't training as hard as he would like and couldn't handle her crises of confidence with enough sensitivity to curb their effects.

Robson needed a coach who understood her and the

challenges of being a top 40 professional *and* a teenager. She put enough pressure on herself without someone else heaping it on too. After nine months, it was clear that Krajan wasn't the right man for her. It was time to move on, and Laura returned to the Adidas coaching team, led by Sven Groeneveld.

She ignored Krajan when he bitterly told the press that she was immature, and responded tactfully that they just had different ways of working: 'We didn't have enough in common and I think you need to really get on with your coach on and off the court... We just didn't click. He's free to say whatever.'

In Madrid, Laura was bloodthirsty for a win. After five first-round exits in three months, she needed the confidence of triumph – and she finally got it by beating Magdalena Rybarikova from Slovakia.

Through to the second round of a WTA event again at long last, she didn't bat an eyelid when she looked over the net to see world No. 4 Agnieszka Radwanska getting ready to take her on in her next match. Radwanska was an epic challenge – just the kind of prized scalp Laura needed to send her back on track. Robson satisfyingly shocked just about everyone by absolutely demolishing the Polish player.

'I'd had enough of losing,' she exclaimed, after handing out the hammering, and the tennis world finally understood: this was why Robson was so exciting – she could lose all year but you could never count her out of the running. You never knew when that comeback would happen and who would crumble beneath her racket.

Without the exacting standards of her former coach, Laura felt the pressure was easing, and it showed. In the third round, she went a set up against Ana Ivanovic, and, although she failed to win, she was happy when she flew on to Rome for the Italian Open.

And, with time to kill before her first match, she took in the sights of the ancient city, smiling for pictures next to the Coliseum and the famous Trevi Fountain. With her hair loose in a side plait, she looked fresh and carefree – a far cry from the troubled soul she had seemed for most of the year.

When the Italian Open began, Laura had a shock when she found out who her first-round opponent would be.

Back when she was ten, Laura had gone to Wimbledon to watch Venus Williams play and had been in awe of the titan ever since. A few years later, when Venus won the junior title, she vowed she would one day take her down. Now, she finally had an opportunity to make good on her promise.

Her mother, on hearing the news, sent her a copy of the interview Laura gave five years before, in which she uttered her monumental challenge to the tennis giant.

'As if I could ever forget saying something so stupid,' she remarked to a reporter.

Laura was overcome with excitement. As the seconds counted down to their clash, she jumped up and down with nervous energy, causing Groeneveld to tell her to calm down. By the time both players stepped out onto the impossibly beautiful Centre Court at the Foro Italico, Laura was practically foaming at the mouth.

Serena Williams watched from the stands as Laura handled the wind and sporadic clay storms far better than her sister was doing. With exquisite timing she broke Venus almost at will, leaving the seven-time Grand Slam winner looking more like one of the kitsch marble statues that dotted the redeveloped court.

In fairness, Venus wasn't playing her best. But that couldn't detract from the poised manner in which Laura took her down – in straight sets, no less.

Robson had beaten a Williams.

It was a legendary win, and one that set Laura up to face Serena in the second round. 'I've never played her and I've always wanted to,' said a bright-eyed Laura after the unbelievable match. 'She is playing probably her best tennis and so it's going to be insanely tough but I'm just going to go out there and do my best.'

Serena was equally apprehensive of the second-round clash. 'She's really young, still,' she said. 'She's just so free and she looks great on the court and she's so smooth and she's a lefty, so that just adds a notch to her whole level. I've never played her before. I've always wanted to. So I have a tough second-round match.'

Laura was enjoying her sport again, and was even smiling when she walked out into the Rome sunshine to find Serena in a vengeful mood. Whatever happened, it would be an amazing learning experience, one she would savour every moment of.

Robson got off to a flying start, breaking in the first game and powering off some dynamite serves to outfox her No. 1 opponent. But Serena was aggressive in her returns, and played tactically, exploiting Robson's still limited movement and outgunning her at every opportunity.

The first set went to Williams.

Laura showcased her classy ballstriking in the second, and even had break points for 3-2, but she couldn't convert them into a win, and a liberal sprinkling of double faults didn't help her case at all. Serena was too much for her, just as she was too much for pretty much every other player in the world, and Laura lost 6-2; 6-2.

She was relaxed in her defeat, understanding that it had been 99 per cent a certainty.

'It was definitely a learning experience,' she said afterwards. 'I had a couple of chances but didn't take them, and she is able to play her best on the big points. She was very dialled in tonight.'

Williams was generous in her summary of the young player, saying: 'I think she has a lot of potential, more potential than I thought before playing her. She is a lefty and a relaxed hitter, plus she has a really big serve.'

In private, Williams was more rattled than she had led the press to believe. Walking back to the players' area to find her coach and boyfriend, Patrick Mouratoglou, she said: 'Now I understand why you warned me that she's good.'

CHAPTER 28

WIMBLEDON GLORY FOR BRITAIN

Facing both the Williams sisters, one after another, had been an amazing experience, and it had given Laura the confidence she so desperately needed as she now prepared for the French Open and her grass-court outing at Wimbledon.

'I'm in a better place now and I'm moving in the right direction,' she said. 'You always want things to happen quickly and I definitely get frustrated sometimes, especially when you lose close matches, but the important thing now is to keep moving.'

And keep moving she did.

In Paris, she faced an intriguing first-round match against Caroline Wozniacki, a former world No. 1 who was ranked 10 at the time. The two players had always got on well and had practised together often, both being Adidas ambassadors, coached by Sven Groeneveld.

He couldn't help either of them in this match though, as it would be a conflict of interest. Instead, Laura was relying on advice from Ian Bates, the new head of women's tennis at the LTA.

Rory McIlroy, Wozniacki's famous golfing boyfriend, was in the crowd to watch the two players face off, and must have found it a tough experience. When he had first started dating Wozniacki it was Robson to whom he chatted in the players' lounge – a familiar face in what was, to him, an unfamiliar world.

But he would be supporting his girlfriend in the match, despite his affections for the youngster. And, under his watchful gaze, Wozniacki triumphed over young Laura Robson, who was struggling with a sore back.

It wasn't the end of the world. The grass season was about to begin and it was by far Laura's best surface.

To prepare for Wimbledon, she cemented a new coaching partnership with Miles Maclagan, a former coach of Andy Murray, and someone who was much more in tune with Laura's needs.

'We're going to start out for a little period over the grass to see how things go,' he told the press, instantly proving himself as someone who wouldn't pressurise the teen with wild predictions of glory. With Maclagan she focused on improving her consistency, and threw herself into training with Wimbledon in mind.

She didn't shine in any of the tournaments she entered in the run-up to the summer spectacular, but she was defiant in the face of any criticism. 'I tend to play well in the big matches,' she told inquisitive journalists. 'So I'm hoping it will stay that way for Wimbledon.'

But when she lost to Wozniacki again in June at the Aegon International in Eastbourne, her temper got the better of her.

'Fucking hit the ball!' she yelled to herself in the middle of the second set, which was a natural response to the fact that she was losing. But it was unfortunately caught by a BBC microphone, and broadcast live to the nation.

'I'll try not to swear so loud next time,' she conceded sheepishly.

As Wimbledon 2013 began, Laura was in a transitional stage of her life. She had just moved into her own flat in South West London, and her family, so long based in Wimbledon, had moved to Athens, taking the dogs Kiri and Ella with them.

A new job in shipping had taken Andrew to the Greek capital, far from their daughter's old London home. Laura was now fully independent – an adult at last, and it was down to her to forge her career alone.

To kick off Wimbledon, Laura arrived at the WTA pre-tournament party looking stunning in Burberry green lace. Unlike the previous year, when she had spent most of the evening perched awkwardly on a stool in her tight dress, she mingled confidently with the cream of the tennis crop.

Kvitova, Sharapova, Azarenka – one after another the glamorous women took their turn in front of the paparazzi, but it was Laura who received the most coverage in the British newspapers.

It was now five years since her Wimbledon debut had thrust her into the spotlight, and it was definitely time for her to live up to the nation's high hopes.

'Time to toughen up, Laura,' said the *Daily Mail* in the days leading to the championships. 'The honeymoon is over. At 19, she's now old enough to face up to her responsibilities.'

Laura had to embrace the expectations, or face being overwhelmed by them. She chose the former, and penned a column for the British newspaper to share her thoughts on the forthcoming tournament and reveal a bit more about herself.

'It's time for my favourite Grand Slam of the year,' she began…

Yes, I'm a bit biased but Wimbledon is the best of the four. It's such a happy place for me.

Once you're down at Wimbledon, it is fantastic. I like to get to the courts early so there's no rushing. It can get quite cramped at some other tournaments, with people on top of each other, but at Wimbledon you can chill out in your own space. I have a little area in the back where I spend some time before matches. I've got a couple of stretching mats there.

Part of my fitness routine means doing press-ups and chin-ups; I'm getting better at them. I used to be able to do only one chin-up but I can now do eight, which I'm pretty happy with. It's still a work in progress, though.

As the game approaches, you have to eat about an hour and a half before. There is a lot of rice, chicken and vegetables: all that boring stuff. Then, during my matches I'll have my gels and electrolytes.

After the match, you have an hour before going to the media centre, during which you shower and stretch. Then after that you go back and have a massage and ice-bath. I have to go up to my neck! I stay in for 10 minutes at a time.

In the evenings, I usually watch TV: the tennis if it's still on or something like *Game of Thrones*, which I love. I don't stay at the club – once I've done press and physio I get straight out of there. I don't go up to the village during the tournament either. It's a bit too busy up there. I prefer the quiet life...

Kathy had been forced to stay at home in Greece to look after the dogs, but when Laura's first match began on Court One she had her brother Nick to cheer her on. He had been employed as a ground coverer for the tournament, and Laura was grateful to have some family around her.

Robson was backed by an excitable crowd as she took on Maria Kirilenko in the first round. The strict silence was punctuated frequently by shouts of 'Come on, Laura!' and enthusiastic clapping whenever she scored a point.

It was a scintillating display that restored British pride on a day that saw every British woman bow out of the tournament – everyone except for Laura, that is.

Her nails were bright pink, her serves were superb and her nerves were in check as she focused on her victory, and when it came, in straight sets, the crowd rose to give her a standing ovation.

Laura was relieved, and graciously accepted the wave of compliments that came her way.

Prime Minister David Cameron tweeted: 'Great to hear Laura Robson beat the number 10 seed Maria Kirilenko at Wimbledon,' while Pat Cash tweeted: 'Just watched a future top 5 and I think a slam winner Laura Robson crush 10th seed Kirilenko.'

In one interview, Virginia Wade added that Laura was

capable of achieving something truly incredible in the next few weeks. Robson laughed when she heard what the British tennis champion was saying. 'Virginia always gets quite excited, doesn't she?' she said, quick to play down expectations. 'I'd love to win a couple more matches but I don't want to get ahead of myself.'

The nation was watching her progress, and she didn't want them to get too excited – especially since she was the only female Brit left in the competition. It was a lot of responsibility, and she was trying as far as possible to ignore the strain of it all.

Her occasional doubles partner, American Lisa Raymond, was quick to point out the pressure Laura was under. 'She reacts phenomenally well to having the weight of a country on her shoulders,' she said. 'My hat goes off to her. She rises to the occasion. She has more eyes on her here than at any other Grand Slam. It's amazing how a girl of 19 can handle that. She's just a kid.

'It's not easy being the next "great one" in British tennis, the next potential Grand Slam champion, but she is mature enough to handle it.'

Laura had never got past the second round of Wimbledon, so her next match, against Mariana Duque-Marino, was an important one.

Support flooded in from all over the world, and even super pop band One Direction sent their personal messages of support, leaving her to face the wrath of their notoriously jealous fans.

'I looked in my replies, and it was just like thousands of these messages, saying, "who is she?" I was wetting myself because it was so funny,' she told reporters.

In the end, her second-round match was delayed by a whole day due to the sheeting rain, and it finally took place under the closed roof on Centre Court.

Laura was a little nervous as the match began, conscious of the millions of people willing her to succeed. But she eased herself gently into the match, and put pressure on her Colombian opponent with the force of her serve and her powerful groundstrokes.

Robson didn't play her best, but it was enough to win – Laura had finally surpassed her previous best and made it through to the third round of Wimbledon. She was pleased with her performance, particularly in dealing with the burden of expectation she was feeling. 'I think I'm handling it pretty well so far,' she said. 'I've had a fair few matches in big stadiums now where I've handled the crowd support perfectly fine. I love it when people get involved.

'Sometimes they do a massive groan if I hit a double fault, but I'm doing it as well. So we're just living it together.'

Laura now had nothing to lose. She had shown progression in reaching the third round, and was building on her achievements step by step. But she wanted to go as far as she could on the hallowed grass, and set herself the challenge of beating her next opponent, the New Zealander Marina Erakovic.

Erakovic won the junior doubles at the 2004 US Open, and turned pro in 2006. She already had a WTA Tour title under her belt, after vanquishing Sabine Lisicki just a few months previously in Memphis. She had celebrated by sky-diving with her coach, Christian Zalhalka.

She was also one of Robson's closest friends on the circuit, and just a week earlier the pair had gone to see The Killers at Wembley together. They frequently went to see gigs together all over the world while on tour, and had even trained together in Florida, so there would be no surprises for either player on court.

Both would have to put aside their friendship in their quest for Wimbledon glory.

The crowd was nervous as Robson dropped the first set in a short 19 minutes of action. They were silently sympathetic as she went 3-5 further down in the second.

But, on the brink of victory, nerves set in for Erakovic, and, seeing her opponent weaken, Robson found herself newly motivated. She grew in stature as Erakovic weakened her grip – both on the match and her racket, which suddenly looked redundant in her hands.

The crowd grew noisier, swelling with excitement as Laura won an incredible eight games in a row to stage an unbelievable comeback. 'Laura, Laura,' they chanted, and Erakovic began to feel very lonely. The match was now so far out of her reach that she had no chance of reclaiming it. Laura delighted the 4,000-strong crowd by securing victory, just when they had thought all hope was lost.

Laura was through to the fourth round of Wimbledon – the first British woman to reach the final 16 since Sam Smith in 1998.

The crowd went wild, and Laura had to fight her way through a tidal wave of fans to leave the court. Security guards quickly leapt to her aid, escorting her through the maze of people, all desperate to congratulate their heroine.

Facing the press a little later, Laura thanked the crowds for inspiring her comeback. 'They helped massively,' she said. 'I thought they were so great, especially at the end of the second and the whole of the third set. I don't think they had much to support in the first set! They were amazing.'

The epic achievement pushed her to No. 27 in the rankings – making her the first Briton in the top 30 since Jo Durie in 1987.

After such an iffy start to the season, Laura was on fire, sparking jubilation across the country.

Andy Murray was also through to the final 16, and for the first time Britain had both a male and female player to cheer on in the second week of Wimbledon.

'Just let her enjoy it,' Murray sternly told the press.

The young tennis star would next be taking on the vastly more experienced Kaia Kanepi, an Estonian with a formidable track record. She prepared for the match with some light practice, physio and an excruciatingly cold ice-bath, and largely stayed away from the media, who were desperately following her every move.

The British newspapers were filled with predictions, both positive and negative, about the match. They recalled every victory and defeat of her career, discussed her cheeky sense of humour and ramped up the public's already high expectations of the youngster.

Laura wisely ignored it all, focusing exclusively on her training.

She had beaten a Maria, a Mariana and a Marina – now it was time to face a Kaia...

On the day, she came so close to success she could almost taste it. But Robson ultimately fell prey to the Estonian's vastly superior experience, losing 7-6; 7-5 and causing a funereal hush to fall over Wimbledon.

Her Bambi brown eyes were wet with tears as she shook

hands with her opponent. Putting her hand to her chest and bowing her head, she was unable to muster the strength to acknowledge the crowd who had so defiantly cheered her on. She walked slowly off court, a heartbreakingly sad sight that moved some of the spectators to tears.

In a voice that barely rose above a whisper, she later told the press: 'It is more disappointing because I put so much pressure on myself...'

It was devastating for the youngster, but yet again she had proven herself worthy of the love of the nation, and consoled herself by shopping her sorrows away. Strolling down Oxford Street a few days later, she was pictured laden down with purchases and sporting a huge grin.

She ventured out to posh nightclub Mahiki that evening, dressed in a foxy pair of hot pants and skyscraper heels, determined to enjoy a night on the town in the wake of her defeat.

Back at Wimbledon, her friend Andy Murray was still going strong, having secured a spot in the final. The nation turned its full attention to the plucky Scot, dreaming of the possibility, barely to be spoken of, that this year could see a British Wimbledon winner.

When Murray faced Novak Djokovic in the final of the 2013 Wimbledon Championships, the whole country watched the showdown.

Laura was one of them.

She smiled as her friend and mentor finally ended Britain's 77-year wait for a men's champion, lifting the trophy he was born to raise. It was more than consolation for her own fourth-round defeat – a spirit-lifting historic display that proved that anything was possible in the world of tennis.

CHAPTER 29

SEEDED AT A GRAND SLAM

Before she made her way to New York for the 2013 US Open, Robson was supposed to play in two other tournaments – the Canadian Open in Toronto and another in Cincinnati. But she pulled out of both in early August with a wrist injury.

She spent the month training and rehabilitating instead, safe in the knowledge that she would be seeded for the first time at Flushing Meadows – at No. 30. In doing so, she would become the first British woman to be seeded at a Grand Slam tournament for 26 years, and was once more following in the footsteps of Jo Durie, who was last seeded in the Australian Open in 1987, before Laura had even been born.

Robson spent her newly acquired spare time watching movies and going to music festivals like the Yahoo Wireless Festival in London, as well as reading a few novels. She flew out to Greece to see her family, before heading out to the

IMG Academy in Bradenton, Florida, for a fortnight's training. With her wrist still in a delicate condition, she couldn't work through the usual drills, so instead she worked on different parts of her game: volleys, slices, serves and she performed plenty of intense aerobic exercises, which was just what she needed to improve her fitness.

By the time she flew to New York in late August, she was in great condition and raring to take on another challenge.

Wearing a pair of fluorescent orange trainers, a matching skirt and wristbands, she looked fully recharged as she faced her first-round opponent, Spain's Lourdes Dominguez Lino, a woman to whom she had lost twice and whom she had never beaten.

Her wrist was heavily strapped and clearly Robson wasn't pain free. But doctors had assured her she was fine to play, and she wasn't going to argue.

Everyone expected her to be rusty after so long a break, but for the most part she proved them wrong. In the opening set, both players committed a string of errors and Robson was clearly a bit nervous taking on this particular opponent. Twice she trailed by a break, but both times hit back right away and battled on, even saving three break points at 5-5.

Powerful groundstrokes outfoxed her Spanish foe, making all the difference as she edged the 12th game to take a crucial one-set lead. But her nerves turned to steel in the second set, and a dispirited Dominguez Lino didn't get a look in as Laura stormed her way to victory without letting the Spanish contender get even one game.

Laura was full of love after the match.

'I love these courts,' she told Sky Sports enthusiastically. 'I love New York and I love the atmosphere.'

Calming herself somewhat, she added: 'I knew I had to pace myself in the rallies – stay aggressive but only go for it when I had the opportunity. Previously when I played her that is what I did quite badly I would say, so today I knew that I had to keep doing that and I managed to throughout the match. I really wanted to win today because I have lost to her twice before.'

It was a great start to the Open, one which gave her a huge rush of confidence for the second round.

Her next hurdle came in the form of a fellow 19-year-old: Caroline Garcia of France. But she barely had time to hit the ball before the skies above them opened and rain began to lash the court. The match was delayed by more than four hours, and all Robson could do was stare outside and will it to stop. She amused herself by taking a few selfies with her pal Eugenie to post on Twitter, but it was a boring wait.

She was bursting with energy once the match finally restarted, but so was Garcia, and the game was a tight one. Point by point they matched each other in the first set, and it looked like it would move on to a tiebreak, until Robson pounced on the first sign of her opponent's weakness: attacking the Garcia backhand at 5-4, she converted the first break point of the match to move ahead.

With the first set safely tucked away, Laura had to take a medical time-out to have her wrist seen to. She took some painkillers to numb the wretched thing and got straight back out to bravely continue the battle. The second set was much like the first, with both girls attacking each other with consistent strength and determination.

Robson was within sight of victory at 5-4, 30-30, but

Garcia produced two killer serves before breaking her opponent and almost bringing Laura to her knees.

The British player slipped to 0-40 and double-faulted for the first time that day, and it looked to everyone as if she would give away the set. But instead she played a stunning game to save two set points, and delivered a series of crushing forehands to force a tiebreak.

Garcia quickly took a 2-0 lead, but Laura rose above it to dominate matters with her forehand. She pushed back with six points in a row, held her nerve when Garcia tried to level things, and snatched victory with a bomb of a first serve.

Exhausted, she managed a broad grin as she waved to her supporters, who rose in their seats to applaud her.

It had been a truly terrific battle and Laura must have felt proud that she didn't crumble under the pressure.

'I thought I played really well and I served really well, and I'm looking forward to the next round,' Robson told BBC Radio 5 live. 'I think she's a great player and she's had some tough matches in the past, where she should have won and nerves have got to her.

'That's kind of what I was focusing on at the end of the second set when she was serving for it – try to play aggressive and let her get a bit nervous.'

Laura was getting the experience that had defeated her so comprehensively when she first began playing on the WTA Tour – it was translating into a new ability to expose her opponents' weaknesses and pounce on their nerves, all the while pushing her own faults down, and not letting her emotions get the better of her.

Her wrist may have been hurting, but she was on fine form mentally, and this determination to succeed was evident.

Exactly 12 months before, she had reached this stage after sending Kim Clijsters into retirement. On a rampant high, she had stomped all over Li Na to make it through to the fourth round of the US Open – the first woman to do so since Samantha Smith.

Now she would face Li Na again, at exactly the same stage of the tournament. Would history repeat itself?

Li Na was out for revenge when she stepped out into the sunshine to face Robson. She had a score to settle with the youngster, and from the first swing of her racket it showed. Robson struggled to fend her off and, with her wrist still hurting, it was a tall order.

There were positive signs in the beginning of the match, but then Robson's potent forehand began to repeatedly land long and Li Na took the first set.

Robson was more ruthless at the start of the second set, and she initially pulled ahead for 3-0. But the Chinese player's serve yielded an audacious 11 aces, and Laura couldn't find a way through her. Despite taking her opponent all the way to a tiebreak, Robson couldn't pull herself back from the brink, and lost 6-2; 7-5.

She hung her head in disappointment, but she had succeeded in making the round she was seeded for and had gone a lot further than she was expected to.

'I'm disappointed and I could have played better but, overall, I'm going in the right direction and my overall game is improving,' she said, sounding a little dejected. 'I will have a bit of rest now and let my wrist settle down completely.'

When Laura was asked if she was satisfied with her season so far, it was clear that she was not, when she said: 'I would say I set my expectations quite high, so for me it's still quite disappointing. I would love to be more consistent at the smaller tournaments. So that's what the plan is for Asia.'

It was onwards and upwards once more for Robson, who flew back to the UK with a not very pleasant experience ahead of her: she needed to have her wisdom teeth extracted before she could get back on the WTA Tour.

Locker-room gossip hadn't helped the nervous teenager prepare for the painful operation, as all her friends unhelpfully had recounted their own nasty experiences. As much as Laura loved a good horror movie, she really didn't need all the gory details of real-life medical procedures.

'All the other girls in the locker room are telling me their horror stories,' she said. 'Like, "Oh, yeah I pulled my gauze out and it was just blood". Jamie Hampton was like, "Oh, I couldn't do anything for three weeks".'

She wryly added: 'But I don't really listen to Jamie.'

The operation went well and despite the gruesome predictions of her pals, Laura was ready for Asia by the end of September. She was looking to finish off her season on a high, but the reality of the situation left her feeling more than a little dejected. First off was the Guangzhou Open in China, where she reached the quarter-finals of the tournament, before losing to home favourite Zheng Jie. And that, unfortunately, was the best result she could muster in the Far East.

At the Toray Pan Pacific Open in Tokyo she suffered a first round exit to Ayumi Morita, who she had both beaten and lost to on previous occasions. At the time Morita was ranked 24 places below Laura, at 62 in the world. Her spirits were temporarily boosted upon arrival in Beijing for the China Open, when she was presented with a tennis-themed cake by a gaggle of grinning fans. She smiled and signed autographs for the excited group, thanking them for their generosity.

In the first round of the tournament she managed to beat a top 50 player for the first time since her Wimbledon run in the summer – by overcoming Czech player Klara Zakopalova. The first two sets were tight, but Laura stormed on to a 7-6; 4-6; 6-1 win against the world No. 33. By this time Laura had herself risen to No. 38.

Sadly, in the second round she suffered a dramatically comprehensive defeat at the hands of Angelique Kerber. The German player was on top form during the match, denying Robson a single break point in the first set. And though Laura battled to break twice in the second, her own serve let her down too often for her to be any kind of threat to Kerber.

Less than a week later, Robson played her last match of 2013: losing in the first round at Osaka to 43-year-old Kimiko Date-Krumm. It was a disappointing end of season run, but apparently it hadn't all been Laura's fault. British newspapers later reported that she had been plagued with various injuries and illnesses throughout the autumn, although she herself rarely let on that she was suffering from anything.

After flying home to London, Laura was poised to make another significant decision in her life: she soon parted ways with her coach, Miles Maclagan, explaining that she wanted to make a clean break before the next season's start.

Looking back on 2013, her time in Asia had seemed an unfair ending to what had often seemed a promising year. The truth was, she'd had some impressive Grand Slam achievements, but she was still struggling to find consistency on the regular WTA Tour. Laura needed to settle into a stronger pattern and she knew it, so she had a lot to think about as she made her way to Nick Bollettieri's tennis academy in Florida for the off-season. In the past, Laura had certainly taken her time when choosing her coaches, often going for long stretches without one. But this time it was less than a month before she announced Maclagan's replacement: Nick Saviano, one of the best-known coaches in American tennis.

The 57-year-old former player was actually Laura's best friend Eugenie's coach, and was expected to act in more of a training and consultancy role, with assistant coach Jesse Witten travelling with her to tournaments instead. Plus, Robson had first worked with Saviano when she was just 12, so she knew the coaching giant well. Everyone involved hoped that the new arrangement would prove successful.

As 2013 turned into 2014, Laura trained hard in the Floridian heat. She wanted the new year to be her best yet and did everything she could to be prepared for it. But, in January 2014, just ahead of her first outing under Saviano's tutelage, she pulled out of the ASB Classic in Auckland – with another wrist injury. This time it was the tendons in her left wrist that were causing her issues.

Barely a week later she was winning in a match against Yanina Wickmayer at the Hobart International when she had no choice but to pull out half way through because of the wrist pain, which hadn't subsided. Her fans were stunned – and very worried. With barely a week to go before the hallowed Australian Open, it was doubtful whether she'd even be able to take part in the important calendar event.

It was yet another blow to the teen, who described it on her Twitter feed as a 'less than wonderful day'. It is generally accepted that wrist injuries are just about the worst thing that can happen to a tennis player – especially at the beginning of a season. Speculation was rife about whether Robson would be ready for Melbourne. Most were doubtful that she would play at all, which would be exceptionally frustrating for her and the team supporting her.

But ahead of her opening match Laura seemed confident that pulling out of Auckland was merely a precautionary move. 'I just wasn't quite ready to play a match and didn't want to make anything worse,' she told the press. 'It seems to be cleared up now. My wrist feels pretty good. I'm not someone who needs a lot of practice to be able to play well… I'm happy with how I'm playing right now.'

And so, despite many people's predictions to the contrary, Laura stepped out on court at Melbourne Park on the very first day of the Australian Open, 2014. There, in the soaring heat, she faced her first round opponent, Kirsten Flipkens, in one of the very first matches to start at the tournament.

In hindsight, maybe she should have given it all a miss, because the next 50 minutes were probably the most painful she had ever experienced at a Major tournament: Laura was swiftly dispatched by her Dutch opponent in straight sets – 6-3; 6-0. And to make it worse, the speedy court exit meant that Laura became the first player to lose at the tournament that year. There were mutterings that it was her wrist that was at the root of her defeat. But stoic Laura refused to make excuses for the loss: 'I'd prefer not to talk about my wrist because then it turns into a massive excuse,' said the teen. 'Practice is a lot different to playing a proper match in Slams. So I would have loved to have had some more points before-hand, but that's what happens sometimes. Really she played better than me.'

Instead of descending into a depression or rage, Laura tried to see the positive in the situation. 'These matches motivate you to do better and be as fit as possible, and that's what I'll do (now),' she explained. 'It's a tough one today, but everyone has those kinds of days and you have to come back from them stronger.'

A few days later, Laura celebrated her 20th birthday. Her teenage years were over. What a decade it had been.

CHAPTER 30

MONEY, MONEY, MONEY

After reaching the fourth round of Wimbledon in 2013, Laura's on-court earnings for the year had topped £317,000. It was a massive sum and had already eclipsed her total earnings for the year before, which were £285,000.

These seem huge amounts until they are compared with the sums raked in by the highest earners in the sport.

Number one in tennis in 2012, and among the richest sports stars in the world, was Maria Sharapova, whose on- and off-court earnings within the year came to more than £17 million. She was catapulted to that figure not only by the amount she won playing in tournaments but by the truly stellar amounts she was paid from sponsorship and endorsements.

In 2011, Maria extended an eight-year deal with Nike. She has her own collection of tennis gear, which gives her a percentage of the sales, set to add up to £50 million by the time the contract expires.

Sharapova also has an arrangement with American clothing, shoe and handbag designer Cole Haan, which nets her a multimillion-dollar sum. She also has endorsements with racket maker Head, water company Evian, watch manufacturer Tag-Heuer, electronics giant Samsung and luxury sports car company Porsche. It has been estimated that more than half of her earnings come from her activities off the court.

Maria Sharapova, in fact, now believes that these off-court deals are of the utmost importance, which, considering that the career span of a top tennis pro is perhaps eight to ten years, is hardly surprising. She has even invested at least £350,000 of her own money to start a business venture selling sweets.

'Sugarpova' sweets have been selling like hot cakes in the USA at the equivalent of £3.70 a packet. Sales have been helped by an innovative marketing strategy that has included such stunts as claiming she intended to change her name to 'Maria Sugarpova' during the US Open.

Maria's success, and her income, and the wealth of others who have followed similar paths, such as the super-rich Roger Federer, stand to inspire others who will increasingly see tennis as a path to huge wealth.

Today, the figures are astounding. The top ten male and female earners, from on-court earnings alone, are said to have pulled in total lifetime earnings of £360 million. That's before the staggering sums they have made from other sources, such as sponsorship.

According to *Forbes* magazine, Federer is also among the top-earning sports stars in the world – rivalling people like multi-major-winning golfer Tiger Woods and basketball superstars like Kobe Bryant. Around £41 million of his £45 million annual earnings in 2012 was from endorsements alone, dwarfing the salary of football's highest earner David Beckham, who only made a total of £30 million.

But, while Federer is at the top of sport's premier league of earners, numerous other stars of the sport are also nestled among its impressive lower divisions. Their massive earning power shows to what extent tennis and money have become synonymous. How, as one of the most widely played sports around the world, and one that is watched by hundreds of millions, it has taken its place at the top table of sports that attract the world's richest money men.

Not everyone regards it as good for the game.

When top-earning players Sharapova, Caroline Wozniacki, Victoria Azarenka, Ana Ivanovic and Maria Kirilenko crashed out of the early rounds of Wimbledon 2013, it was suggested that maybe players were being dazzled by the dollar signs placed in front of their eyes.

Several of the women had multiple sponsorship deals and would have had to fulfil a number of the obligations that go with a big money business arrangement – leaving them limited time to focus on the tournament.

Some of the players blamed the slipperiness of the grass. Others decided to slope off from the tournament without making excuses, their silence perhaps speaking volumes. But the sheer number of high-earning stars who crashed out in the early rounds of Wimbledon 2013 led many to suggest that some of the players had got their priorities wrong.

One woman who managed to get a grip on her sponsorship as well as on Wimbledon's grass in 2013 was China's Li

Na, who, after becoming the first Chinese woman to win a Grand Slam event in Paris in 2011, was propelled into the top echelons of female earners through a series of sponsorship deals with firms back home.

After she won Paris, she struggled to repeat that level of success until well into 2013. The problems she faced coming to terms with the extra pressures of sponsorship underline how difficult it now is for women to capitalise on their court success.

Former British No. 1 Annabel Croft, who had to reinvent herself after dropping out of the circuit, told the *Sunday Express* in June 2013 that tennis was no longer the gentle pastime it once was. In order to succeed, she stated, women have to be as effective off the court as they are on it.

'The game itself is still as intense as it always was,' Annabel said. 'It is a gladiatorial, one-on-one contest but it has certainly changed in terms of the off-field pressures.

'The prizes on offer are so astronomical; and [players are] having to live up to the expectations of sponsors. The money that has been invested is quite something.

'Sharapova is someone who has coped exceptionally well. Li Na struggled for a while after she won the French Open but has been able to come to terms with it. The game, in that respect, has changed dramatically.'

During the 1970s, almost all the money earned by stars came from what they won on court. The differences between then and now are huge, but there were still substantial amounts to be made if a player managed to stick around and keep winning.

When Virginia Wade, the last British woman to win a Wimbledon singles final, held the trophy aloft in 1997, she took home £13,500 – way behind the £23,500 players took home for going out in the first round in 2013. But, despite what seem like such moderate earnings, Virginia Wade remains the highest-earning British female player ever, with a lifetime winnings pot of just under £1 million.

It shows how much players earn now compared to the 1970s that Laura has already earned more than half of that in just two years on the professional circuit – for reaching Wimbledon's fourth round in 2013, she won £105,000.

This has been helped by the boost to women's winnings that came when the major tournaments started to pay the same amount to females as to males. It wasn't until 2006 that men and women at Wimbledon received equal prize money – before then, women earned on average about 15 per cent less. In 2013, women's singles champion Marion Bartoli won the same £1.6 million as Andy Murray.

Because of this, the amount Laura has earned so far has already put her into the top earners in women's sport. In 2012, the £285,000 she pulled in made her the fourth highest-grossing female sports star after heptathlete Jessica Ennis, on £1 million, Olympic cyclist Victoria Pendleton, on £900,000, and swimmer Keri-Anne Payne on £500,000.

All of them were way behind David Beckham and Britain's other highest-paid sportsmen. Andy Murray, on nearly £10 million a year, didn't even make it into the top five. Second was Lewis Hamilton on £16.5 million, third was Wayne Rooney on £14.5 million, and fourth and fifth were golfer Luke Donald and Jenson Button on £14.4 million and £13.9 million, respectively.

Having managed to get into the women's top five at just 18, and with such huge amounts on offer, it is no wonder that last year Laura was pursued by the best talent agencies in the country.

Until 2012, she was represented by Octagon, an offshoot of a big American sports agency. But, in 2013, a bidding war erupted for her signature between XIX, which represents Murray, and IMG, which used to include Roger Federer and Tiger Woods among its top draws.

Robson chose to go with IMG, where she would work with agent Max Eisenbud, who also represents Sharapova and Na.

According to John Lloyd, being a Brit in itself is guaranteed to help push Laura to the top of female earners. Lloyd, the former British Davis Cup captain and a former British No. 1 himself, told the *Mail on Sunday*: 'It's a very cut-throat world. The prize money in tennis is the same no matter where you come from in the world. But being inside the top 50 in the world and coming from Britain, as Laura does, she will make vastly more than an American ranked in the top 50, where it means nothing. Britain is one of the hottest places in the world to be a top tennis player with the kind of potential Laura undoubtedly has.'

Making a championship-winning player does not come cheap, either. It has been estimated that in order to produce a world top 50 player it costs parents, or whoever pays for the person's development, up to £250,000. In addition to weekly coaching sessions, they have to pay for tennis holidays, summer camps, and tournament fees and then more intensive training as their protégé approaches the world top 500.

In recent years, but only relatively recently, some of that money has come from the LTA. But, in providing it, staff and committees at the LTA have to decide which players to give it to. Many have claimed that there has been a bias towards families who the LTA knows are able to help with those costs – in other words, those already wealthy enough to pay for travel to tournaments – and often people who live close to the LTA's base in London.

Some believe that the reason why Britain has struggled to find winners is because the huge amount of money the LTA has had to spend has ended up going to the wrong people.

Tim Henman has told *The Sunday Telegraph*'s money section that he was able to make it only because he was lucky enough to have parents who were comfortably off. He said that he may have struggled if his parents had not been prepared to support him, but, ultimately, he rose to the top because he loved playing the game so much.

He said: 'I had a very middle-class upbringing and was given lots of opportunity to play sport as a youngster. I was fortunate enough to never have struggled with paying for the costs of tennis, which can be quite high. I do remember when I was playing in junior tournaments that we'd have to fork out £25 here and £50 there, but that was never a problem.

'Money was never a dictating factor in me playing tennis, unlike some players nowadays. I did it because I loved playing the sport. I have been lucky to earn lots of prize money but if I hadn't this wouldn't have changed my attitude towards playing tennis. I did it because I loved it.'

Tim is another person who believes that the success of some of the players who have come though from Eastern Europe is down to the fact that many of the most successful started out with little and had to work hard for what they have earned.

'Money can be a very strong motivator, especially when you don't have it. We have seen this with some of the Eastern European countries producing some great players in recent years.

'As a 17- and 18-year-old playing away in tournaments for six weeks at a time it can be quite tough paying for expensive hotels, flights and other costs. This was a struggle and you really need support from the Lawn Tennis Association [LTA].

'At times ... you have to have an inner belief that you are doing the right thing and that it'll be worth it in the end. But I think here lies one of the problems with British tennis. There is a lot of money invested in the game and sometimes the young [British] players are a little too comfortable. So they don't have the hunger to succeed as much as in other countries.'

Laura has been one of those helped by the LTA, but there is still much debate whether the success she is now achieving has come despite the money she has received or because of it.

Her will to win at all costs was something admitted and admired by the former head of the LTA Roger Draper, who, as far back as 2007, in an interview with the *Guardian* held her up as a shining example to other professionals who had failed to achieve.

He said: 'She's abroad four months a year and hitting four hours a day and has her own personal tutor. A lot of people might say, "Oh God, that's a bit hairy and scary", but if we want to produce more winners, that's the way it's got to be. To succeed in tennis, you have to be on a more or less full-time programme by the time you are nine or ten. If not, you have no chance of getting into the world top 100.

'What we have to do is convert more athletes to play

tennis at a younger age, get them on proper programmes and then make sure that those costs of £30,000-or-so-a-year are subsidised.

'The sacrifices parents have to make are far different than in any other sport. Our challenge is to remove the excuses. Desire and hunger are essential. We have got the talent without a doubt but we have to channel it in the right direction. Whether we like it or not, Tim and Andy were accidents, in a way. There wasn't really a system. We need a group of players pulling and pushing each other through.'

As up-and-coming players like Laura have demonstrated, tennis faces immense challenges. Not enough players have been coming through to stand a chance of making it at the top level. It is perhaps inevitable that a lack of champion players – who are seen to earn footballer-sized wages – to emulate means youngsters have little to inspire them.

It could explain why only a fraction of those who play football bother to pick up a racket on a regular basis. A recent survey by Sport England found that, in some parts of the UK, football is played regularly by 67 per cent of under-16-year-old boys and by 17 per cent of under-16-year-old girls. Tennis, by comparison, is only played by 10 per cent of boys and 12 per cent of girls regularly outside of school.

Andy Murray, who has been shown to succeed despite not coming from tennis's traditional tennis-playing English middle classes (although with the added advantage of a mother who is a top tennis coach), has come through to triumph. Laura has the potential to do so too.

Laura believes it's not about the money, it's about the winning. But she is also smart enough to know not to waste a good thing.

In 2012, Laura spoke to the *Daily Mail*, revealing how her growing fortune was being well managed by her father Andrew.

'At the end of the season, he was nice enough to give me a bonus,' she joked, before admitting that her cash windfall was spent almost immediately on a shopping expedition.

In the years after she had won junior Wimbledon in 2008, up to 2012, her father had made sure a financial adviser was brought in to watch over her burgeoning bank account.

'When we had a meeting at the bank the other day, I was told that 30 per cent of footballers end up bankrupt,' Laura told the *Daily Mail*. 'I think my dad is being very cautious; not that I would ever go crazy. You just have to be aware that it's a short career and do as much as you can to save for as long as possible.

'I am not overly interested in what I am worth because I don't get to spend it anyway. But I am becoming more involved. Dad wanted to wait until I was 18 or interested in what to do with what I earn. I have become interested, so I'll keep going to meetings and learn from them.'

She revealed that, despite the temptations to spend her earnings, she didn't possess any credit cards, and only had one debit card in her bag. Her foresight to become a good manager of money could stand her in good stead. In 2013, after making it to the fourth round of Wimbledon, she was ranked 40th out of the top 50 most marketable sports stars in the world by Sportspro.

With her good looks, skill on court and bubbly personality off court, experts are saying she is looking increasingly like commercial gold dust – an appeal that will only grow as she wins bigger events. They estimate that, if she was able to win

Wimbledon, especially with her interest in fashion to attract sponsorship, her potential earnings could rival many of those at the top of tennis.

And, as she earns more money, there will be many who look on and wonder if they too could achieve such success.

Now, with a burgeoning star in the making, despite all that has held it back over the last century, British tennis is hoping that Laura's monetary and on-court success will inspire a new generation to wonder if they too have what it takes to reach the heights and success of Maria Sharapova, the Williams sisters and Laura herself.

In the meantime, it is up to Laura to continue reaping the rewards of all the hard work she has put in, and fulfil her potential to become the true heroine of British tennis.

It will be a tall order. But if there's one thing that we have learned about Laura, since her explosive arrival on the tennis scene in 2008, it's this: she certainly loves a challenge.